JOHN WESLEY

K.S. WOERNER
AFTER
ROMNEY

JOHN WESLEY

By ARNOLD LUNN

Author of "Roman Converts," "The Harrovians," Etc.

With a Foreword by
S. PARKES CADMAN, D.D.

LINCOLN MAC VEAGH
THE DIAL PRESS
NEW YORK · MCMXXIX
LONGMANS, GREEN AND CO., TORONTO

PRINTED IN THE UNITED STATES OF AMERICA
BY THE VAIL-BALLOU PRESS, INC., BINGHAMTON, N. Y.

To

WILLIAM HOLDSWORTH LUNN

CONTENTS

CONTENTS

FOREWORD

Why another book on Wesley? He has been portrayed from almost every possible viewpoint, by men of different political and religious beliefs. Nevertheless, here is a volume which every admirer of Wesley should read, and which all who would know more of the foremost Englishman of his century cannot afford to neglect. It presents the great ecclesiastical statesman and evangelist as he appears to a man of culture, insight and sympathy, who at the same time is committed to the methods of realistic biography.

So far as religious literature is concerned Mr. Arnold Lunn is to the manner born. His father, Sir Henry Lunn, is well known to many American Churchmen as the brilliant and versatile Editor of "The Review of the Churches," and to American scholars as one of the best informed Englishman of our day on questions relative to the early history and constitutional development of the United States. On his maternal side, Mr. Lunn is the grandson of the late Canon Moore, the Headmaster of an Anglican School in Ireland, of which Father Tyrrell was once a pupil. By his marriage he is linked into the families of Dean Farrar of Canterbury and the Victorian statesman, Lord Iddesleigh.

One of his first books, "The Harrovians," introduced Mr. Lunn to a wide and appreciative constituency. It showed that he had intelligent convictions, and expressed them with a courage and a clarity that commanded attraction. Among other notable contributions of his pen

"Roman Converts" has won a large hearing for similar reasons. Now comes this work on Wesley, containing some hitherto unpublished matter, and displaying a blend of critical appraisal and deserved reverence for its subject which augments its value.

I do not propose to anticipate its pleasures and profit by discussing it. Enough to suggest that its readers will find in its pages what may be termed the twentieth century estimate of Wesley, and one more than likely to prevail with the oncoming generation.

S. PARKES CADMAN.

INTRODUCTION

"We are only saved from describing the age of Walpole in the words which Porson once applied to an individual, as 'mercantile and mean beyond merchandise and meanness,' by the reflection that the age of Sunderland, of the second George, and of Walpole is also that of Berkeley, of Wesley, and of Pitt. . . . The earlier half of the eighteenth century in England is an age of materialism, a period of dim ideals, of expiring hopes. Before the middle of the century its character was transformed. There appeared a movement headed by a mighty leader, who brought water from the rocks to make a barren land live again . . . Berkeley among philosophers, Law among divines, all derived new thoughts, evoked new harmonies, or caught new inspirations from the age. But more important than any of these in universality of influence and range of achievement were John Wesley and the religious revival to which he gave his name and his life."

H. W. Y. Temperley in the *Cambridge Modern History, Vol. VI.*

Dr. Parkes Cadman must share with the author the responsibility for this book; for it was Dr. Cadman who urged me to write it. He believed that there was still room for a new Life of Wesley written by a man not a Methodist, but who had a Methodist background, and who might, therefore, be expected to combine a sympathetic interest in John Wesley with a certain detachment of outlook. I only hope he is right.

As an Anglican who was duly confirmed while at school, I suppose I possess the necessary detachment, and perhaps it is easier for those with a Methodist background to understand Methodism and to appreciate its founder.

xi

My father is a Methodist, and my mother an Anglican: as
a small boy I attended the Methodist service in the morning and the Anglican service in the evening. Perceiving
that two forms of the same faith under the same roof
doubled my attendance at church, I soon became a passionate advocate of Church Re-union.

I began this book with a faint prejudice against Wesley,
the normal reaction against a man whose virtues had been
impressed upon me by my grandfather. One's grandfather's heroes are seldom one's own. It is, indeed, difficult to exaggerate the reverence with which Methodists,
like my grandfather, spoke of John Wesley. Wesley had
been dead for a century when I was a boy, but my grandfather would have thought it an unpardonable liberty to
refer to him as anything but "Mr. Wesley."

Long before I had finished reading Wesley's Journal,
the lingering traces of youthful prejudice had disappeared.
Page after page in this Journal is as dull as a physician's
notebook, yet the cumulative effect is fascinating.

As you read, there gradually emerges the portrait of
one of the most remarkable men that ever lived.

The dreadful sameness of the human race is a depressing fact. It is only too easy to pigeonhole the average
saint or the average sinner. Rare indeed, are those specimens which demand a label to themselves. Wesley was a
genuine eccentric, a unique specimen. He has no dupli-
cate in eccelesiastical history.

The literature of love, for instance, runs into some
millions of volumes, but there is no love story the least
like Wesley's Georgia romance.

Autocrats are common enough, but few of them strike
out a new line in autocracy. It is only the exceptional
genius, a Wesley or a Mussolini, who does not run absolutely true to type. Mussolini cured Communism with
castor oil, a stroke of creative genius. The Communists

swallowed castor oil because they had to, but Wesley dosed his people without the aid of bayonets. "I thought," he says, "of a kind of desperate experiment. I would prepare and give them physic myself." And he did.

Wesley had even less respect for doctors than for bishops. He prescribed freely for his people, and to please him his devoted followers swallowed concoctions far less pleasant than castor oil. He was obeyed because he was loved. He was loved because he was absolutely disinterested, and because he was disinterested few resented his autocracy, and fewer still challenged the decisions of this precise and masterful little man. Wesley's portrait suggests, not a despot, but an ascetic High-Church Don, which indeed he was, an eighteenth century Liddon rather than an eighteenth century General Booth.

John Wesley was, perhaps, the greatest Englishman of his age. He founded a Church, which is to-day by far the largest Protestant communion in the world, numbering as it does over twenty million adherents. His influence, however, must not be measured merely in terms of church statistics. His effect on the social life of England was profound and far-reaching. Lecky, the rationalistic historian, considered that Methodism had saved England from revolution. Among modern historians, that distinguished French scholar Halévy finds in Methodism and in the Evangelical revival one of the most potent factors in shaping the life of England in the early nineteenth century.[1]

Again, it was Methodism which paved the way for the Romantic Revival.

Dr. Leger, in his preface to Père Piette's great work "La Réaction du John Wesley dans l'Evolution du Protestantisme," comments on "la filliation spirituelle du

[1] "A History of the English People in the Ninetenth Century," by Elie Halévy.

Mouvement Oxford avec John Wesley," and Miss Sheila Kaye-Smith, who is an Anglo-Catholic, attributes the Catholic revival in the Church of England to the joint effect of the Evangelical Revival and the Romantic Movement. And the Romantic Movement itself was made possible by the emotional revolt of Methodism against the formalism of the eighteenth century. Just as Wesley stands half-way between the prosaic Latitudinarians of the early eighteenth and the romantic Tractarians of the early nineteenth century, so his hymns and his brother's hymns herald the release of poetry from the formal fetters of their age.

Of these hymns, Dr. Leger, a brilliant French critic of Wesley, writes, "The smooth, correct, regular heroic couplet of Pope and his school is superseded by endlessly varied combinations of metre and stanzas; lines freely encroach upon each other; verse and language strive to picture the manifold impulses of the soul, the vehement rush of religious emotions. Cowper, it must be remembered, came under the influence of Methodism. Both in this more refined fashionable garb, and in the more uncouth form of the Society hymn-books, a new kind of poetry here rises before us, instinct with a more ardent flame, alive to every pulse of individual sensibility: the truly lyrical poetry. To this degree, Methodism did perhaps pave the way for romanticism in literature. To a high degree, it was spiritual romanticism, or lyrical religion." [2]

Indeed, nothing but a snobbish prejudice against hymns as literature would have excluded the finest of Charles Wesley's religious hymns from a representative collection of English lyrics. It is surprising that Sir Arthur Quiller-Couch, whose "Hetty Wesley" showed such sympathetic

[2] "Wesley's Last Love," by Augustin Leger, D. Litt.

understanding of Methodism, did not see fit to include
Charles Wesley's "Wrestling Jacob" in the "Oxford Book
of English Poetry," and at least one of Mrs. Wesley's
letters in the "Oxford Book of English Prose."

Wesley's Journals should be studied, not only for their
intrinsic interest, for the light which they throw on the
political and social conditions of the time, but also for
their indirect evidence of the reality of things unseen.

Religion is said to be on the decline. It may be so. It is
certainly true that the churches are no longer patronised
by the type of person who slept through the sermon in
Victorian days. Church attendance is largely a matter of
convention, and therefore varies from age to age, but
it is doubtful whether the small proportion of genuinely
religious people changes greatly from one generation to
another.

The interest in religious problems is as great as ever.
It is, perhaps, a more active, a more intelligent and a
more scientific interest. Dogmas are no longer accepted on
trust, not even the dogmas of the scientists. The Victorian
Bishop who averted his gaze from the fossils in the rocks,
fossils whose existence could not be reconciled with
Genesis, is, of course, out of date, but he is no more dated
than the scientist who refuses to examine the facts of
religious experience, lest his simple faith in a godless universe might be shaken. There is a growing respect for
the attitude which deserves to be called scientific, the
determination to take account of all facts, and to follow
out every possible line of research, physical and psychical.
Every fact must be taken into account, not only the facts
which can be weighed and tested in a laboratory, but all
the evidence, baffling and contradictory though it may be,
of religious and mystical experience.

Utrum Deus sit, the second problem debated in the *Summa Theologica,* is the greatest of all problems, and the study of religious revivals is one of many modes of approach to solution.

Wesley's evidence was of value because he was an accurate observer. He was never carried away by the emotions which he aroused in others. He loved truth, and he hated "guile" and inaccuracy. His Journals often record his impatience with those of his own people who had exaggerated the effect of the Revival. Here is a characteristic entry. "I returned to Cork and met the classes. Oh when will Methodists learn not to exaggerate? After all the pompous accounts I had had of the vast increase of the society it is not increased at all; nay, it is a little smaller than it was many years ago."

Wesley was often deceived by individuals, but he was pessimistic rather than sanguine in his estimate of the effect of his work on communities. By temperament he was a sceptic. He had that particular type of scientific *pietas* which is rarer among scientists than it should be, a deep reverence for facts and a deep distrust of theories unsupported by evidence.

He was impressed, as well he might be, by the Revival of which he was the architect. He had seen too many cases of men whose whole lives had been permanently changed to doubt the validity of religious experience. Nothing is easier than to produce a temporary revival, a fleeting condition of religious exaltation. Nothing is more difficult than permanently to transform character, for character and personality are intensely conservative.

Now historians of all creeds and of none are agreed that the Evangelical Revival produced permanent results. In that brilliant book "The Psychology of the Methodist Revival," Mr. Dimond writes as follows: "Methodism may well be content to accept the verdict of history as to the health and sanity of its influence on the life of the people."

Facts are stubborn things, whether they be the facts of chemistry or the facts of conversion. To dismiss an inconvenient fact which does not fit into your system is unscientific, whether that fact be a fossil in the rocks or a change of heart and of life. Nothing, for instance, could be less scientific than the impatient generalizations with which that conscientious agnostic Leslie Stephen attempts to dismiss the problem of conversion. "What, they seemed to have tacitly enquired, is the argument which will induce an ignorant miner or a small tradesman in a country town to give up drinking and cock-fighting? The obvious answer was: Tell him that he is going straight to hell-fire to be tortured for all eternity. Preach that consoling truth to him long enough, and vigorously enough, and in a large crowd of his fellows, and he may be thrown into a fit of excitement that may form a crisis in his life."

I cannot believe that Leslie Stephen himself was satisfied with this feeble caricature of a solution. He was exceptionally well-read in religious history, and must have known that men are seldom reformed by fear. Throughout the Middle Ages, the horrors of hell formed the staple topic of medieval sermons, but there were few cases of men being thrown into "fits of excitement" by such sermons, and still fewer cases of such fits proving an important crisis in their lives.

Facts, as I said before, are stubborn things. Had Leslie Stephen checked his theory by the facts, he would have discovered that Wesley only preached one sermon on hell, whereas he preached rather more than forty thousand times on his favourite theme, the love of God freely offered to all mankind. It was, indeed, his invariable custom to select for his sermons what he himself called "comfortable words."

The problem remains. I shall not attempt to impose my solution on the reader. If he studies Wesley's Journals, he will doubtless discover his own solution, which may not be identical with Wesley's, but which can hardly help being more plausible than Leslie Stephen's.

I have not added a bibliography of Wesley at the end of the book for the very good reason that a complete bibliography would be longer than the book itself, and an incomplete bibliography would have little value. "The Works of John and Charles Wesley" edited by the Rev. Richard Green is a bibliography with which all students of Wesley are familiar. It is both complete and accurate. There is an excellent bibliography of books about Wesley and Methodism at the end Père Piette's admirable study of John Wesley (see below). I shall therefore content myself with acknowledging my indebtedness to the books which I have found most useful.

"The Works of the Rev. John Wesley."
"The Journal of John Wesley." (Standard Edition). By Nehemiah Curnock.
"John Wesley and the Religious Societies."
"John Wesley and the Methodist Societies."
"John Wesley and the Advance of Methodism."
"John Wesley the Master Builder."
These four works are by John S. Simon, D.D.
"A New History of Methodism." Edited by W. J. Townsend, D.D., H. B. Workman, M.A., D.Litt. and George Eayrs, F. R. Hist. S.
"The Letters of John Wesley." Edited by George Eayrs. (Contains a valuable introduction and also an excellent chapter by Augustine Birrell, K.C.)
"The Life of John Wesley." By C. T. Winchester.
"Wesley's Legacy to the World." By J. Ernest Rattenbury.

"La Réaction de Wesley dans l'Evolution du Protestantisme." By P. Maximin Piette.

"The English Church in the Eighteenth Century." By
C. J. Abbey and J. H. Overton.

"The Living Wesley." By the Rev. J. H. Rigg, D.D.

"The Psychology of the Methodist Revival." By S. G.
Dimond.

"John Wesley's Last Love." By Augustin Leger.

"John Wesley." By W. H. Hutton. D.D.

"The Three Religious Leaders of Oxford." By
S. Parkes Cadman.

"Charles Wesley." By D. M. Jones.

"The Holy Lover." By Marie Conway Oemler.

I have not included in the above list the earlier biog-
raphies such as those by Southey, Tyerman and others,
for if I once began to enumerate my indebtedness to the
earlier writers on Wesley, I might as well attempt a
formal bibliography.

I am also deeply indebted to that great scholar, Dr.
Workman, who read this book in manuscript. Others who
have struggled through the manuscript are Miss D. M.
Jones, Dr. Cadman, my father and my wife. To one
and all I offer my best thanks for valuable criticisms and
suggestions. My father's book *Chapters from my Life*
contains a valuable study of Lincolnshire Methodism
during the sixties and seventies of the last century.

Finally I should like to thank my secretary, Miss G. H.
Leigh, whose assistance has not been confined to the
mechanical work of transcribing the manuscript.

ARNOLD LUNN.

JOHN WESLEY

CHAPTER I

"A BRAND PLUCKED FROM THE BURNING"

IT was midnight—February 9th, 1709.

The Vicar of Epworth had fallen asleep when his daughter rushed into his room. Fragments of lighted wood had fallen on to her bed. Fire! The Vicar bundled his wife and daughter downstairs, dashed into the nursery where he aroused five of his children, and collected his family in the hall. So far, so good, but unfortunately the front door was locked, and the keys were in one of the upper rooms. A waste of precious moments. When at last the keys had been discovered, the staircase was on fire. The Vicar threw open the door, but a strong easterly wind hurled back the flames, and against that tidal wave of fire they could not stand. The children tumbled out of the windows. The Vicar's wife, who was pregnant, could not climb through the window, and after being driven back three times she at last succeeded in wading through the sea of fire "which did me no further harm than a little scorching my hands and my face."

The family re-assembled outside. One was missing, a small boy who was asleep in an upper room. The Vicar dashed back into the house, and leapt up the burning staircase. It collapsed beneath him and he was cut off from the upper storey by a furnace of flame. He could do no more. He threw himself on his knees, and in an agony of prayer commended the soul of his child to God.

Meanwhile, the child awoke and found the room full of light. He thought that it was day, and called to his nurse. No one answered. He looked out of his curtains and saw tongues of flame creeping along the ceiling. He jumped out of his bed and ran to the door, threw it open and looked out on to an inferno of blazing walls. Back to the window. He climbed on to a chest, and was seen from the yard below. A man in the crowd shouted that he would run to fetch a ladder. "No time for that," growled another. "Here, I have thought of a shorter way. I will fix myself against the wall; lift a light man and set him on my shoulders." The house was low and the human ladder sufficed to reach the window and just as the burning roof collapsed, the child was delivered from a terrible death. That child was John Wesley, the Father of Methodism, "a brand plucked from the burning" as he liked to describe himself in later years.

II

The Vicar of Epworth wandered sadly through the ruin of his house. Had the fire been an accident, his loss would have been easier to bear, but even so it would have stunned a less courageous man. "We have now," he wrote to a friend, "very little more than what Adam and Eve had when they first set up housekeeping."

But as he pondered on the sequence of events, he could not evade the conclusion that the fire was the last of a long series of calculated outrages. For years his parishioners had been hostile. Not only had the Vicar been too outspoken in his condemnation of their failings, but he had also taken the unpopular side in the local election. The men of the isle had vowed vengeance. They had assembled under his windows, and had "complimented him all night long with drums and guns." Three cows had been stabbed in one night though none of them had been killed outright. The poor house-dog had his leg almost chopped off by an unknown hand.

The fire could hardly have been an accident. It started in the depth of winter, when the inflammable roof covering was in the worst possible condition to be lighted by accident. It broke out at night, when all fires in the house had been extinguished for hours. It did not break out in any lower room, but in the thatch of the roof, which must therefore have been lighted from outside.

Few things undermine a man's courage more rapidly than secret and anonymous persecution. A weaker man would have surrendered, would have applied for a new living, and would have turned his back on the brutal peasantry whom he had tried to tame and to civilise. But Samuel Wesley was no quitter. They had burnt his home over his head. Well, he would rebuild his home, and perhaps they would burn that too. Something caught his eye—lying among the charred foundations of his home—his treasured Polyglot Bible. Sadly he picked it up. He ought never to have bought it,—an unjustifiable extravagance. As he turned over the scorched leaves, one sentence and one sentence only was legible. *Vade; vende omnia quae habes, et attolle crucem, et sequere Me.* "Go; sell all that thou hast; take up thy cross and follow Me."

III

Private judgment is no more common among Protestants than among Catholics. "There is not," writes Milton, "any burden that some would gladlier post off to another than the charge and care of their Religion. There be, who knows not that there be, of Protestants and profes-

sors" (i. e., Puritans) "who live and dye in as arrant
an implicit faith as any lay Paptist of Loretto."

John Wesley inherited from both his parents a critical
attitude to "implicit faith." Dissent was in his blood,
dissent, that is, from any received beliefs. His paternal
great-grandfather was an Anglican clergyman ejected
from his living by the Act of Uniformity. His father
Samuel Wesley had been brought up as a Dissenter but
had left the Dissenters for the Church of England. His
maternal grandfather Dr. Samuel Annesley was an Anglican priest, who also had suffered ejectment under the
Act of Uniformity. His mother Susannah at the age of
thirteen examined the whole controversy between the
Established Church and the Dissenters and adopted the
Creed of the Church of England.

Wesley's family tree translated into ecclesiastical terms
might be represented as follows:

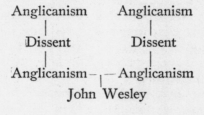

Anglicanism Anglicanism
| |
Dissent Dissent
| |
Anglicanism — — Anglicanism
|
John Wesley

IV

Most people would admit that moral courage is a characteristic of religious folk, but it is less generally realised
that physical courage is almost invariably associated with
religious leadership.

Missionaries share with mothers-in-law the privilege
of providing mirth for the proletariat. But when one
has sucked the last dregs of humour from comic repre-
sentations of cannibal feasts, it is as well to remember

that a missionary who faces the risk of providing the cannibal with a hearty meal, probably possesses many of those qualities which evoke tumultuous applause from the Pit when exhibited by the V.C. hero of the cast.

The man who took a hostile world for his parish did not come of coward stock. His father Samuel Wesley was a man of great moral and of great physical courage. One sees him against a sullen background of hostile parishioners, cheerful and undismayed, daunted neither by poverty nor boycott nor the debtor's gaol. He did not know the meaning of fear.

He was dining one day at a London coffee house. A Guards officer strolled in, ordered a drink, and favoured the company with a succession of choice expletives. Wesley called for the waiter, told him to bring a glass of water, and in a clear, resonant voice ordered him to "carry it to that gentleman in the red coat; and desire him to wash his mouth after his oaths."

The officer was furious, and would have set upon Wesley had not his companions restrained him. "Nay, Colonel! You gave the first offence," they said. "You see the gentleman is a clergyman. You know it is an offence to swear in his presence."

A few years later, Wesley was accosted in St. James's Park by a stranger, none other than the Colonel of the Guards. "Since that time, sir," said the colonel, "I thank God I have feared an oath, and everything that is offensive to the Divine Majesty; and as I have a perfect recollection of you, I rejoiced at seeing you, and could not refrain from expressing my gratitude to God and you."

This is, of course, the sort of thing which goes down well in a tract, but life seldom conforms to copybook standards. There is, however, no reason to doubt the authenticity of this edifying anecdote, which is, therefore, a striking tribute to Samuel Wesley's personality.

In real life, nothing is less calculated to reform the erring than a public and devastating rebuke. Wesley was not only in the right, which was irritating enough, but he scored decisively, and it was long odds that the colonel would subside into sulky resentment and seize the first opportunity for revenging his discomfiture on the barrack square. The colonel's conversion was probably less due to godliness than to the gallantry and the wit of Wesley's rebuke.

One's heart bleeds for the poor colonel in the first crushing shock of his humiliation. It is easy to understand his feelings. The little man in the clerical collar looked so inoffensive and there seemed no risk of trouble to be feared in that quarter. And then suddenly the parson had trumped his ace and exposed him to public ridicule and contempt. . . . He had done it so neatly, had not turned red like a turkey-cock and protested in a shrill clerical voice against blasphemy. . . . He had dropped the parson, his retort was monstrous neat, the most famous wit could not have bettered it. The little man had a stout heart, he might have been run through the body for his insolence . . . He had shown a very proper spirit. He was a man of parts.

Samuel Wesley's sturdy independence did not desert him in his dealings with the great. It is difficult for the modern reader to realise the reverence with which great nobles were regarded in the eighteenth century. The peerage was worshipped as a semi-divine order of exalted beings. Men who were normally sane disgraced their books with fulsome and servile dedications to their aristocratic patrons. Nor was this mere common form. These flattering addresses were only too sincere, only too accurate an index of the relations between literature and the aristocracy. The social and political power of the peerage had never stood so high.

The patron of Wesley's first living was the Marquis of Normanby, a great noble. His mistress called on Mrs. Wesley secure in the conviction that the mistress of a marquis took precedence of the wife of the Vicar. Samuel Wesley walked up to her, took her by the arm and bundled her out of the room to the great displeasure of her noble patron.

Samuel Wesley had need of all the courage with which he was endowed, for life did not spare him and a weaker man would never have survived the buffetings of fate to which he was exposed.

He was born at Whitchurch, Dorset, in 1662 and was brought up as a Dissenter, and was educated at Stoke Newington, a famous Dissenting Academy.[1]

While he was studying at this Academy, he was required to write an answer to some attacks on Dissenters, but according to John Wesley "this set him on a course of reading which soon produced an effect very different from what had been intended. Instead of writing the wished for answer he himself conceived, he saw reason to change his opinions; and actually formed a resolution to renounce the Dissenters, and attach himself to the Established Church."

Having paid his debts, he got up one morning and walked to Oxford where he entered himself as Pauper Scholaris at Exeter College. There he maintained himself by his own exertions, took his degree and left Oxford with a pound or two more to his credit than when he entered.

He married as a curate on thirty pounds a year. He kept out of debt until the autumn of 1690 when he was

---

[1] These Dissenting Academies played an important rôle at that period. Daniel Defoe was a fellow student of Samuel Wesley's, as was also a certain Timothy Cruso, later a famous preacher, whose name Defoe borrowed for his greatest romance. Bishop Butler of the "Analogy" was also educated at a Dissenting Academy.

appointed rector of the little village of South Ormsby.
As Vicar of South Ormsby his income rose to the munif-
icent figure of fifty pounds a year. Meanwhile, the family
was increasing at the rate of one child per annum. Samuel
Wesley was no quietist relying on Providence to feed his
family. He contrived, Heaven alone knows how, to send
his sons to good schools and to Oxford. He survived
catastrophes which would have killed a weaker man.

In 1701, Wesley's barn collapsed. In 1702, part of the
Rectory was burnt. In twelve months his entire growth
of flax was burnt, in 1709 the Rectory was entirely destroyed by fire, and in 1710 Samuel Wesley was thrown
into prison for debt.

He resumed the struggle with undiminished cheerfulness. He carried on without bravado. He was not the sort
of man who "thanked whatever gods there be" for his
"unconquerable soul." Real courage is seldom self-
conscious; it is only the weakling who advertises that his
head is "bloody but unbowed." Like Mr. Britling, Samuel
Wesley saw it through. Unlike Mr. Britling, he struck
no attitudes.

His sense of humour never deserted him. A cheerful
whimsical man with a neat gift for repartee and a fond-
ness for a good joke, he conquered "the fell clutch of circumstance" by sheer good humour. There is a good story
of a miser who lived near Epworth and who had never
been known to give a friend a dinner, or to relieve a
relation in distress. Once and once only he yielded to a
momentary impulse and invited Wesley and some other
friends to dinner. Wesley returned thanks with the following impromptu Grace:

> "Thanks for this feast! for 'tis no less
> Than eating manna in the wilderness.
> Here meagre famine bears controlless sway,
> And ever drives each fainting wretch away;

Yet here,—O how beyond a saint's belief!
We've seen the glories of a chine of beef:
Here chimneys smoke which never smoked before,
And we have dined where we shall dine no more."

The old miser listened attentively, nodded his approval at the last line—"And we have dined where we shall dine no more"—and remarked with gloomy conviction, "No, gentlemen; for it is sadly too expensive."

Samuel Wesley was something of a poet. His work was just good enough to attract the notice and the scorn of Pope. Like many a country parson, he amused himself by writing books, some of which were published and some, perhaps, even read.

Anglicanism is often represented as reaching its nadir in the eighteenth century but a church which could produce country parsons like Samuel Wesley or like Wesley's father-in-law could not have been quite so black as it was painted. Samuel Wesley was what we should now call a High Churchman. His piety was never forced, and his devotion to the Church was unimpaired and unembittered by the contrast between his own poverty and the wealth of absentee bishops. He never lost his courage, never compromised with his principles and his gallant humour never degenerated into bitterness.

v

Had Dr. Annesley been content with a modest family of two dozen, England would have been the poorer of one of the most remarkable women that the century had produced, and Methodism would have been robbed of its Founder.

For Susannah Annesley, John Wesley's mother, was the twenty-fifth child of her father, and the twenty-fourth child of her father's second wife. Even in those days a family of twenty-five aroused some comment. "How many children has Dr. Annesley?" asked a friend of Thomas Manton who had just baptised the last arrival. "I believe it is two dozen," he replied, "or a quarter of a hundred."

"This reckoning of children by dozens," sagely remarked the eccentric John Dunton, "is a singular circumstance; an honour to which few persons ever arrive.

Susannah Wesley was the daughter of Dr. Samuel Annesley, and was the great-niece of the first Earl of Anglesea, for Dr. Annesley's father was a brother of Arthur, first Earl of Anglesea.

John Wesley therefore, came of good stock on both sides of his family. He was a gentleman and a scholar and a descendant of gentlemen and scholars. But no man attached less importance to social rank, perhaps because he had no reason to suffer from that inferiority complex which finds expression either in snobbery or in aggressive contempt for breeding. He could meet and mix with men of all stations in life knowing that no man would ever patronise him twice. His maternal grandfather, Dr. Samuel Annesley, was a man of character and education. He was born at Kenilworth in 1620 and educated at Queen's College, Oxford. In 1644 he was ordained chaplain of His Majesty's ship "Globe." He left the Navy and settled at Cliff in Kent in the place of a minister "who had been sequestered for scandalous conduct." The inhabitants were so attached to their sinful leader that they assailed Dr. Annesley on his appearance "with spits, forks and stones." He told them that "Let them use him as they would, he was determined to stay with them till God should fit them by his ministry to profit by one better, who might succeed him; and solemnly declared, that when they became so prepared, he would leave the place." It was therefore not only from his father that John Wesley inherited his courageous contempt for opposition.

Dr. Annesley was ejected from his vicarage by the Act of Uniformity and became a Non-Conformist.

Like John Wesley he lived and died a poor man, and like John Wesley he left very little to his heirs. Here is an extract from his will:

"Of what I shall leave behind me, I make this short disposal,—

"My just debts being paid, I give to each of my children one shilling, and all the rest to be equally divided between my son Benjamin Annesley, my daughter Judith Annesley, and my daughter Ann Annesley, whom I make my Executors of this my last Will and Testament; revoking all former, and confirming this with my hand and seal this 29. March, 1693."

VI

The Mother of the Wesleys had no claims to great beauty, but her features were good and her figure slight and graceful. Her face was grave and thoughtful, her expression serene rather than vivacious. We have all met women who could sail into a drawing room wearing a dowdy frock and last year's hat, and yet make the most beautifully dressed woman present look undistinguished. Mrs. Wesley must have been that sort of woman. She possessed the inborn dignity which compels respect. She ruled over her family and her household by sheer force of personality. The present age, so we are told, is an age of feminine emancipation. Women have broken the fetters of the past, and have sallied forth free and fearless to claim their rights and to redress their wrongs. And the contrast is pointed by a picture of bygone dames fainting at the sight of a mouse, tapping their "beau" with their fans, archly murmuring, "You Quiz!" and content with the modest rôle of the dainty ·playmate for those hours of ease when the Lords of Creation relax.

But it is doubtful whether the modern woman plays a more important rôle in life than her mother, grandmother and great-grandmother. She can vote, and if her husband has died, been raised to the peerage, or unseated for corruption, she will probably capture the seat in Parliament which he has lost. But few would be rash enough to assert that Parliament has been affected for good or for evil by the women M.Ps.

Women like Mrs. Wesley have exerted a far greater influence on the destinies of the race, an influence all the more potent because it does not depend on legal right or political privileges.

Mrs. Wesley was not, of course, a Xantippe, and her husband was far from being the hen-pecked spouse of the comic stage. The alliance was never endangered by the violation of those spheres of influence established less by formal treaty than by tacit understanding. No married life is unclouded, but the storms were shortlived, for both Wesley and his wife were ready, not only to defend their own territory, but equally quick to retreat when they had been caught trespassing.

Mrs. Wesley's sympathies, to quote one instance, were Jacobean, but when she refused to join in the prayers for the Hanoverian King, her husband settled the issue with a decisive stroke. "Sukey," he said, "if we are to have two kings, we must have two beds." Samuel did not have a monopoly in this matter of issuing ultimatums. He was once absent for some weeks in London, and his wife decided to supplement the parish services by personal ministrations. The curate who was left in charge of Wesley's two parishes was a poor preacher and an indifferent pastor. Mrs. Wesley organized the services in the vicarage, read a sermon and said the prayers. The curate scented danger in this feminine diarchy and appealed by letter to the absent Vicar. He complained that Mrs. Wesley was setting up an irregular conventicle. Samuel Wesley supported the curate, and Mrs. Wesley replied with a cogent defence of her action.

"If you do, after all," she concluded, "think fit to dissolve the assembly, do not tell me that you desire me to do it, for that would not satisfy my conscience. Send me your positive command in such full and express terms as may absolve me from the guilt and punishment of neglecting the opportunity of doing good when you and I shall appear before the great and awful Tribunal of our Lord Jesus Christ."

The "positive commands" were withheld, and the irregular conventicle continued until Samuel Wesley returned.

John Wesley was his mother's son, and it was from Susannah, rather than from Samuel Wesley, that Methodism received its imprint and traces its descent.

Samuel Wesley was a devout Christian and a faithful shepherd of his flock, but it was from his mother that John inherited his sense of vocation.

It was said of Manning that the word "sacerdos" was written on his brow. The same could have been said of John Wesley.

There are men who bear this stamp from birth, men who seem set apart from their fellows to bear witness to the unseen, conscripts of the Most High, dedicated to His service as the one compelling preoccupation for every waking moment. Such was John Wesley.

His mother was one of Nature's Methodists. It was from her he inherited his executive gifts, his methodical genius for making the best of poor material. The care which Mrs. Wesley displayed in organizing the scanty resources of the Epworth vicarage so that "strictly speaking nobody did want for bread" was inherited by her son. From his mother John Wesley inherited his iron will. He had none of his father's sense of humour, but he had his mother's sense of irony, which is as common as humour is rare among great religious leaders. The man whom fate has selected for religious leadership is indeed unlikely to succeed if his sense of vocation is disturbed by a sense of humour. He must never for a moment doubt the importance of his mission, or his own supreme fitness to impress his gospel on his generation. For humour is an elfin sprite which pokes fun at movements and men, and which loves to insinuate subtle doubts as to the supreme importance of anything or anybody. The man whose emotional reactions are complicated by humour is apt to suspect his own credentials as a prophet of the Most High. And such suspicion is fatal to effectiveness.

Irony, on the other hand, is an asset to the prophet, for it helps him to see life *sub specie aeternitatis,* and to detect the folly of attaching undue importance to the little things which bulk so large in little lives. Irony exalts the eternal by emphasising the absurdity of the ephemeral. Humour derogates from the eternal by suggesting that there is a funny side even to eternity.

We find no traces of humour in Mrs. Wesley's letters and very few in John Wesley's journal, but we find abundant evidence of irony. Here, for instance, is Mrs. Wesley's account of Archbishop Sharp's visit to their vicarage.

"Tell me, Mrs. Wesley," said Archbishop Sharp, "whether you ever really wanted bread."

"My Lord," replied Mrs. Wesley, "I will freely own to your Grace that, strictly speaking, I never did want bread. But then, I had so much care to get it before it was eat, and to pay for it after, as has often made it very unpleasant to me. And I think to have bread on such terms is the next degree of wretchedness to having none at all."

"You are certainly in the right," replied his Lordship, and made her a handsome present, which she had "reason to believe afforded him comfortable reflections before his exit."

John Wesley and his mother were true children of the eighteenth century, in their distrust of emotionalism and in their suspicion of fine talk.

John Wesley was a grave, reserved, little man, donnish in appearance and in tastes, an Evangelist on whom Oxford had set her seal. The contrast between Wesley and another great Oxonian Methodist is interesting. Whatever manner Whitefield had, it was certainly not the Oxford manner. He had the cheerful vitality and the unabashed emotionalism of the lower orders from which he sprang. Oxford neither made nor marred him. Wesley was a gentleman by birth, and in spite of democratic sympathies, he never lost the hall-mark of the scholar and the gentleman. Facts change, fashions change. The trim and modish landscape gardening which delighted our eighteenth century forebears finds little favour in our eyes. The romantic revival restored Gothic to its pride of place, not only in architecture but in scenery, for the beauty of mountain scenery, a discovery of the Romantic revival, is in essence Gothic.

Each age has its qualities. The restraint of the Parthenon and the luxuriant beauty of Gothic and Baroque architecture satisfy different aesthetic needs. The eighteenth century, classic rather than Gothic, emphasised the importance of restraint, of balance and of proportion. And it is to the eighteenth century that we owe many of our most enduring characteristics. The English reserve, or "phlegm" as our Latin friends term it, is an inheritance from the days when "enthusiasm" was a term of abuse. Even the Romantic revival owed much of its success to the tradition of restraint which lingered on into the nineteenth century, and which prevented sentiment degenerating into sentimentalism. The English are an emotional race, but they learned from their eighteenth century forebears that emotion obeys the law of diminishing returns, and that the most moving effects in prose and in poetry are only produced with a due economy of emotional appeal.

Biographers of Wesley have been so concerned to prove that Mrs. Wesley was a good woman that they have forgotten that Mrs. Wesley was a good writer. And good writers are even rarer than good women. Her journal and her letters were not written for publication, and they betray no conscious striving for literary effect. She wrote down her own creed and her own reasons for that creed and produced passages which ought to have found a place in any representative anthology of eighteenth century prose. Characteristic of the eighteenth century in their sober tone and temper, all her writings are marked by perfect balance of phrase, and by unconscious and unforced rhythm of expression. No colour, no high notes, but an easy effortless mastery of the written word. They prove once again that Greek restraint can be as potent in its effect as the more luxuriant appeal of unfettered emotion. Let me quote one example. John Wesley had expressed in a letter his affection for his mother in language which to the severe taste of the day seemed suspiciously enthusiastic. He announced that he could not face the prospect of surviving her. Mrs. Wesley replied with a grave and tender rebuke.

"You did well to correct that fond desire of dying before me; since you do not know what work God may have for you to do ere you leave the world. And besides, I ought surely to have the preeminence in point of time,

and go to rest before you. Whether you could see me
die without any emotions of grief I know not; perhaps
you could; it is what I have often desired of the children,
that they would not weep at our parting, and so make
death more uncomfortable than it would otherwise be to
me. If you or any other of my children were like to reap
any spiritual advantage by being with me at my exit, I
should be glad to have you with me. But as I have
been an unprofitable servant, during the course of a long
life, I have no reason to hope for so great an honour, so
high a favour, as to be employed in doing our Lord any
service in the article of death. It were well if you spake
prophetically, and that joy and hope might have the
ascendant over the other passions of my soul in that important hour. Yet I dare not presume nor do I despair,
but rather leave it to our Almighty Saviour to do with
me both in life and in death what He pleases, for I have
no choice!"

Set this letter with its unstudied effects and easy effortless rhythm beside the acknowledged masterpieces of English prose, masterpieces written for publication by men
conscious of their gifts and interested in their command
over words. Mrs. Wesley's letter, composed for no other
eyes than her son's, is at ease in such company.

VII

In her later years, Mrs. Wesley summarised briefly
the principles which had guided her in bringing up her
family.

"When turned a year old, (and some before), they were
taught to fear the rod, and to cry softly, by which means
they escaped abundance of correction which they might otherwise have had; and that most odious noise of the crying of
children was rarely heard in the house: but the family

usually lived in as much quietness as if there had not been a child among them."

Nor were the little Wesleys encouraged to be dainty about their food. The financial resources of the vicarage did not lend themselves to dietetic experiments. Wesley's children ate what was set before them with the admirable result that when they were ill, they swallowed without demur the most unpleasant medicines, "though some of them would presently throw it up." "This I mention," adds Mrs. Wesley, "to shew that a person may be taught anything, though it be never so much against his stomach."

Wesley's formal manner may well have been acquired during his childhood. The Wesley children were never permitted to call each other by their proper names "without the addition of brother and sister." They were taught to treat each other with a nice regard for their respective rights. Promises had to be strictly observed and "a gift once bestowed, the right passed away from the donor, be not resumed, but left to the disposal of him to whom it was given; unless it were conditional, and the condition of the obligation not performed." We are not told whether the exchange of a doll against a white mouse was duly regularised by a formal contract.

"None of the children," Mrs. Wesley tells us, "were taught to read until they were five years old. One day was allowed the child wherein to learn its letters; and each of them did in that time know all its letters, great and small, except Molly and Nancy, who were a day and a half before they knew them perfectly; for which I thought them very dull." After learning their letters the children were taught to spell out the first chapter of Genesis, with the happy result that long before they were six years of age they were able to read. The working hours were from nine until twelve, and from two until five, six hours of school. "And it is almost incredible," writes Mrs. Wesley, "what a child may be taught in a quarter of a year, by a vigorous application, if it have but a tolerable capacity, and good health."

Good health was, doubtless, a factor of some importance, for six hours a day seems rather long for a child of five, and it is perhaps not surprising that of Mrs. Wesley's nineteen children, ten died in infancy.

John Wesley, himself, was the fifteenth child of his mother. He was born on June 28th, 1703. We know little of his childhood, but the little that we do know fits into the picture which Wesley himself has painted in his Journal. Even as a child, Wesley seems to have guided his life by reason. "Sweetheart," said Samuel Wesley to his wife, "I profess I think our boy Jack would not attend to the most pressing necessities of nature unless he could give a reason for it." John Wesley to the life!

The child, no less than the man, seems to have had no moods and no unregulated impulses.

VIII

John Wesley was sent to Charterhouse at the age of ten and a half, his admission to that famous school being due to the friendly services of the Duke of Buckingham.

In those days, life at a public school was Spartan and severe, but Wesley bore the customary hardships bravely, and the affection which he retained through life for his old school was a tribute all the more striking because it was not dictated by convention; for the public school spirit had not been invented in the eighteenth century.

The older boys at Charterhouse confiscated the younger boys' allowance of meat. As a result, Wesley lived on bread during his earlier years at Charterhouse, and was, perhaps, none the worse for this simple diet.

Of this period in his life, John Wesley wrote in later years, "Outward restraints being removed, I was much more negligent than before even of outward duties, and almost continually guilty of outward sins which I knew to be such, though they were not scandalous in the eyes of the world. However, I still read the Scriptures and said my prayers morning and evening. And what I now hoped to be saved by, was—1. Not being so bad as other people. 2. Having still a kindness for religion. And, 3, reading the Bible, going to church and saying my prayers."

Wesley was, perhaps, a little too anxious to believe that he, like many of the great saints, had passed through a stage of lurid wickedness. "Terrible is the danger," remarks his biographer, the Reverend Luke Tyerman, "when a child leaves a pious home for a public school. John Wesley entered Charterhouse a saint. He left it a sinner."

This sounds interesting, but neither Wesley nor Tyerman produces any evidence to support this theory.

Wesley, according to a story almost certainly apocryphal, spent most of his time with his juniors, and on being asked why, replied, "Better to rule in Hell than to serve in Heaven."

John Wesley never suffered from a sense of inferiority as far as his fellow beings were concerned. He abased himself before God, but not before men. Humility was never his failing, though pride may have been his danger. It is the vain rather than the proud man who prefers to rule in hell.

There is another story of Wesley in his youth, which is true and which certainly rings true. Wesley had called on the famous Dr. Sacheverell with a letter of introduction from his father.

"I found him," said Wesley who told the story many

years later to Alexander Knox, "as tall as a maypole and as proud as an archbishop. I was a very little fellow. He said, 'You are too young to go to the university. You can know no Greek and Latin yet; go back to school.' I looked at him as David looked at Goliath and despised him in my heart. I thought, if I do not know Greek and Latin better than you I ought to go back to school indeed. I left him and neither entreaties nor commands could have brought me back to him." There speaks the real Wesley. "I looked at him as David looked at Goliath." It was thus that Wesley looked at the world.

IX

When Wesley was at school there were certain strange happenings at the Epworth rectory.

During 1716, the family at Epworth were constantly being disturbed by loud knocks which were supposed to be due to an invisible spirit. The children soon learned to regard the invisible spirit with good-humoured contempt. "Old Jeffrey" as they called him was a Jacobite, and he was never so obstreperous as during family prayers. When Samuel Wesley read the prayer for the Hanoverian King, a knocking began all round the room, and a thundering knock attended the "Amen." John Wesley has given us an account of these phenomena: "Old Jeffrey did not confine himself to noises. Sometimes he would playfully thrust back the door of the Vicar's study, as the Vicar entered, with such violence as had been likely to have thrown him down." Nancy Wesley used to hear old Jeffrey behind her when she swept the chambers, only "she thought he might have done it for her and saved her the trouble."

"By this time," wrote Wesley, "the family was so accustomed to these noises that they gave them little attention. A gentle tapping at their bedheads used to begin between nine and ten at night. They then commonly said to each other: 'Jeffrey is coming, it is time to go to sleep.' "

The whole story is puzzling, and admits of no easy explanation.

To the Spiritualist, of course, the Epworth ghost is one of the best authenticated cases of the poltergeist phenomenon. The poltergeist, according to the Spiritualists, is a low-grade spirit with a half-wit intelligence who takes a childish delight in throwing furniture about and in making meaningless noises.

There is no *a priori* reason why spiritual beings, both inferior and superior to man in their intelligence should not exist in the universe, and there is no scientific law which forbids us to believe in the existence of the poltergeist. On the other hand, it is quite possible that science may discover a plausible and non-supernatural explanation for the phenomena such as those which disturbed the Epworth household, phenomena which cannot be easily explained either as the result of fraud or hallucination. Meanwhile, the supernatural explanation, though far from proven, is, at least, plausible, and it is no reflection on Wesley's intelligence, as certain writers seem to suggest, that he accepted without demur the supernatural explanation of phenomena for which no modern writer has been able to produce an equally plausible natural explanation.

CHAPTER II

WESLEY AT OXFORD

JOHN WESLEY left Charterhouse with an Exhibition of forty pounds per annum—and was entered at Christ Church, Oxford, on June 24th, 1720.

According to the late Mr. A. D. Godley, the intellectual life of Oxford was never at a lower ebb than between the years 1714 to 1760.

There were no Honours Schools and no inducements for research. Mr. Godley sums up the situation as follows:

"The eighteenth century had but little adventitious stimulus to learning. It was a period of conventions. Oxford gave her degrees really for residence, on the basis of the plausible and pleasing convention that Universities, being places of study, are inhabited by students, and that residence implied the habit of serious study. No doubt this attractive theory was at variance with the obvious facts of life; still, those who entertained it may at least have the credit of maintaining a theory which is nothing if not respectable, and the few who did actually try to verify it must be the more laudable for the lack of incentive. In the absence of honour examinations and even of pass examinations other than merely farcical, they did nevertheless teach and learn." [1]

Gibbon entered Oxford some forty years later. Here is his verdict on the university:

"To the University of Oxford I acknowledge no obligation; and she will as cheerfully renounce me for a son, as I am

[1] A. D. Godley's "Oxford in the Eighteenth Century."

23

willing to disclaim her for a mother. I spent fourteen months at Magdalen College; they proved the fourteen months the most idle and unprofitable of my whole life. . . . The fellows or monks of my time were decent easy men, who supinely enjoyed the gifts of the founder; their days were filled by a series of uniform employments; the chapel and the hall, the coffee-house and the common room, till they retired weary and well satisfied, to a long slumber. From the toil of reading, or thinking, or writing, they had absolved their conscience; and the first shoots of learning and ingenuity withered on the ground, without yielding any fruits to the owners or the public. As a gentleman-commoner, I was admitted to the society of the fellows, and fondly expected that some questions of literature would be the amusing and instructive topics of their discourse. Their conversation stagnated in a round of college business, Tory politics, personal anecdotes, and private scandal: their dull and deep potations excused the brisk intemperance of youth."

Little is known of Wesley's undergraduate life. In spite of his limited financial resources, he does not seem to have lived the life of a recluse. A Christchurch contemporary described him as "a very sensible, active collegian, baffling every man by the subtleties of his logic, and laughing at them for being easily routed; a young fellow of the finest classical tastes, of the most liberal and manly sentiments, gay and sprightly with a turn for wit and humour."

We owe to Dr. Whitehead a tantalising glimpse of a Wesley very different from the Wesley of the Holy Club. Dr. Whitehead unearthed a translation which Wesley had made of a Latin poem, a poem in honour of Chloe's flea. As Juno had a favourite peacock, such is the theme of this edifying ode, and Venus a favourite dove, so Cloe had a favourite flea whose bliss it was to crawl about her person.

Dr. Whitehead was severely criticised by the Methodists for publishing this effusion. The Reverend Luke

Tyerman on the other hand, whose well-known Life of Wesley appeared in 1870, was grateful to Dr. Whitehead for this timely disclosure. The vital importance of conversion is the key-stone of Methodist doctrine, or at least, of Methodist doctrine as preached in the days of Tyerman. It was, therefore, essential for Wesley, as the founder of Methodism, to exhibit in his own person the miracle of an unimpeachable conversion. Now conversion is only impressive against a background of a lurid past. In order, therefore, to glorify the doctrine which Wesley preached, it was necessary to libel the life which Wesley led. One sympathises with Mr. Tyerman, for no man ever worked harder to discover a background of sin, and no man ever built up a more impressive case on weaker evidence.

Wesley, it is true, wrote a poem about a flea. This is bad. But worse is to follow. Wesley is convicted out of his own mouth.

"I still said my prayers," wrote Wesley as he looked back in later life on his undergraduate days, "both in public and in private, and read with the Scriptures several other books of religion, especially comments on the New Testament. Yet I had not all this while so much as a notion of inward holiness; nay, went on habitually and for the most part very contentedly, in some one or other known sins, though with some intermissions and short struggles, especially before and after holy Communion, which I was obliged to receive thrice a year."

Wesley, like Mr. Tyerman, no doubt felt it desirable to emphasise the importance of his conversion. Dr. Piette pointed out the interesting parallel between the phrases he uses to describe his iniquitous life at Charterhouse, and those in which he painted in sombre colours his undergraduate career. And, as Dr. Piette remarks, this verdict would have been more impressive if Wesley had produced some detailed evidence as to his alleged career of sin.

All the available evidence proves that Wesley as an undergraduate lived a life of self-discipline and self-denial. His scholarship was worth no more than forty pounds a year, and the fact that he contrived to complete his university career, to keep his terms and to take his degree, is a tribute not only to his heroic family at Epworth, who stinted themselves of everything that makes life worth living in order to keep him at Oxford, but also to John Wesley himself who must have kept down his expenses to the irreducible minimum. He worked hard, he had no vices, and he gave every evidence of being deeply religious. Poor Mr. Tyerman!

In 1725, Wesley began seriously to consider the problem of taking orders. His father urged delay, and warned him against entering the priestly office "just to have a piece of bread," but his mother with a deeper understanding of her son warmly approved of his decision.

During 1725, Wesley read "The Imitation of Christ" and Jeremy Taylor's "Holy Living and Dying." He revolted against the predestinarian theology of the "Imitation," and put his difficulties to his mother in a series of letters. A letter from his mother provided him with most of the arguments which he used many years later in a sermon which he preached at the height of his controversy with Whitefield on the subject of predestination.

II

In 1725, Wesley began to keep his famous diary.

Wesley wrote both diaries and journals; the distinction is important. Wesley published long extracts from his Journals which were, in the main, written for publication, but he took elaborate precautions to protect the privacy of his diaries.

The diaries were written partly in cipher, partly in abbreviated longhand, and partly in shorthand. They were written for his eyes alone, and were intended as a check on his conduct. Had Wesley been a Catholic, his diary would have provided him with the material for his weekly confessions. Day by day he recorded in intimate detail, his own shortcomings from the rigorous standard of conduct carefullly defined in the diary itself.

The first diary opens with the following page of rules and resolutions written down in Wesley's exquisite penmanship.

A GENERAL RULE IN ALL ACTIONS OF LIFE

Whenever you are to do an action, consider how God did or would do the like, and do you imitate His example.

GENERAL RULES OF EMPLOYING TIME

1. Begin and end every day with God; and sleep not immoderately.
2. Be diligent in your calling.
3. Employ all spare hours in religion; as able.
4. All holidays (holy-days).
5. Avoid drunkards and busybodies.
6. Avoid curiosity, and all useless employments and knowledge.
7. Examine yourself every night.
8. Never on any account pass a day without setting aside at least an hour for devotion.
9. Avoid all manner of passion.

Friday, March 26. I found a great many unclean thoughts arise in prayer (or devotions), and discovered these temptations to it:

    a. Too much addicting myself to a light behaviour at all times.

    b. Listening too much to idle talk, or reading vain plays or books.

    c. Idleness, and lastly—

Want of devotion—consideration in whose presence I am.

From which I perceive it is necessary
  a. To labour for a grave and modest carriage;
  b. To avoid vain and light company; and
  c. To entertain awful apprehensions of the presence of God.
  d. To avoid idleness, freedom with women, and high-seasoned meats;
  e. To resist the very beginnings of lust, not by arguing with, but by thinking no more of it or by immediately going into company; lastly

To use frequent and fervent Prayer.

GENERAL RULES AS TO INTENTION

  1. In every action reflect on your end;
  2. Begin every action in the name of the Father, the Son, and the Holy Ghost;
  3. Begin every important work with prayer;
  4. Do not leave off a duty because you are tempted in it."

In the first year following his ordination, Wesley adopted a method of self-examination, with the help of his diary, which was probably the model from which the Methodist Band Meetings developed.

"His standard," writes Mr. Curnock in his masterly introduction to the Standard edition of John Wesley's Journal, "takes the form of rule and resolution. Sometimes, both at Oxford and Wroote he holds a Saturday night 'private band' with his own soul; he reads his resolutions, makes rigid inquest upon his own thoughts, upon his conversation, studies, and amusements during the week; he brings all his most secret motives and emotions to the test, making confession to himself at the bar of his own conscience. Questions and confessions are written in the remorseful Diary. He binds his tortured soul to the horns of the altar, and the flames play around it. He has no mercy upon himself. Not once does he excuse himself or enter a single plea in extenuation. When the record is more humiliating than usual, his only remedy is a pathetic strengthening of the outward standard or a new emphasis added to an old rule, and always with a cry to God in the sacred tongue (Κύριε Βοήθει). More law, more methods; a new cord to the flagellant's whip, or a new knot in the old cord. As we read from page to page we expect to find this self-upbraiding candidate for saintliness in the grip of despair. Nothing, however, daunts him. Saturday night finds him in the depths, but on Sunday morning he is bravely beginning again. Defeat and failure always seem to stimulate Wesley to new effort."

Wesley was constitutionally lazy. He liked his bed, but he trained himself to rise at 4 o'clock every day, and seldom rose later than 5 o'clock, and when his diary records as a black mark against his record "immoderate sleep" or "intemperate sleep," we may deduce that Wesley so far forgot himself as to get out of bed at 5.30 or 6 a. m.

Wesley used his diary not only as a check on his spiritual progress, but as an index of his mental and physical fitness. By the help of this remorseless record he trained himself never to waste a minute of time or a pound of energy.

Here is a specimen page from his diary during a voyage to America:

Diary on Board the *Simmonds.*

1735.   Saturday, October 18.

4.30.   Dressed; prayed; began Genesis 6. Deacon ¾; writ to Varanese.

7.   Miss Sally Andrews, Sister Emilia.

8.   Talked; writ to Salmon and

9.   Clayton.

10.   Falcon with Tackner; baptized him!

11.   Delamotte senior; read Whiston's Catechism.
1.30.   Dinner.
2.30.   On Board. Conversed.
3.30.   German. 4 cabin.
4.   Writ to Sister Kezia, Mr. Vernon, Mr. Hutche-
         son, my Mother.
5.   Rivington.
5.30.   Talked.
6.15.   Devotion.
6.30.   Sung.
7.   German with Tackner.
7.   Conversed.
9¼.   Prayer.

Wesley was not born with a strong constitution, and
in middle life he all but died of consumption. His marvellous vitality even in old age, is a striking tribute to the
virtues of simple diet and asceticism. For the asceticism
revealed in every page of his diary forged the weapons
which Wesley needed in his long campaign, the weapon of
a mind which never slackened in its concentrated energy,
and of a body which never surrendered to fatigue or
discomfort.

Wesley was elected a Probationary Fellow of Lincoln
College, Oxford, during March 1726. The gallant old
man at Epworth had only five pounds left to keep his
family until after the harvest, but the good news of his
son's election was all the reward that he needed for the
privations which he had endured to send his son to Oxford.

"What will be my own fate, God only knows," he
wrote. "Sed passi graviora. Wherever I am, my Jack is
fellow of Lincoln." Wesley owed a great debt to Lincoln,
for he continued to draw his emoluments as a Fellow until
he married twenty-five years later.

Lincoln College was founded in 1427 by Richard Fleming, Bishop of Lincoln. Fleming had been suspected of sympathising with the Lollards, but the Committee appointed by the King acquitted him of heresy, and shortly afterwards his orthodoxy was officially recognised by the great prize of the bishopric of Lincoln.[2] It was, perhaps, to settle once and for all any lingering doubts which might still remain of his orthodoxy that Fleming founded Lincoln to be "a little college of theologians to help in ruining heresy." An oath against heresy was exacted from its Fellows, who were bound to take priest's orders.

Little did Fleming dream that the "little college of theologians" which he had founded "to help in ruining heresy" was destined to send forth into the world an evangelist far greater than Wycliffe, and far more dangerous to that older faith which Lincoln College was founded to preserve.

Wesley settled down to his academic duties with characteristic energy.

"Leisure and I," he wrote to his mother, "have parted company," and as Mr. Winchester remarks, "they never met again." Mondays and Tuesdays he gave to Greek and Latin; Wednesdays to logic and ethics; Thursdays to Hebrew and Arabic; Fridays to metaphysics and natural philosophy; Saturdays, to oratory and poetry; Sundays to divinity. He was appointed Greek lecturer and Moderator of the classes, a position which involved taking the chair at the daily debates which were an important feature in the intellectual life of Lincoln.

Wesley was a born logician, and he looked back with real pleasure to these debates in later life.

"I could not avoid," he wrote, "acquiring hereby some

[2] "John Wycliffe," by Herbert B. Workman, D.Litt. Vol. ii, page 364.

degree of expertness in arguing, and especially in discovering and pointing out well-covered fallacies. I have since found abundant reason to praise God for giving me this honest art."

Wesley, perhaps, was always a little too deferential to a syllogism, but his logical training undoubtedly saved him from many pitfalls. Many of the leaders of the Evangelical revival, notably Whitefield, would, perhaps have been all the better for a little study of "this honest art."

III

Wesley left Oxford during August 1727, in order to help his father who had charge, not only of the parish of Epworth, but also of the neighbouring parish of Wroote. His father was feeling his age, and John Wesley agreed to take up his residence at Wroote.

Wroote lies in a dismal country which at that time was surrounded by bogs, and for many months of the year was only accessible by boat. Wesley's brilliant sister Hetty summed up his new parishioners, in two stinging lines:

> "High birth and virtue equally they scorn,
> As asses dull, on dunghills born."

Wesley was neither conspicuously successful nor an obvious failure during the two years that he passed at Wroote, but it was probably with profound relief that he received from the Rector of Lincoln College the summons back to Oxford.

William Law's "Serious Call" which was published in 1728 profoundly influenced Wesley. This book convinced him that it was impossible to be "a half-Christian." He did not realise that the Church would soon be reduced to an exclusive "Holy Club" if "half-Christians" were refused admission.

Wesley, in the Oxford period, was, perhaps, too much of an ascetic. His religion was too solitary, and too selfish to be effective. He quietly rebuffed the approaches of those who were not in complete sympathy with his ideals. "I resolved," he wrote, "to have only such acquaintances that would help me on my way to Heaven." He was courteous to callers, but he did not return their visits; with the natural result that before long half-Christians left him alone. And yet he does not seem to have been unpopular with his colleagues. A Lincoln Fellow wrote to him during his long absence at Wroote, and commented on his reputation for courtesy, and expressed his regret at the absence of so congenial a companion.

CHAPTER III

THE OXFORD METHODISTS

CHARLES WESLEY, who might perhaps be described as the Founder of Oxford Methodism, was born on December 18th, 1707. Four years younger than his brother John, he was the eighteenth child of his parents.

Charles Wesley entered Westminster school at the age of nine. His elder brother Samuel had married the daughter of the Reverend John Berry, who kept a boarding house for Westminster boys, and thanks to this marriage he was able to offer Charles a home and education. A little later, Charles became a King's Scholar, thereby relieving his father of any further expense.

The best-known incident recorded of his schooldays was a fight in which he championed a small Scotch boy, John Murray, who was being bullied by the other boys for being a Jacobite. Charles, like his brother Samuel, who lost the headmastership of Westminster for his convictions, was a keen Tory and a High Churchman. John Murray, later Lord Mansfield, often referred to this fight in after years.

Charles Wesley was Captain of the school in 1725. After leaving Westminster, he was called upon to make a decision which was destined to have a far-reaching effect on the history of England.

Garrett Wesley, a member of the Irish branch of this ancient family which traces back its pedigree to the Battle of Senlac, had no heir. He wrote to the Vicar of Epworth,

34

his remote kinsman, and asked him if he had a son called Charles, and offering, if such were the case, to adopt him as his heir.

During Charles's career at Westminster, Garrett Wesley helped regularly with his school expenses, and at the close of his school career Charles Wesley received a visit from Garrett Wesley, who repeated his offer to make him his heir.

To the younger son of a poverty-stricken parson, this offer must have seemed very tempting. He appealed to his father for advice, but his father refused in any way to influence his decision. Charles thought the matter over and finally declined the offer.

Garrett Wesley then adopted a maternal kinsman, Richard Colley, who was descended in the female line from the Wesleys. Richard Colley assumed the Wesley name, and was raised to the peerage as Lord Mornington. He was the grandfather of Arthur Wesley, the great Duke of Wellington, who in 1805 decided to resume the original form of the family name—Wellesley. The Duke of Wellington had Wesley blood in his veins, and on the female line was closely related to the family by frequent intermarriages.

Had Charles Wesley accepted his kinsman's offer, there might have been no Methodists, and there would certainly have been no Iron Duke. Seldom has a schoolboy made a more momentous choice.

II

Charles Wesley left Westminster with a scholarship for Christ Church in the autumn of 1726. He revelled in the freedom of Oxford after the restrictions of Westminster. His brother was a little perturbed. There was no vice in the boy, for Charles's amusements were harmless enough, but life was short and eternity was long, and to his sober, serious brother, Charles seemed to be drifting gaily through life without a thought for ultimate realities. John remonstrated with Charles, and Charles replied petulantly, "Would you have me become a saint all at once?" Perhaps he realised that his revolt was foredoomed to failure. Perhaps his petulance was provoked by the thought that he was merely a prisoner on parole, and that the rollicking happiness of carefree youth was a phase which would pass all too soon. John was then, as always, the steadying influence on his life. "Charles was as eager and abrupt in manner as his brother was calm and deliberate. He would burst in on John in his rooms at Lincoln, recite scraps of poetry, turn over the papers on the desk, peer among them with his near-sighted eyes for what he wanted, and pour out a stream of questions and remarks without waiting for the answers. He was orderly in nothing but in his handwriting, which was exquisite. All the more, therefore, he looked up to his grave, self-controlled, and methodical senior." [1]

One of the original Oxford Methodists, John Gambold, described Charles Wesley as follows:

"I never observed a person have a more real deference for another than he constantly had for his brother. Indeed, he followed his brother entirely. Could I describe one of them I should describe both. And therefore I shall say no more of Charles than that he was a man made for friendship, who by his cheerfulness and vivacity would refresh his friend's heart, with attentive consideration would enter into and better all his concerns."

At the end of Charles's first year John Wesley left Oxford for the parish of Wroote. But though he had gone his influence remained, and indeed it was perhaps more potent because of his very absence.

[1] "Charles Wesley: A Study," by D. M. Jones.

At the beginning of January 1729, Charles wrote a letter to his brother, a letter which was the foundation stone of a partnership which was only dissolved by death.

"God has thought fit (it may be to increase my wariness) to deny me at present your company and assistance. It is through Him strengthening me I trust to maintain my ground till we meet. And I hope that neither before nor after that time I shall relapse into my former state of insensibility. It is through your means, I firmly believe, that God will establish what He hath begun in me; and there is no other person I would so willingly have to be the instrument of good to me as you. It is owing in great measure to somebody's prayers (my mother's most likely) that I am come to think as I do, for I cannot myself tell how or when I awoke out of my lethargy, except that it was not long after you went away."

III

John Wesley had to pass through a phase of solitary religion. Charles was essentially a "clubbable man," and the "Holy Club" was the natural result of his religious activities.

Among his friends there were three or four young men who shared his views on the importance of regular attendance at the Sacrament. This little group decided to communicate weekly in the cathedral at Oxford, which is also used by Christ Church as a College chapel. Charles and his friends did not parade their religion, but the spectacle of young men communicating regularly, treating the statutes of the university with respect, and displaying an unprecedented devotion to their studies was bound to invite comment. A cheerful undergraduate of "the House" caught sight of the little group on their way to the cathedral and exclaimed, "Here is a new set of

Methodists sprung up." The word "Methodist" occurs
in seventeenth century literature, but like many other
famous words, only caught on when applied as a nickname. It was many years before John Wesley could bring
himself to use this nickname without a qualification, but
he tells us that the nickname caught on at once and spread
all over the university.

IV

On October 21st, 1729, Dr. Morley, the Rector of
Lincoln, informed John Wesley that it had been decided
that the junior fellows of the college must, in future,
attend to their duties in person, and he sent Wesley a
cordial invitation to return to Oxford.

John received a warm welcome from the members of
the Holy Club.

"They had thought of him," writes Dr. W. H. Hutton,
"in his country retirement as the young Oriel men a
century later thought of the brilliant John Keble working in the villages between Cotswold and Thames. And
John came at once to be the director of the Holy Club,
as it was already called. His accession to it was like that
of Pusey, to the writers of the "Tracts for the Times."
For he came with a weight of reputation and authority
which the younger men could not possess." [2]

From the fens of Lincolnshire, Wesley returned with
a new attitude to religion. He had hoped to save his soul
as a recluse, only to learn from a "serious person" whom
he had met by chance in the country that he was on the
wrong road to salvation.

"Sir, you wish to serve God and go to Heaven," the
"serious person" had said, "remember you cannot serve

[2] "John Wesley," by W. H. Hutton. D.D., Dean of Winchester.

Him alone, you must try to find companions or make them. The Bible knows nothing of solitary religion."

A few words will sometimes alter a man's whole life. These words sunk into Wesley and became the motto of his life.

V

Oxford continued to find new nicknames for the Methodist group, most of which such as "The Sacramentarians," the "Bible Bigots" and "Bible Moths" enjoyed only an ephemeral success, but the "Holy Club" was a happy hit, and like "Methodists" spread rapidly through the university.

In 1730, William Morgan, a member of the Holy Club, visited a man in the Castle who had been condemned to death for killing his wife. He was impressed by the terrible condition of the prisoners, and he persuaded the Wesleys and other members of the Holy Club to join him in a regular gaol ministration.

This good work among the prisoners was followed by charitable work among the poor of Oxford. The Holy Club set up a school, and helped by voluntary contributions, they clothed the children and paid the mistress. Wesley was careful not to trespass on the preserves of others, and obtained the permission of the Bishop to preach in the prison, and of the parish priests to visit the poor of the parishes under their charge.

John Gambold of Christchurch, a member of the Holy Club, has recorded his view that the Methodists were unpopular not so much because of their frequent communions and fasting, but because of their charitable ministrations to the poor and the sick. Oxford began by laughing at the Holy Club, but their amusement gradually turned to alarm. A nameless gentleman of whom all we know for certain is that he was "a gentleman eminent for learning and well-esteemed for piety" was much distressed by the habits his nephew had contracted. The nephew was a member of the Holy Club and was alleged to attend Holy Communion every week. The uncle threatened to turn him out of doors, and finally took him by the throat and shook him violently. This treatment seems to have been at least partly successful, and was no doubt followed by other gentlemen "well-esteemed for piety."

This private suasion was supplemented by quasi-official action. Early in 1731, a Meeting of some of the senior members of one of the colleges was held, the business before the Meeting being the necessary action to be taken in order to check the distressing outbreak of "enthusiasm." The University learned with pleasure that the Censors had decided "to blow up the Godly Club." But alas, the rumour proved to be unfounded.

John Wesley's father was wholeheartedly in sympathy with his sons and gave them good advice. "Bear no more sail than is necessary, but steer steady." John wrote to his brother Samuel at Westminster, who replied judiciously:

"I do not like your being called *a club;* that name is really calculated to do mischief. But the other charge of *enthusiasm* can weigh with none, but such as drink away their senses, or never had any. For surely activity in social duties, and a strick attendance on the ordained means of grace, are the strongest guards imaginable against it."

In 1732, William Morgan died, yet another blow to the Holy Club. Morgan's father thought that his son's death had been caused by the austerities which he practised as a Methodist.

Wesley's Journal opens with the letter which he addressed to Morgan's father, a letter which contained a convincing defence on the main indictment, and a well-reasoned apology for the Oxford Methodists. Mr. Morgan was persuaded that neither Wesley nor the Holy Club could be blamed for the death of his son, and he gave sincere proof of this belief by entrusting his younger son to Wesley's care at a later date.

The fortunes of the Holy Club varied with the personal attention which Wesley was able to give the Club, and when the Wesleys left Oxford the Club soon expired. The last notable recruit was George Whitefield.

It is not easy to understand the opposition which the Oxford Methodists provoked in Oxford.

As Dr. Godley says:

"The means they employed were what most ages would have called purely beneficent; never, one might have supposed, did any revival lay itself so little open to adverse criticism. There was no vulgarity, no sensational appeal to the emotions of large and excitable audiences—in Oxford, at any rate. All that the Methodists did was to encourage each other to virtuous living and good works. They were diligent in religious observance; they fasted with the over-asceticism of a new enthusiasm; they started schools for the poor, they relieved the sick, they visited the prisoners in jail. And they were consistently and uninterruptedly derided, abused, and even punished. The mass of undergraduate opinion would have none of Methodism. . . . Perhaps we should not judge a learned University by its foolish youth. But the attitude of the authorities towards a wholly blameless and virtuous movement is really not explainable; it seems to justify all the hard things that have been said of the century. . . . The hostility of Oxford to the Wesleyan movement, in its fully developed activity, is easy enough to understand. It is less easy at first sight to account for the intolerance of 1730; yet it was not out of keeping with the narrow formalism and party bitterness of that rather inexcusable period." [3]

[3] "Oxford in the Eighteenth Century," pp. 266–69.

VI

The Holy Club did not entirely monopolise Wesley's interest during his life at Oxford. Shortly after his election as a Fellow of Lincoln, he met Miss Betty Kirkham, the sister of an Oxford friend Robert Kirkham, and the daughter of a clergyman in Staunton. Wesley was soon on terms of intimacy with the family, and it was clear that the family, or at least the young lady's brother, would have welcomed a match.

"Often have you been in the thought of M. B." (Miss Betty), wrote young Kirkham, "which I have curiously observed by her inward smiles and sighs, and by her abrupt expression concerning you. Shall this suffice? I caught her this morning in a humble and devout position on her knees . . . I must conclude, and subscribe myself your most affectionate friend, *and brother, I wish I might write,* Robert Kirkham."

Such a letter would have startled the average young man into a proposal of marriage, or at least, into an abrupt termination of a compromising friendship. But Wesley throughout his life remained deaf to hints of this description. Even Leap Year would have presented no terrors for him. It is recorded of Sir Richard Burton that he was once asked by an anxious parent to define his intentions towards her daughter, and he replied without a moment's hesitation, "My intentions are strictly dishonourable."

Wesley, as we shall see, was quite capable of replying under similar circumstances that his intentions were strictly spiritual.

Wesley continued to correspond with Miss Kirkham for four years, at the end of which time we find Miss Betty Kirkham married to a Mr. Wilson.

The Kirkhams introduced Wesley to one of the most brilliant women of the day. Mrs. Pendarves had been married at the age of eighteen to a gouty old gentleman of sixty who did not long survive his wedding day. She was a niece of Lord Lansdowne and was described by Burke as "the highest-bred woman in the world." In the course of her social career, she met most of the leading figures of the century. Her friendships ranged from Jonathan Swift to Samuel Johnson. She enjoyed the intimate friendship of King George III. Eventually, she married Dr. Delaney, the Dean of Down.

Mrs. Pendarves corresponded with Wesley for many years signing herself "Aspasia," Wesley being "Cyrus" and Betty Kirkham "Varanese." The letters are stilted in expression, and are written with the formal courtesy and sentiment characteristic of the age.

Wesley was very fond of "Aspasia" and "Varanese," but the great love of his life was yet to come.

VII

Wesley was never more completely happy than at Oxford. Oxford gave him a group of friends with like outlook and life, and provided him with ample leisure for study and with ample opportunity for his work of charity.

Nor was this all. Wesley had little aesthetic sense, but though he dismissed Cologne cathedral [4] as "mere heap upon heap, a huge misshapen thing," though he desired that his own chapels should be octagonal in shape in order that the pulpit might be in the centre and the preacher heard in all corners, he could not resist the enchantment of the Oxford towers. "I went to Oxford," he wrote as an old man of seventy-five, "and having an hour

[4] In justice to Wesley, it must be remembered that Cologne cathedral had not been restored in his day, and was little more than a ruin.

to spare, walked to Christ Church for which I cannot but
still retain a peculiar affection. What lovely mansions are
these." Indeed, through life, Oxford was the standard by
which he measured all other places. After describing with
enthusiasm the beauty of some Dutch town which he had
visited at the age of eighty, he adds, "After all, there is
nothing to compare with St. John's or Trinity Gardens,
much less with Magdalen river walk or Christ Church
Meadows."

Wesley's biographers have sometimes tried to minimise
the influence of Oxford in order to emphasise the contrast
between Wesley the High Church don and Wesley the
great evangelist of Methodism. But the attempt to divide
Wesley's life into two parts divided by his conversion in
Aldersgate Street, produces, as we shall see, a false and
foolish dichotomy. Wesley remained to the end an Oxford
Methodist. Oxford had set her seal on him, and none of
Oxford's sons have loved her better.

Towards the end of his long life, when the battle had
been won, when Methodism was firmly established, and
when opposition had virtually ceased, he wrote to his
brother Charles: "I often cry out, Vitae me redde priori:
let me be again an Oxford Methodist!"

VIII

Wesley's love of Oxford was soon to be tested.

His father was drawing to the end of his long life.
He urged John to apply for the living at Epworth, for
there was reason to fear that the living might fall to a
fox-hunting parson. "The prospect of that mighty Nimrod
coming here shocks my soul," wrote his father, "and is
in a fair way to bring down my grey hairs in sorrow to
the grave."

His son produced twenty-six methodical reasons for

staying at Oxford. At Oxford he was undisturbed by
worldly persons and lukewarm Christians. He could be
most holy at Oxford, and could do most to promote holiness in others, and so on and so forth. His father brushed
these reasons aside, and applied the common sense of the
century to his son's arguments:

"Your state of the question and only argument is: The
question is not whether I could do more good to others, there
or here; but whether I could do more good to myself; seeing
wherever I can be most holy myself, there I can most promote holiness in others. But I can improve myself more at
Oxford than at any other place.

To this I answer, first, it is not dear self, but glory of
God, and the different degrees of promoting it, which should
be our main consideration and direction in the choice of any
course of life.

Second. Supposing you could be more holy yourself at Oxford, how does it follow that you could more promote holiness in others there than elsewhere? Have you found many
instances of it, after so many years' hard pain and labour?

Third. I cannot allow austerity, or fasting, considered by
themselves, to be proper acts of holiness, nor am I for a
solitary life. God made us for a social life; we are not to
bury our talent; we are to let our light shine before men,
and that not merely through the chinks of a bushel for fear
the wind should blow it out."

Wesley was torn between his love of Oxford and his
love of his father. He loathed the prospect of returning
to the Lincolnshire fens, and the stubborn Lincolnshire
folk, whose affection he had failed to win during the time
he had been at Wroote. A few weeks before his father's
death, he applied for the living, but too late. The "mighty
Nimrod" got the living, but does not appear to have
troubled the parish with his presence.

Samuel Wesley died in the presence of his two younger
sons, and just before his death he used a phrase which

was destined to play a great rôle in Methodism. Turning to John, he said, "The inward witness, my son, that is the proof, the strongest proof of Christianity," and to his son Charles, "Be steady. The Christian faith will surely revive in this kingdom. You shall see it though I shall not."

CHAPTER IV

GEORGIA

SAMUEL WESLEY had spent the last weeks of his life in a feverish attempt to pass through the press his magnum opus "Dissertationes in Librum Jobi," a vast volume of 600 pages. The last letter that Samuel ever wrote to John Wesley was entirely taken up with the book. He approved with the agreement that had been made with the engraver. "But I would have leviathan's rival, that is, the whale, as well as the crocodile. As for the elephant, he is so common that he need not be added. I am glad the tombs want no more than retouching, . . . 'Job in Adversity' I leave to your direction, as likewise the frontispiece, which Mr. Virtue is doing, who now duns me pretty hard for money for it."

A few weeks later, the gallant old man had escaped for ever from duns. John Wesley came up to London, personally to present the book to Queen Caroline, to whom it was dedicated and inscribed by permission.

The Queen was playing with her maids of honour when John Wesley was introduced. He dropped on his knees and handed her the book. The Queen glanced at the cover. "It is prettily bound," she remarked graciously, and placed Job on a window seat without so much as a glance at "the leviathan's rival, that is, the whale."

But the Dissertations on Job produced an effect more momentous than the old vicar had ever dreamt, for it was on this visit to London that John Wesley was introduced to James Oglethorpe, the founder of the new colony of Georgia.

II

James Edward Oglethorpe, the son of Sir Theophilus Oglethorpe, entered the army at twenty-two and served as secretary and Aide-de-Camp to Prince Eugene. In 1722, he succeeded to his father's estates and took his seat in Parliament.

He was one of the outstanding figures of the day. Hannah More, who saw him as an old man, declared that he was "the finest figure ever seen, heroic, romantic, full of old gallantry."

In 1728, a friend of Oglethorpe's was thrown into the Fleet prison for debt. Oglethorpe visited him regularly and was filled with indignation by the stories that he was told of the treatment of the prisoners. He moved in the House of Commons for a Committee to inquire into the conditions of the English prisons, and acted as chairman of a Commission which disclosed the full horrors of prison life. The late and acting wardens of the Fleet were prosecuted, and legislation was introduced to reform the more flagrant abuses of the system. Many of the prisoners were set at liberty and the problems of their future livelihood had to be solved. Oglethorpe decided to ask the Government to make a grant of land in America for their settlement. He was a statesman, no less than a philanthropist, and he realised what the mere transport of men who had failed in business from one continent to another would not of itself solve the problem. He was therefore anxious to secure a more solid kind of emigrant as a backbone to the colony.

He intended his colony to prove a refuge for the persecuted Protestants in Europe who might act as a centre of missionary enterprise among the Indians. At that time, over 20,000 Protestants had been expelled by the princely Bishop of Salzburg, and Oglethorpe persuaded the Trustees of the new Colony to extend a general invitation to these expatriated Salzburgers. The invitation was promptly accepted.

Oglethorpe founded his Colony in 1732, and then returned to England. He was anxious to discover some young man to serve as parson to the English community and as missionary to the Indians. Dr. Burton, of Corpus Christi College, introduced John Wesley to him, and Oglethorpe promptly offered him the chaplaincy. Wesley went down to Epworth, for he had decided to leave the decision to his mother. She did not hesitate. "If I had twenty sons, I should rejoice that they were all so employed, though I never saw them more."

Benjamin Ingham and Charles Delamotte decided to accompany him, as did also his brother Charles, who had just been ordained.

Wesley's reasons for going to Georgia were much the same as those he had used a year previously for staying in Oxford.

"My chief motive is the hope of saving my own soul . . . I cannot hope to attain the same degree of holiness here which I may there."

Like most of his contemporaries Wesley was a wholehearted believer in the myth of the noble savage. The idealization of the primitive, which finds its most complete expression in the works of Rousseau, was, of course, the normal reaction against the more artificial features of the age. In religion, this tendency was responsible for an artless confidence in the inspiration of the illiterate. The Anabaptists of Zwickau conscientiously refused to open the commentaries of learned divines on the Bible, and applied to ignorant peasants to explain to them the hidden meanings which lurked behind the gospel text. Wesley entertained a similar hope. The Red Indian, he trusted, would prove to be the ideal exegete.

"They have no comments to construe away the text (of the gospel)," he wrote, "no vain philosophy to corrupt it; no luxurious sensual, covetous, ambitious expounders to soften its unpleasing truths. They have no party, no interest to serve, and are therefore fit to receive the Gospel in its simplicity. They are as little children, humble, willing to learn, and eager to do, the Will of God."

Two years later, he penned a more accurate description of these same Indians whom he summed up as "gluttons, thieves, dissemblers, liars, murderers of fathers, murderers of mothers, murderers of their own children."

III

On October 14th, 1735, the Wesleys embarked on the "Simmonds." On the 21st, they set sail from Gravesend, but for various reasons the ship was delayed, and it was not until December 10th that they sailed from Cowes. They were at sea from December 10th till February 5th. Wesley, in fact, took about three times as many days as Lindbergh took hours to cross the Atlantic.

The passengers on the ship included twenty-six devout Moravians and their Bishop David Nitschman. Wesley began to learn German a few days after embarking. He had hardly been on board a day before he had mapped out an inhuman programme of spiritual exercises and hard work. A specimen page of his Diary, quoted on page 29 of this book, may be taken to represent almost any one of the hundred days which he spent on board ship.

Few people on board escaped Wesley's tireless administrations. Amongst others a "gay young woman" who having casually heard Wesley speaking on the nature of Christ, "appeared to be much affected." "Good company," adds Wesley, "soon restored her to her former gaiety." But that gay young woman was destined to give John Wesley a great deal of trouble. She was the wife of Dr. Hawkins, a surgeon, and a pretty, unprincipled Jezebel.

On December 10th, they set sail, and John Wesley's Diary for the day strikes a very human note.

"Sailed from Cowes.
Not Sick."

and then follows:

"Mrs. Lambert much affected"

(not by sea-sickness, of course, but by Wesley's spiritual advice)

"Mrs. Hawkins twice in tears.
Oglethorpe opened his heart."

Mrs. Hawkins's tears are described in great detail. She had been listening with flattering attention while Wesley "spoke closely on the head of religion," and afterwards said with tears, "My mother died when I was but ten years old. Some of her last words were 'Child, fear God, and though you lose me, you shall never want a friend.'"

Mrs. Hawkins squeezed Wesley's hand, looked up into his eyes and said, "I have now found a friend when I most wanted and least expected one."

Certainly, she had found a friend, certainly she needed one, for the Atlantic Ocean was monstrous tedious, and after all any man was better than none. Mrs. Hawkins did not despair. Even parsons are human, and though Wesley might prove to be a St. Anthony, he would still be useful as a step to more exalted quarry. For Mrs. Hawkins had discovered that General Oglethorpe held Wesley in great respect. She had heard him administer severe ratings to some sailors who had been lacking in courtesy to Wesley and his friends.

"Do not take these gentlemen," Oglethorpe had said, "for tithe pig parsons. They are gentlemen of learning and respectability; they are my friends, and whoever offers an affront to them insults me."

Yes, decidedly, John Wesley was worth cultivating.

Mrs. Hawkins was not alone in finding Wesley curiously attractive. There were Mrs. Lawley and Mrs. Welch and Mrs. Moore. All of them seemed in trouble about their souls. Wesley wandered round, praying with them and reading with them. We see Beata Hawkins pretending to be ill, sitting up in her cabin propped up on her pillows while Wesley reads to her. What was the book? "Christian Prudence." Wesley, thought Mrs. Hawkins, had more than his fair share of that commodity. Mrs. Lawley, on the other hand, was treated to a daily dose of "Christian Perfections" with excellent results. "Mrs. Lawley," writes Wesley in his Journal, "seems every day more earnestly to pursue the one thing needful." But then Mrs. Lawley and Wesley would not have agreed as to what constituted "the one thing needful."

Wesley, like a physician of souls, notes daily in his Diary the spiritual temperature of his patients.

"Mrs. Hawkins affected . . . Mrs. Hawkins very open and affected . . . serious and open . . . Mrs. Welch seriously affected," and so forth.

Charles Wesley was called upon to admire Mrs. Hawkins's steady progress towards the Light. He was not impressed. Charles thought that John was making a fool of himself, and Charles said so. He was horrified by John's decision to admit Mrs. Hawkins to the Sacrament.

Charles once said that his brother was made to be the victim of knaves. John retorted: "I believe in everybody. Charles believes in nobody, yet he is often more deceived than I."

Before long, the women began to quarrel, and Wesley tried to make peace. His technique of reconciliation was original. He insisted on telling Mrs. Hawkins exactly what Mrs. Welch had said about her, and in telling Mrs. Welch exactly wherein she had failed to meet with Mrs. Hawkins's approval.

Wesley always practised absolute frankness, and believed in telling people what he thought about them, and what other people thought about them. There would, of course, be less scandalmongering if everybody followed his example. Malignant gossip is only possible because the scandalmonger is protected from reprisals by the convention that confidences should be respected. But why should A be allowed to make remarks detrimental to B without B being given an opportunity of refuting those criticisms, and of cross-examining the man who made them? This was the principle on which John Wesley acted throughout his life. "Openness" was a quality to which he attached supreme importance. Transparently honest himself, he suffered from a constitutional inability to keep a secret. Many years later he remarked to a friend, "If I go to America, I must do a thing which I hate as bad as I hate the devil." "What is that?" he was asked. "I must keep a secret."

And so when his brother, Bishop Nitschmann and others protested against his intention to admit Mrs. Hawkins to the Holy Communion, he promptly informed Mrs. Hawkins, with that "openness" on which he laid such stress of the exact charges against her. Mrs. Hawkins wept, and "was desperately affected and open." But she neither forgot nor forgave.

IV

Then came a great storm. Wesley was ashamed. He saw the waves break across the ship, and discovered that he was unwilling to die. This unholy reluctance distressed him keenly.

He stepped out of the cabin door. "The sea did not break as usual, but came with a full, smooth tide over the side of the ship." Then comes a fine phrase. "I was vaulted over with water in a moment, and so stunned, I scarce expected to lift up my head till the sea should give up her dead."

The storm increased in violence. In the height of its fury, a child which was privately baptized, was brought to Wesley to be received into the Church. "It put me in mind," wrote Wesley, "of Jeremiah publicly buying the field when the Chaldeans were on the point of destroying Jerusalem, and seemed a pledge of the mercy God designed to show us, even in the land of the living."

And still the storm raged. Even the stoutest hearts began to waver. But there was one little group who went about their business as if they were on dry land. The Germans began their evening service at 7 p. m. They sang a psalm. Suddenly the sea broke across the ship, split the mainsail in pieces and poured in between the decks as if the great deep had swallowed them up. But above the din, the straining of timbers, the roar of the waters, and the screams of the English women and children, Wesley heard the voices of the Moravians calmly and soberly singing their psalm, a psalm which praises the power of God. They did not pause even when the mainsail broke.

"Were you not afraid?" asked Wesley. "No," said the Germans.

"But were not your women and children afraid?" persisted Wesley. And the Germans answered mildly, "No, our women and children are not afraid to die."

"From them," continues Wesley, "I went to their crying, trembling neighbours and pointed out the difference in the hour of trial between him that feareth God and him that feareth Him not."

v

On Feburary 15th, the *Simmonds* anchored in the Savannah River. Oglethorpe took boat for Savannah leaving the emigrants in charge of Wesley. The crew and some of the passengers celebrated the safe conclusion of their voyage by getting drunk. Wesley's reaction was characteristic. He first took a private vow of abstinence from flesh and from wine, and then publicly staved in the rum casks that had been brought from England, an action of doubtful wisdom which widened the breach between him and his fellow passengers.

On landing, Wesley was welcomed by August Gottlieb Spangenberg, who had arrived in Georgia with the first party of Moravians. Spangenberg had been a scholar of Jena, and a lecturer at the university of Halle. Wesley and Spangenberg became friends at first sight. A few days later, Wesley asked his friend's advice as to the attitude he should adopt towards his new parishioners. Spangenberg, who had listened sympathetically, suddenly put a few personal questions. "Do you know yourself?" Wesley was taken by surprise, and remained silent. "Do you know Jesus Christ?" Spangenberg continued. "I know," replied Wesley, "He is the Saviour of the world." "True," said Spangenberg, "but do you know He has saved you?" Wesley temporised. "I hope He has died to save me." Spangenberg was not satisfied. "Do you *know?*" Wesley replied, "I do," but in recording the conversation he added, "I fear they were vain words."

This conversation made a great impression on Wesley.

VI

Spangenberg left for Pennsylvania, and Oglethorpe was planning to go south. Wesley was, therefore, left without the two men whose advice and encouragement would have been useful to him in those early days in Georgia.

Oglethorpe knew that Spain had a better title than England to Georgia, and he hated Spain with Elizabethan hatred. It was his ambition to give England a safe southern frontier, and with this in view, he kept pushing steadily southward. He had seized Savannah to protect Carolina, and Althama to protect Savannah. His Scots were at Darien. He had just built Frederica, fronting the tideway and the marsh, England's southernmost outpost. Huts had already been built at Frederica for the encouragement of about fifty emigrants and their families. Oglethorpe therefore left Georgia for Frederica, and with him went Charles Wesley as his secretary, Benjamin Ingham as Minister . . . and Mrs. Hawkins.

VII

Wesley was left at Savannah where he opened his public ministry on March 7th, 1736. He made it clear from the first that he would permit no laxity as far as the observance of the rubrics was concerned. He informed his parishioners that he would admit none to Communion unless they had previously given him notice. He baptized by immersion all children who could endure it, and said that he would accept none as godparents who were not communicants.

Wesley based his practice on what he believed to be the customs of the Early Church. In his strict obedience to the rubric and canon law, Wesley was a High Churchman, and he was soon to discover that Georgia did not provide a hopeful field for High-Church experiment. His parishioners were a motley crew, Scotch Highlanders, adventurers and debtors, worthy artisans, and a sprinkling of saintly Moravians.

And then, of course, there were the Indians. Wesley had come to Georgia to convert the Indians, but he was disappointed to discover that Oglethorpe had no intention of allowing him to waste his time in missionary enterprise among the Indians. He met Tomochcichi, a friendly chief, and broached the subject of conversion. Tomochcichi replied: "Those are Christians at Frederica, those are Christians at Savannah. Christians lie, Christians steal, Christians beat men. Me no Christian."

The other chiefs were less aggressively candid, but were no less evasive. For the moment, they explained, they had too much fighting on their hands to bother about anything else. But a little later, perhaps, they would look into the matter.

Shortly before Wesley left Georgia, he confessed that he had never heard of any Indian who had the least desire to be instructed in the Christian verities.

Meanwhile, Charles had been getting into trouble. Frederica meant different things to different people. To General Oglethorpe, Frederica was a city of destiny, England's southern outpost against the Spaniards. To Charles, Frederica was the germ of a theocratic state. The citizens were to worship God with the simplicity and the earnestness of the Early Christians. To Mrs. Hawkins, Frederica was a miserable hamlet of palmetto huts and tents. The storehouse acted as the base of general assembly and as the church. Life at Frederica, as she fore-

saw, could be devastatingly dull, and to make matters
worse, that impossible parson, Charles Wesley, seemed
anxious to inflict Puritanical restrictions upon the settlers.
The Wesleys seemed to be very influential with the General. Mrs. Hawkins detected their hand in the ordinance
forbidding Sunday sport. During Oglethorpe's temporary
absence, Charles had actually caused her husband, the
surgeon of Frederica, to be arrested for shooting on Sunday.

Mrs. Hawkins and Mrs. Welch got together, and
hatched an ingenious plot. They persuaded Charles Wesley
that they had committed adultery with Oglethorpe, and
they confessed to Oglethorpe not only that they had been
seduced by Charles, but that he had unjustly accused
Oglethorpe of illicit relations with Mrs. Hawkins.

Charles was very upset. "Horror upon horror," he
wrote in his Diary, "never did I feel such an access of
pity. I gave myself up to prayer for her. Mr. Ingham
soon joined me."

Charles's artless consternation might have amused the
General in another mood. Once before, he had lightly
hinted at some earlier gallantry. John had not understood
at first, and when he did understand he had been so
genuinely distressed, that Oglethorpe was careful never
again to offend his pudicity.

Oglethorpe was a soldier, and he had not lived the life
of a monk, but he had left that side of his life behind
him when he set sail for Georgia. Georgia was his mistress. He hated Spain, and he loved Georgia too passionately to neglect her for lighter loves. He would not have
weakened his influence in the young colony or have compromised the dignity of his office by an affair with the
wife of the surgeon. Oglethorpe, again, had great respect
for the cloth. Parsons, he held, should be chaste. Chastity
was one of those inconvenient obligations which a man

assumed on ordination, just as a soldier undertook to die at his post if need be. He was therefore shocked at Charles's supposed lapse, and furious that this pharisaic young parson should try to cover his own fall from virtue by libelling his chief.

He did not wish publicly to expose Charles, because he still had a high respect for his brother. He showed his disgust by treating Charles with the utmost unkindness and severity. The Colonists were delighted and took their cue from Oglethorpe.

Charles fell ill, and his colleague Ingham wisely decided to send for John Wesley. Wisely, because Oglethorpe never wavered in his respect for John. John arrived, and set about the task of reconciliation with his customary sanguine hopefulness. He still persisted in believing that Mrs. Hawkins was not wholly bad, and he did his best to disentangle a complicated network of lies and deceit. His diary records the rise and fall in public temperature.

"Mon. 12. Mrs. Welch open! resolved to change.
    Oglethorpe friendly, soft.
    Horton soft, friendly, serious.
    Oglethorpe came out of the house, very angry
     with her!
Tues. 13. Mrs. Hawkins civil.
    Mrs. Welch soft, open and affected.
    Mrs. Hawkins at prayers. She open and mild.
Fri. 16. Mrs. Welch and Mrs. Hawkins came to me in
     the field.
    Oglethorpe seemed quite open, and in an excitable temper.
    Mrs. Hawkins and Oglethorpe seem innocent!
     Amen!
    She quite angry.
    Mrs. Welch in a swoon. Open my eyes!"

It was some time before Oglethorpe and Charles Wesley were completely reconciled. "Nothing in all this strange story," remarks Miss Jones in her life of Charles Wesley, "is stranger than the fact that two men of high character were ready to believe the worst of each other on the word of a worthless woman."

VIII

But John Wesley had not done with Mrs. Hawkins.

It was August. Charles was on his way back to England to report to the Trustees of Georgia. John had taken his place at Frederica. He was recovering from malaria, and he went along one morning to Dr. Hawkins for a decoction of bark. Now Hawkins had intercepted a letter from Charles to John, a letter which contained two Greek words which accurately described Mrs. Hawkins and Mrs. Welch, who were not, however, mentioned by name.

Dr. Hawkins was not at home, but his wife received John Wesley.

"All the women in the town," she told him, "are uneasy and affronted at the two Greek words in your brother's letter. They think them a general reflection on them all. Pray tell me, who do they mean?"

Wesley replied that he was not responsible for what his brother said, that his brother's opinion had recently changed, and that the Greek words were supposed to apply only to Mrs. Hawkins and to Mrs. Welch. Mrs. Hawkins promptly started up, and exclaimed that John Wesley was a "villain, a scoundrel, a pitiful rascal." At this point, the doctor came in and joined her in abuse of Wesley. "That dog Charles Wesley meant me by those damned words."

"Did he indeed!" shouted the doctor, not to be undone, "we'll unfrock the pair of them."

"The sooner, the better," said Wesley and left them to go and find Oglethorpe.

Oglethorpe was by now thoroughly sick of the Hawkins-Wesley imbroglio, but he did his best to calm things down.

A few days later, Mrs. Hawkins sent Wesley a note asking him to call on her on a matter of importance. Wesley asked the servant whether she knew what her mistress wanted, and receiving an answer in the negative, he remarked, "If a parishioner desires my company, I must go; but be sure, stay you within."

When he went in, Mrs. Hawkins asked him to sit down. She had her hands behind her back, and when Wesley had sat down, she said, "Sir, you have wronged me, and I will shoot you through the head this moment with a brace of balls."

"I caught hold of the hand," writes Wesley, "with which she presented the pistol, and at the same time of her other hand, in which she had a pair of scissors. On which she threw herself upon me, and forced me down upon the bed, crying out all the while, 'Villain, dog, let go my hands,' and swearing bitterly, with many imprecations both on herself and me, that she would either have my hair or my heart's blood. I was very unwilling either to cry out, which must publish to all the world what, for her sake, I desired should be more private; or to attempt rising by force, which could not have been done without hurting her. Just then the maid came in, whom she ordered to reach a knife, swearing she would be the death of her if she did not."

Eventually, a constable put in appearance, followed by Dr. Hawkins, who "asked what that scoundrel did in his house" and commanded the constable at his peril not to touch his wife.

Much encouraged by her husband's loyal support, Mrs. Hawkins put her teeth into Wesley's cassock and "tore both the sleeves of it to pieces."

Mrs. Hawkins was finally removed by her husband, and Wesley went off to find General Oglethorpe. Oglethorpe persuaded Wesley not to bring action. He spoke, "largely of the necessity of union among ourselves, how we were surrounded with enemies, of the many divisions already in the town, and the probability that this would increase them." Finally, "something like an agreement was patched up, one article of which was that we should speak to each other no more."

To all this Wesley, of course, agreed with wholehearted relief.

Wesley always refused to shirk any responsibilities which he considered that he had incurred as a pastor in charge of a cure of souls. Spangenberg, his brother and many others had warned him to leave Mrs. Hawkins to her own devices. He had been tempted to take their advice, for his fastidious soul recoiled instinctively from Mrs. Hawkins's hopeless vulgarity. He persisted, however, in the hopeless task of attempting to convert her, until the Governor of the Colony, whose authority he recognised, freed him from all further obligations. The sincerity of his relief finds expression in the *cri de cœur* which closes the Mrs. Hawkins incident.

"Something like an agreement was patched up, one article of which was that we should speak to each other no more. Blessed be God who hath at length given me a full discharge, in the sight of men and angels, from all intercourse with one 'whose heart is snares and knots and her hands as bands.'"

Those who are tempted to overestimate the importance of Wesley's "conversion" should reflect that he was an Evangelist long before he was converted. "We think of

Wesley," writes Mr. Nehemiah Curnock "as a soul-saving Evangelist from the hour of his 'evangelical conversion,' but the spirit of the Evangelist, mounting into what the world regarded as a mania, was in him long before he reached Aldersgate Street. The Diaries prove, beyond possibility of question, that, from the 'boy' who served in his house to the Governor whom he himself served, he faithfully strove to save every man, woman, and child who crossed his path."

CHAPTER V

WESLEY'S FIRST LOVE

WESLEY'S love story is recorded in Wesley's Journal, and has recently inspired a brilliant novel, "The Holy Lover" by Marie Conway Oemler. This novel combines great imaginative power with fidelity to historic facts. Miss Oemler's description, for instance, of Wesley's appearance could hardly be bettered.

"He was a beautiful little man," she writes, "under medium height like all the Wesleys, very slender and spare of body, but so justly proportioned that his lack of height wore the aspect of an added grace. In company with larger men, he compared as might a rapier against a sword. He wore his dark hair rather long, curling slightly at the ends, and brushed to a burning glossiness. His large, dark blue eyes had that clear cold light which expresses will and the autocratic intellect; for he had not yet attained the sweet patience which made his later years so gracious. In his ascetic and intellectual face, one feature alone did not jibe with the rest; the firm chin was cleft. Unexpectedly, delightfully, as if Ariel had lightly touched the chin of the Sphinx, and left a baffling, fairy fingerprint, John Wesley's chin was cleft.

"The precision of his mind expressed itself in a sort of austere dandyism. He could bear nothing out of order, nothing amiss, nothing careless. His clothes, of which his

64

supply was just sufficient for his needs, were spinsterishly neat. His hand was fine, nervous, delicate, very strong, like all perfectly made things, his leg in his plain hose very shapely. And nothing, not the macerating fasts, the merciless hours, the terrific strain, the strenuous endless labour, nor the inhuman exposure to all sorts of weather ever marred the beauty of his complexion, which had the pure freshness of a young child's. He had the strength of tested steel; he could stand fatigues and overstrain which would have killed a stronger man. Used to the society of elegant and accomplished women, his manners had the incommunicable simplicity of fine art; it had taken generations to produce the polished naturalness of John Wesley."

But in spite of his "polished naturalness," Wesley himself despised "the softness of a genteel education." In his Journal, he expresses great scorn for "that vulgar error concerning the hurtfulness of the rains and dews of America."

"I have been thoroughly wet with these rains more than once, yet without any harm at all. And I have lain many nights in the open air, and received all the dews that fell; and so I believe might any one, if his constitution was not impaired by the softness of a genteel education."

Wesley was an open air man. He could walk his thirty miles a day without showing the least sign of fatigue. He liked using an axe against the woodland trees, and he was happiest, perhaps, in his own garden. "He was ever at his best in his garden," writes Miss Oemler, "and when Sophy thought of him, it was against the green background of trees and shrubs and flowers and grass, under the blueness that was the Georgian sky. Wesley's garden always had a lovely touch of homeliness."

II

Such then, was John Wesley at the age of thirty-three, when he first met Sophia Christina Hopkey.

Miss Hopkey was the niece of Mrs. Causton, the wife of Thomas Causton who was the Magistrate of the Colony, a position to which he should never have been appointed, for he had left England in disgrace after practising a fraud on the public Revenue. Two years after the events chronicled in this chapter, he was expelled from his offices in Savannah, and his certified accounts were refused as incorrect.

Sophy was young and beautiful, and had already been ardently wooed by a handsome young man called Tom Mellichamp. Mellichamp belonged to a good family, but he had a reputation of being a dangerous young man, violent when roused and likely to get into trouble before long.

He had threatened her. "I mean to have you," he said, "and if by chance somebody else blunders in between us, there will be a funeral instead of a wedding."

And then Sophy met Wesley. What a contrast. She was overawed by his holiness. At first, there was no room for any emotion other than a profound respect for this grave, distinguished scholar and saint.

To Wesley, Sophy was both a parishioner and a pupil. He gave her spiritual advice and taught her French every day.

Causton, knowing well the high esteem in which Wesley was held by Oglethorpe, watched the affair develop complacently. His niece, so long as she remained unmarried, was an encumbrance, but his position in the Colony would be strengthened if only his niece could be induced to marry Wesley.

Weeks passed. Charles left for England, and Oglethorpe was quite relieved to see the last of this well-
meaning but blundering saint. John came to Frederica
to take Charles's place, and acted as Oglethorpe's Secretary and as his second-in-command. Oglethorpe was
more and more impressed by his judgment and by his
sagacity. It would never do to lose John. He must be
securely anchored to the Colony by a wife.

Oglethorpe sounded Causton. As a result Causton
suddenly discovered that Sophy really ought to pay a
visit to a friend of hers in Frederica. She went south, and
resumed her lessons in French with John Wesley, and
the friendship ripened slowly, until Wesley was recalled
to Savannah, where he remained for three months. Then
once again, he returned to Frederica. Before setting forth,
he called on Causton to ask "what commands he had to
Miss Sophy." His Journal records the conversation which
followed.

"The girl will never be easy till she is married." I
answered, "Sir, she is too much afflicted to have a thought
of it. . . ." He said, "I give her up to you. Do what you
will with her. Take her into your own hands. Promise
her what you will. I will make it good."

On his return to Frederica, he learnt with dismay that
Morning and Evening prayers had been discontinued, and
that most of his parishioners had "thrown off the form
as well as the power of godliness." Even Sophy had lapsed
from grace. "Most of her good resolutions were vanished
away" and she startled Wesley by announcing that she
intended to return to England.

"I am resolved," said Miss Sophy, "to leave America
with the first ship that sails."

One glance at Wesley, and her heart leaped. He
minded! Undoubtedly he minded.

Wesley reasoned with her and argued but with no

success. He then dropped the argument and fell back on
his favourite remedy for distressed ladies. "I read her
some of the most affecting parts of the 'Serious Call' and
of Ephrem Syrus." Very affecting, no doubt, but the
"affecting parts" seemed to have lost their magic. Miss
Sophy seemed distraite. "I was at first a little surprised
and discouraged; but I soon re-collected my spirits, and
remembered my calling."

A few days later Oglethorpe returned. He greeted
Horton effusively, but he ignored Wesley. It is not
clear why. Probably Wesley read an accidental slight as a
deliberate insult. He mentioned the incident to Miss
Sophy, and added, "Now Miss Sophy, you may go to
England, for I can assist you no longer; my interest is
gone."

"No," replied Miss Sophy softly, "now I will not stir
a foot."

Wesley was on the point of returning to Savannah, and
next day he had an interview with Oglethorpe. Oglethorpe suggested that perhaps it might be best if Miss
Sophy also returned to her home.

Wesley went back to Sophy and told her what had
been said. She burst into tears and said that she could
not bear the thought of returning home.

"Do not be distressed," said Wesley, "your uncle Mr.
Causton engaged himself to make good whatever I
should promise you. You have only to make your own
terms."

Sophy glanced up sharply. She tried to read his face.
No, he was not paving the way for a proposal. The dear,
naïve, innocent man was repeating Mr. Causton's words
without the least sense of their true significance.

Next morning Wesley went to Oglethorpe, and
asked him in what boat Miss Sophy was to travel. Oglethorpe replied with assumed casualness, "She can go in

none but yours, and indeed there is none so proper."

Wesley flushed. A sudden tumult of happiness possessed him. And yet . . . He dreaded Sophy. "I saw the danger to myself, but yet had a good hope I should be delivered out of it, (1) because it was not my choice which brought me into it; (2) because I still felt in myself the same desire and design to live a single life; and (3) because I was persuaded should my desire and design be changed, yet her resolution to live single would continue."

For Sophy had informed Wesley at an early stage of their friendship that the married state had no attraction for her, and that she proposed to die an old maid. Wesley did not realise that this sort of remark is common form when friendship begins to ripen into love. To the end of his life he persisted in accepting the remarks of his lady friends at their literal face value.

III

They set out at noon. There was the usual boat's crew, but Wesley and Sophy were the only passengers. Oglethorpe had arranged it so. It was clear that Miss Sophy's "resolution to live singly" was to be subjected to a severe test.

It was October. The wooded shores past which they drifted were golden with autumnal glories. Sophy's eyes wandered from the shore to the river, and then her glance stole across to the grave, earnest face of her companion, who was busily engaged in reading aloud to her. What was he reading? She neither knew nor cared. The words passed over her.

("The afternoon we spent reading the first volume of Fleury's 'History of the Church,' a book I chose for her sake chiefly as setting before her such glorious examples of truth and patience in the sufferings of those ancient worthies, 'who resisted unto blood, striving against sin.' ")

In the evening they landed and spread a sail over four stakes driven into the ground, to keep off the night dews. Wesley lay between Miss Sophy and the servant. The east wind was piercingly cold, but Miss Sophy "complained of nothing, appearing as satisfied as if she had been warm upon a bed of down."

And so the days passed, and the more Wesley observed her, the more he was "amazed." "Nothing was ever improper or ill-timed. All she said and did was equally tinctured with seriousness and sweetness."

Poor Sophy! She was doing her best. She concealed her weariness during "a close conversation on Christian holiness." Nay more. "The openness with which she owned her ignorance of it and the earnest desire she showed for fresh instruction, much endeared her to me, so it made me hope she would one day prove an eminent pattern of it."

Wesley seldom found it difficult to sleep, but one night he lay awake till the small hours. The fire was still burning brightly, and as he turned over on his side, the light from the flickering flames lit up Sophy's dear face. She too was wide awake. Suddenly he turned to her and said: "I should think myself very happy if I was to spend my life with you."

He says in his Journal that "this was the expression of a sudden wish, not of any formed design."

His sudden wishes were often sound where the other sex were concerned, but his "formed designs" were incredibly inept.

Sophy burst into tears and said, "I am in every way unhappy. I won't have Tommy for he is a bad man. And I can have none else."

She was thinking of Tom's threat, and of the vengeance he vowed on any man who might supplant him.

"Sir" she added, "you don't know the danger you are in. I beg you would speak no word more on this head."

Wesley remained silent. She had asked him not to continue the conversation. Clearly she did not want the conversation continued. Sophy looked up, and after a pause added: "When others have spoken to me on the subject, I felt an aversion to them. But I don't feel any to you. We may converse on other subjects as freely as ever."

The gods who watch over our wooing had done their best. The dark woods, the silent stars, the river's ancient song, the camp beneath the stars, was there ever such a setting for love?

"Both my judgment and will acquiesced in what she said," writes Wesley, "and we ended our conversation with a psalm."

Pan put up his flute with disgust, for his flute was never meant to accompany psalm tunes. The gods abandoned Wesley in despair.

IV

They were nearing home, and Sophy was feeling depressed. This enchanted interlude was coming to an end, and Sophy was suffering by anticipation all the torments of that form of homesickness which attacks its victims— at home. Suddenly she could bear it no longer, and expressed the strongest uneasiness and an utter aversion to living with Mr. Causton, saying with many tears, "I can't live in that house: I can't bear the shocks I meet with there."

Wesley turned to her and said, "Don't be uneasy, Miss Sophy, on that account. If you don't care to be at Mr. Causton's, you are welcome to a room in our house."

Sophy flushed. At last, at last. But no. Merely another instance of the incredible monumental gaucherie of that strange beloved simpleton. . . . The parsonage was often used as a guest house, and Wesley was offering her not a home, but an asylum.

"Or perhaps," Wesley continued, in the same maddeningly prosaic voice, "it would be best of all, and your aunt once proposed it, if you went to live in the house with the Germans."

With the Germans! And so that was to be the end. A procession of memories passed before Sophy. . . . Long days on the tidal river, and the longer nights. The camp fire edged by the great trees on which the flames spun a flickering web of light and shadow, the haunting scent of burning cedarwood, the boat sail spread over four sharpened stakes, the sail which rose and sank with the wind, the semi-tones of the water splashing against the bank . . . and the dim shape of her queer inarticulate lover lying beside her.

But above all, the haunting, all-pervading sense of ancient urge and desire, no less potent because unavowed, tamed but not extinguished by daily doses of Law's "Serious Call."

Those days and those nights were over, and the tears came into her eyes, as the lover who had lain beside her beneath the stars, offered her, not the shelter of his arm, but the alluring prospect of living with the saintly Moravians, as indeed her aunt had at one time proposed.

Such was the offer, and Wesley in his Journal has recorded the interesting fact that "to this offer she made no reply."

V

Twelve months later, Wesley was sitting in his old rooms at Lincoln. He had just left his mother and he had come down to Oxford to see his brother Charles who was seriously ill.

He sat down at his old desk to write the story of his relations with Miss Sophy. The narrative was, in all probability, intended for his mother, for he employed none of his customary abbreviations, and formed his letters with particular care as if he were writing for one whose eyes were already dimmed with age.

He turned over the first page, and wrote in a firm hand at the top, "Oh give me not up unto my own heart's lusts, neither let me follow mine own imagination." On the blank fly-leaf he inscribed the memorable words, "Snatched as a brand out of the fire." . . .

An hour passed and he was still writing. He had just finished describing the enchanted journey to Savannah, and memories crowded in upon him fast. He forgot the foolish trouble which had precipitated his departure from America. He remembered Sophy only as he had learned to know her during the long months of their friendship.

Before bringing the story to its tragic curtain, he sat down and wrote a pen-portrait of Miss Sophy.

From the Journal of John Wesley.
Nov. 1. Mon. She was eighteen years old. And from the beginning of our intimate acquaintance till this day, I verily believe she used no guile: not only because even now I know no instance to the contrary, nor only because the simplicity of her behaviour was a constant voucher for her sincerity; but because of the entire openness of all her conversation, answering whatever questions I proposed, without either hesitation or reserve, immediately and directly. Another thing I was much pleased with in her was, that whenever we were conversing or reading, there was such a stillness in the whole behaviour, scarce stirring hand or foot, that "she seemed to be, all but her attention, dead." . . .

Nor did she at all favour herself on account of that weakness; she could not remove, she would not indulge it. Softness and tenderness of this kind she would not know, having left the delicacy of the gentlewoman in England. She utterly despised those inconveniences which women of condition in

England would think worse than death. With bread to eat and water to drink she was content; indeed she never used any drink beside water. She was patient of labour, of cold, heat, wet, of badness of food or of want; and of pain to an eminent degree. . . . And she was equally careless of finery in other things. It was use she considered, not show; nor novelty either, being as little concerned for new as for fine or pretty things. The same disregard she had for what are called diversions, such as balls, dancing, visiting; having no desire either to see or be seen, unless in order to be wiser and better. . . . Her apprehension was so quick that there was scarce ever need to repeat a thing twice to her, and so clear as to conceive things the most remote from common life without any mistake or confusion. But she was by no means fond of showing her sense; seldom speaking when she could decently avoid it, and then in few words, but such as were clear and pertinent, and contained much in little compass. . . . The temper of her heart towards God is best known by Him "who seeth in secret." What appeared of it was a deep, even reverence, ripening into love, and a resignation unshaken in one of the severest trials which human nature is exposed to. The utmost anguish never wrung from her a murmuring word. She saw the hand of God, and was still. She said indeed, "If it be possible, Father!" But added, "Not as I will, but as Thou wilt!"

Such was the woman, according to my closest observation, of whom I now began to be much afraid.

VI

"Of whom I now began to be very much afraid. . . ."

Why afraid? Perhaps the answer is to be found in Kenneth Hare's epigram:

"The Puritan through Life's sweet garden goes,
He plucks the thorn and casts away the rose,
And thinks to please by this peculiar whim,
The God who fashioned it and gave it him."

"My desire and design," continued Wesley, "still was

to live single, but how long it would continue, I knew not."

Meanwhile, Miss Sophy was coming to his house every day. The time was spent partly in learning French, partly in reading devotional literature. And so the weeks passed. Then comes a characteristic entry (February 3rd). Wesley considers marriage, but he made no direct proposal. "For indeed it was only a sudden thought, and had not the consent of my own mind. Yet I firmly believe, had she closed with me at that time, my judgment would have made but a faint resistance. But she said 'she thought it was best for clergymen not to be encumbered with worldly cares, and that it was best for her, too, to live single, and she was accordingly resolved never to marry.' I used no argument to induce her to alter her resolution."

"Upon reflection," adds Wesley, "I thought this a very narrow escape."

He went to Mr. Töltschig, the pastor of the Moravians, and asked him for his advice. Mr. Töltschig appears to have been a sensible person. On being asked whether Wesley ought to break off "so dangerous an acquaintance" he replied, "What do you think would be the consequence if you should?" Wesley said, "I fear her soul would be lost."

"And what do you think," said Töltschig, "would be the consequences if you should not break it off?"

"I fear," answered Wesley gloomily, "I should marry her."

Tölschig replied shortly, "I don't see why you should not."

"I went home," says Wesley, "amazed to the last degree."

Unfortunately, neither Delamotte nor Ingham agreed with Mr. Töltschig. Delamotte worshipped Wesley and was certainly jealous of Sophy. He loathed the possibility of her breaking up the Holy (and celibate) Club, and he therefore did his best to discourage Wesley's intention.

A few days later, Wesley informed Sophy that he was resolved not to marry till he had been among the Indians. Sophy remarked inconsequentially that she did not think that she would come to his house any more.

"I don't think it's dignified," she added, "for me to learn French any longer."

The Journal thenceforwards is painful reading, painful and maddening in its tantalising suggestions of happiness within reach and yet ever perversely declined. If only Wesley's mother, or some sensible woman, had been with him in this crisis, to shake a little sense into him, his whole life would have been changed. Instead he fell back upon Delamotte.

More than once, matters appeared to be working up to their final climax.

"Calling at Mrs. Causton's she was there alone. This was indeed an hour of trial. Her words, her eyes, her air, her every motion and gesture, were full of such a softness and sweetness! I know not what might have been the consequence had I then but touched her hand. And how I avoided it I know not. Surely God is over all!

"After all the company but Miss Sophy was gone, Mr. Delamotte went out and left us alone again. Finding her still the same, my resolution failed. At the end of a very serious conversation, I took her by the hand, and, perceiving she was not displeased, I was so utterly disarmed, that that hour I should have engaged myself for life, had it not been for the full persuasion I had of her entire sincerity, and in consequence of which I doubt not but she was resolved (as she had said) never to marry while she lived."

Unfortunately, he learnt too late that a woman in love should never be taken at her word.

Meanwhile, the good Delamotte was getting more and more uneasy, and he urged Wesley to decide one way or another without delay. Wesley decided to invoke the decision of God by drawing lots. Ingham, Delamotte and Wesley met together. Wesley made three lots. On the first was written "Marry," on the second "Think not of it this year" and on the third "Think of it no more."

"We prayed to God to give a perfect lot." Delamotte rose, put out a shaking hand, drew a piece of paper towards him, opened it and in a voice tense with emotion read out the words "Think of it no more."

But Delamotte was taking no chances. He insisted that they should draw again to decide whether Wesley should ever hold converse with Sophy again. Delamotte's luck was in. "Only in the presence of Mr. Delamotte," replied the oracle, a reply which gave Mr. Delamotte every satisfaction.

From Wesley's Journal.

March 4. Fri.

"I saw and adored the goodness of God, though what He required of me was a costly sacrifice. It was indeed the giving up at once whatever this world affords of agreeable—not only honour, fortune, power (which indeed were nothing to me, who despised them as the clay in the streets), but all the truly desirable conveniences of life—a pleasant house, a delightful garden, on the brow of a hill at a small distance from the town; another house and garden in the town; and a third a few miles off, with a large tract of fruitful land adjoining to it.[1] And above all, what to me made all things else vile and utterly beneath a thought, such a companion as I never expected to find

---

[1] Miss Sophy possessed property in her own right. Her "lot" is frequently referred to. She was also heiress presumptive to the Caustons, who held an estate, or lot, at Hogstead, a few miles from Savannah, and also a large town house.

again, should I live one thousand years twice told. So that I could not but cry out: *O Lord God, Thou God of my fathers, plenteous in mercy and truth, behold I give Thee, not thousands of rams or ten thousands of rivers of oil, but the desire of my eyes, the joy of my heart, the one thing upon earth which I longed for! O give me wisdom, which sitteth by Thy throne, and reject me not from among Thy children!"*

VII

Miss Sophy did not wait to learn from Wesley himself his resolve to desert her. She accepted the addresses of another suitor, a certain Mr. Williamson. But even then, the issue was not decided. At the eleventh hour, Wesley had only to say the word, to dash the cup of happiness from Mr. Williamson's lips.

Wesley at first could not bring himself to believe that of all men, Williamson had been selected by Sophy as her mate, for Williamson, so Wesley thought, was "not remarkable for handsomeness, neither for greatness, neither for wit or knowledge or sense, and least of all for religion." It would, perhaps, be unreasonable to expect from Wesley a dispassioned verdict on Williamson, but it seems clear that the worthy Mr. Williamson was undistinguished and uninteresting.

Wesley sought out Sophy who was together with Mr. Williamson. Williamson greeted Wesley with surly defiance.

"I suppose, Sir, you know what was agreed on last night between Miss Sophy and me."

"I heard something," said Wesley, "but," he added bluntly, "I could not believe it unless I should hear it from Miss Sophy herself."

Sophy replied, "Sir, I have given Mr. Williamson my consent—unless you have anything to object."

Wesley adds, "It started into my mind, 'What if she means unless you will marry me?' But I checked the thought with, 'Miss Sophy is so sincere: if she meant so, she would say so.'"

A good instance of a favourite blunder.

Williamson was most uneasy. He had caught Sophy on the rebound between the persistent Mellichamp, and the maddening indecisiveness of Wesley. And he did not trust Wesley.

Next day Sophy came round to the Parsonage for prayers. Williamson begged her not to stay on after he had gone. Sophy dismissed him, but Williamson had a valued ally in Delamotte. The oracle had said that Wesley was not to speak to Sophy excepting in Delamotte's presence, and Delamotte grimly determined not to disappoint the oracle.

And so while Williamson paced up and down outside the house, Delamotte sat tight with his eyes glued on Wesley and Sophy.

Wesley reminded Sophy that she had promised to take no steps in anything of importance without first consulting him. She answered earnestly. "Why, what could I do? I can't live in that house. I can't bear these shocks. This is quite a sudden thing. I have no particular inclination for Mr. Williamson. I only promised if no objection appeared. But what can I do?"

Mr. Williamson then came in abruptly and put an end to the conversation.

"Had Delamotte left us alone," Wesley naïvely reflected, "I know not what might have been the event."   ·

Mr. Williamson's nerves were beginning to give way under the strain. Next morning he saw Wesley and said, "Sir, you shall speak with her no more till we are married. You can persuade her to anything. After you went from the Lot yesterday, she would neither eat nor drink for two hours; but was crying continually, and in such an agony she was fit for nothing."

Wesley replied, "To-morrow, sir, you may be her director, but to-day she is to direct herself."

Wesley went into the garden to Sophy and asked her whether she was fully determined. She replied, "I am."

"Take care," said Wesley, "you act upon a right motive. The desire of avoiding crosses is not so. Beside you can't avoid them. They will follow and overtake you in every state."

Perhaps, but there are crosses which it is our duty to avoid. . . . On the cross of celibacy, Wesley crucified the one great love of his life, and the one and only romance in the life of "Miss Sophy."

Wesley met "Miss Sophy" on March 12th, 1736. On March 12th, 1737, Sophy was married to Mr. Williamson and on March 12th, 1738, Wesley finished transcribing the story of his lost love.

VIII

Weeks passed, weeks of torment. Every time Wesley saw Sophy he suffered in every fibre of his being. He could not, would not admit that he had blundered, that he was paying the penalty of his own egregious folly. Had he not appealed to God? Would it not have been impious to have disputed the verdict of the lots? Is not sortilege an infallible method of determining the intentions of the Most High? No, he had acted throughout for the best, but he had been deceived, he had been injured.

They met again, and Wesley poured out a torrent of reproaches based on no surer foundation than some old wives' tale to the effect that Sophy was still in love with Tom Mellichamp. She listened amazed. He did worse. He put pen to paper and wrote her a letter which no self-respecting woman could have received with patience from an old lover:

"If the sincerity of friendship is best to be known from the painful offices, then there could not be a stronger proof of mine than that I gave you on Sunday: except that which I am going to give you now, and which you may perhaps equally misinterpret.

Would you know what I dislike in your past or present behaviour? You have always heard my thoughts as freely as you asked them. Nay, much more freely; you know it well, and so you shall do, as long as I can speak or write.

In your present behaviour I dislike (1) your neglect of half the public service, which no man living can compel you to; (2) your neglect of fasting, which you once knew to be a help to the mind, without any prejudice to the body; (3) your neglect of almost half the opportunity of communicating which you have lately had.

But these things are small in comparison of what I dislike in your past behaviour. For (1) You told me over and over you had entirely conquered your inclination for Mr. Mellichamp. Yet at that very time you had not conquered it. (2) You told me frequently, you had no design to marry Mr. Williamson. Yet at the very time you spoke you had the design. (3) In order to conceal both these things from me, you went through a course of deliberate dissimulation. Oh how fallen! How changed! Surely there was a time when in Miss Sophy's life there was no guile.

Own these facts, and own your fault, and you will be in my thoughts as if they had never been. If you are otherwise minded, I shall still be your friend, though I cannot expect you shall be mine.

To Mrs. Williamson, July 5."

On August 7th Wesley repelled Sophy from the Communion Table, the reason "specified in my letter of July 5th," and "for her not giving me notice of her design to communicate." And then he wrote to her yet another incredible letter.

"At Mr. Causton's request, I write once more. The rules whereby I proceed are these:

So many as intend to be partakers of the Holy Communion, shall signify their names to the Curate, at least some time the day before. This you did not do.

And if any of these . . . have done any wrong to his neighbours, by word or deed, so that the congregation be thereby offended, the Curate . . . shall advertise him, that in any wise he presume not to come to the Lord's Table until he hath openly declared himself to have truly repented.

If you offer yourself at the Lord's Table on Sunday, I will advertise you, as I have done more than once, wherein you have done wrong. And when you have openly declared yourself to have truly repented, I will administer to you the mysteries of God.

JOHN WESLEY."

This curious letter is striking evidence of the torments through which Wesley was passing. Never before or after did his common sense so signally desert him. "So that the congregation be thereby offended." . . . What was the evidence of this extreme sensitiveness of the congregation so far as Sophy was concerned? Whom had she offended save Wesley himself? Why was he offended? Because he knew that he had lost one whom he still passionately desired. . . .

IX

Savannah was in an uproar. Oglethorpe was in England and there was nobody of the least influence left to befriend John Wesley. He had made himself unpopular on all sides. His austerities had repelled his parishioners. The references to their pet failings in his sermons infuriated them. His rigid sacerdotalism aroused their liveliest suspicions.

"We are Protestants," one of his parishioners had remarked, "but as for you, we cannot tell what religion you are of. We never heard of such a religion before. We know not what to make of it."

Then again, he was the champion of unpopular causes. He fought against the introduction of spirituous liquor into the Colony, and he resisted to the last the attempts to evade the veto laid by the Trustees of the Colony on negro slavery. The Colonists resented this veto. The neighbouring colony of Carolina was slave-owning. The good people of Savannah did not see why they, too, should not employ slaves, and they did their best to evade the law by a system of indenture. Wesley hated slavery with all his soul, and he fought it in every form and disguise. In this his record is infinitely finer than Whitefield's, who compromised with the evil thing.

x

Wesley was indicted before the Grand Jury on one of the oddest Bills which a Grand Jury has ever been required to find true. Causton, the prime mover in this affair, was in charge of the proceedings, and the Jury included a Frenchman who did not understand English, a Roman Catholic who did not understand Anglicanism, a professed infidel, three Baptists, and sixteen Dissenters.

Sophy presented an elaborate affidavit, and in addition Wesley was charged with a fine, confused selection of ecclesiastical offences. He had altered the version of the psalms, he had refused to baptise infants excepting by immersion, he had tried to inflict penances and to institute confession for those who desired to communicate. He taught wives and servants "that they ought absolutely to follow the course of mortification, fastings, and diets of prayers prescribed by him, without any regard to the interest of their private families, or the commands of their respective husbands and masters," and so on and so forth.

"This odd Presentment," Wesley tells us, "was at first both opposed and defended with much warmth. But it was soon agreed to lay it aside; perhaps not so much for the notorious falsehood of many parts, as for the extreme uncouthness of the whole."

The indictments were cut down to ten, and the Jury obligingly found a True Bill on each of these ten indictments.

Wesley was summoned and pointed out with the patient tolerance of the expert to the blundering amateur, that they were not entitled to take cognisance of nine out of ten of the indictments, "they being matters of an ecclesiastical nature, and this not being an Ecclesiastical Court."

The tenth indictment charged him with speaking and writing to Mrs. Williamson "contrary to the desire and command of him, the said William Williamson, which proceedings did occasion much uneasiness between the said Williamson and Sophia Christiana Williamson his wife." This charge was all that they were competent to try.

Wesley moved for an immediate trial at Savannah. The Court was puzzled, and did not know how to proceed. Meanwhile, Wesley went on with his work. In spite of his trouble, he found time to preach to the German, French and Italian emigrants in their own languages. He also learnt enough Spanish to pray in that language. Throughout his tribulation, he was at work on those hymns which have found their way into almost every Christian hymnal.

Meanwhile, the quarrel dragged on. Wesley's enemies began to lose grasp of the situation. Nothing is more remarkable than the way in which this young man of thirty-three towered above his fellow colonials. They were uneasy. They bragged and threatened, but they were beginning to regret that they ever proceeded against him.

His congregation, of course, dwindled to a few loyal supporters, and finally Wesley decided to leave Georgia, to return home and to lay his case before the Trustees. A faint show of restraining him was made, but in their heart of hearts they were all only too glad to see him go. For the last time he conducted prayers for a few faithful friends. "And as soon as evening prayers were over, about eight o'clock, the tide then serving, I shook off the dust of my feet, and left Georgia, having preached the gospel there (with much weakness indeed and many infirmities) not as I ought, but as I was able, one year and nearly nine months. (Oh that thou hadst known, at least in this thy day, the things which make for thy peace.)"

"He knew not what lay ahead of him," writes Miss Oemler, "of good or ill. He had not yet found himself, he had not, as he counted it, been converted. His future was as dark to him as the river on which he was journeying under a sky without stars. Behind him, dry in the dust, was left the dew of his youth, the glamour of his heart, the rose of love's desire.

"Never, no matter what great hour might lie ahead; never, no matter what high destiny, what great and holy mission God might have in store for him; never, never more to know such joy, such love, such ecstasy, such high tide of ardour, and emotion, and despair.

"He was never to see her face again, nor hear her speak, nor touch her hand that had held in its palm the one love of his life. John Wesley was to beget no babe of Sophy's bearing. Instead, the little indomitable man, wrapped in his cloak, his eyes sombre in his white face, his lips a line inflexible and uncoercible, went forth to sow in the womb of the waiting future the seed of the gigantic, one child of his begetting, the seed of the Methodist Church." [2]

[2] "The Holy Lover," by Marie Conway Oemler.

CHAPTER VI

FORGOTTEN SLOGANS

FOUR hundred years ago, a monk might have been observed painfully climbing on his knees the steps which Christ descended after His trial before Pilate. These steps, of course, are no longer in Jerusalem, but they are carefully preserved at S. Giovanni Laterano in Rome, and the Pope accords an indulgence of no less than a thousand years to those who ascend them on their knees reciting prayers.

The monk had travelled halfway up the stairs, and he was still on his knees. Suddenly he heard a voice as if from Heaven, "the just shall live by faith." By faith? . . . Not by works? . . . Not by pilgrimages to distant shrines? . . . Not by crawling painfully up marble steps on one's knees?

The monk stood up. He brushed the dust from his knees, and like a free man he strode down the stairs up which he had crawled on his knees and turned his face northwards, to where, in imagination, he could see the snowy barrier of the Alps, and beyond the Alps the Germanies from which he came.

The monk's name was Martin Luther, and justification by faith was his battle cry.

It is always difficult to understand the magic of forgotten slogans. The dust lies deep on those portly folios which define and debate the truth about justification by faith, and imputed righteousness. And yet those ponderous phrases made the wars of religion, and sent great armies thundering across Europe. The modern reader, misquoting Marlowe, might well ask, "Is this the phrase which launched a thousand ships?" for those ancient battle cries have lost their power to stir the hearts of men. The change in mental climate has transformed the jungle of theological conflict. The luxuriant vegetation which flourished in the tropical age, has not survived the ice age of sceptical indifference.

It is impossible to understand the evangelical revival without disturbing the cobwebs of forgotten debates, and without making some effort to understand the backwash of Lutheranism on the religious life of England.

II

Justification by faith expressed in doctrinal terms the revolt of Protestant individualism against the excessive solidarity of Rome; for Rome always strove to realise her great ideal, the unity of all the faithful in one world state ruled by Pope and Emperor—*una chiesa in uno stato*. This ideal found imperfect expression in that Holy Roman Empire which, as Voltaire remarks, was neither Holy, Roman nor an Empire.

The Roman tradition was preserved by the Church as a figment in the Holy Roman Empire, and as a fact in that imperial organization and *esprit de corps* which Catholicism had inherited from Rome; *Civis Romanus sum* was at once a boast and a surrender, implying as it did the subordination of individual will, no less than the pride of imperial citizenship. Both traditions were preserved in the Roman Church.

The fanatic hatred with which heresy was pursued proved how deeply the medieval mind had been impregnated with the Roman ideal of unity and uniformity. The

heretic was the old barbarian come again. His disintegrating doctrines threatened the imperial unity of Rome
and the prosperity which was based on the pax Romana.
Once again, the Goth was knocking at the gates of Rome.
The Holy Office and the Roman Empire represented two
aspects, practical and idealistic, in which the medieval
mind attempted to protect and to realise religious and
secular unity. "In the Roman Church," writes Dr. Workman,[1] "the individual *qua* individual had little or no place.
His salvation was conditioned from first to last by his belonging to a corporation, in whose privileges and functions he shared; through whose sacraments his life
was nourished; by whose graduated hierarchy, though but
the meanest servant of the Church, he was linked on
to the supreme head; whose saints shielded him by their
merits and intercessions. Through this corporation alone
was he brought into touch with his Saviour; outside the
corporation his soul was lost. In this corporation all national distinctions were obliterated; the Church was
majestically one in creed, ritual, discipline, and language.
The grandeur of the idea few will dispute; its extraordinary hold for long centuries upon the consciences of men
testifies to the strength of its appeal. . . . Against this
exaggeration of solidarity the Reformation was a many-
sided protest. In place of the Holy Roman Empire we see
the rise of separate nations, each determined to work out
its life, political and religious, on its own lines. . . . Instead of a salvation conditioned by corporate relations,
we find the assertion by Luther of the paramount importance of the inner life of the individual. For whatever else
justification by faith may mean it stands for the claim
that between the individual and his Saviour no corporation, no priest, no sacrament, no saints may intervene.

[1] "A New History of Methodism," page 7.

The diverse creeds of the Reformation—and their very diversity was one of the fruits of this resurrection of individualism—agree at any rate in this fundamental position."

In its noblest form, the doctrine of justification by faith was a great piece of idealism, and as such, a tremendous uplifting power. "You must believe," as Mr. F. H. Bradley writes, "that you really are one with the divine, and must act as if you believe it. In short, you must be justified not by works, but solely by faith. This doctrine, which Protestantism to its eternal glory has made its own and sealed with its blood, is the very centre of Christianity; and where you have not this in one form or another there Christianity is nothing but a name." [2]

But the doctrine had its dangerous side. To preach justification by faith too often led to contempt of good works. The believer happy in the conviction that he had at last achieved a justifying faith, was only too apt to assume that it was no longer necessary to fight against sin. What did sin matter so long as a man believed? This theory, of course, led straight to the bottomless pit of antinomianism, to the doctrine that the true believer was indeed beyond the law. "Christ died," so ran the argument, "to pay the penalty of human sin. The sinner who has faith can therefore discharge his debt vicariously. He can impute his sins to Christ, and he can impute Christ's righteousness to himself. The problem of salvation is reduced to a simple book-keeping transaction. Christ's sufferings on the Cross are transferred to the sinner's side of the ledger. Of course, good works are useless. Man is vile, and cannot hope to please God by feeble attempts at 'good works.' He is saved in so far, and in so far only, as he has faith. He may continue to sin, but even sin cannot

[2] "Ethical Studies," page 290.

harm him so long as he is clothed in Christ's righteousness."

Luther's own teaching is not free from dangerous
ambiguity. There are passages in his letters and in his
sermons which might be taken as a direct incitement to
antinomianism. There is, for instance, his famous letter
to Melanchthon, "Sin and sin boldly, but the more firmly
believe." The same sentiment finds even stranger expression in his letter to Jerome Weller.

"Poor Jerome Weller, you have temptations; you must
get the better of them. When the devil comes to tempt
you—drink, my friend, drink deeply; make yourself
merry, play the fool, and sin, in hatred of the Evil One,
and to play him a trick. If the devil says to you, 'you
surely will not drink,' answer him thus, 'I will drink
bumpers because you forbid me. I will enjoy copious potations in honour of Jesus Christ.' Follow my example. I
should neither eat, drink, nor enjoy myself at table so
much were it not to vex Satan. *I wish I could discover
some new sin* that he might learn to his cost that I laugh
at all that is Sin, and that I could not consider my conscience as charged with it. Away with the Decalogue,
when the devil comes to torment us! When he whispers in
our ear . . . 'You will be damned in the next world,'
that is false; I know that there is One who has suffered
and satisfied for me . . . and where He is, there shall I
be also."

One suspects a strain of irony in this letter. Weller,
like Melanchthon, was probably a spiritual hypochondriac
always worrying about the state of his soul. Luther's
impetuous retort was no doubt provoked by a querulous
and despondent outburst. Luther, like so many of the
prophets, delighted in paradox and hyperbole. His letters
abound in picturesque and grotesque exaggerations; and
to appreciate their true significance one needs a sense of

humour. No one who is familiar with his life as a whole, would maintain that he made light of sin, but it is easy to understand how certain extracts from his writings might be used to justify antinomian doctrines. Dollinger, the great Catholic historian, declared that Luther's doctrine of sin and salvation had bewildered and corrupted the religious conscience of mankind for two centuries. This is a gross exaggeration, but though Dollinger's verdict is unfair to Luther, it is by no means unjust to that caricature of Lutheranism which was often preached by his more extreme followers.

I have quoted the tribute of a great Oxford philosopher, Mr. Bradley, to the doctrine of justification by faith. The other side of the picture has been painted by a famous Oxford historian, J. A. Froude, who thus describes an evangelical meeting in the fifties:

"We were told that the business of each individual man and woman in the world was to save his or her soul; and we were all sinners together—all equally guilty, hopeless, lost, accursed children, unable to stir a finger or do a thing to help ourselves. Happily, we were not required to stir a finger; rather we were forbidden to attempt it. An antidote had been provided for our sins, and a substitute for our obedience. Everything had been done for us. We had but to lay hold of the perfect righteousness which had been fulfilled in our behalf. We had but to put on the vesture provided for our wearing, and our safety was assured. The reproaches of conscience were silenced. We were perfectly happy in this world, and certain to be blessed in the next. If, on the other hand, we neglected the offered grace; if, through carelessness, or intellectual perverseness, or any other cause, we did not apprehend it in the proper manner; if we tried to please God ourselves by 'works of righteousness,' the sacrifice would then cease to avail us. It mattered nothing whether, in the common acceptance of the word, we were good or bad; we were lost all the same, condemned by perfect justice to everlasting torture. . . . When the first address was over, the congregation sang the following singular hymn, one of a collection of which, it appeared from the title page, many hundred thousand copies were in circulation:

"Nothing, either great or small,
　　Nothing, sinners, no;
Jesus did it—did it all
　　Long, long ago.

It is finished, yes, indeed,
　　Finished every jot:
Sinners, this is all you need,
　　Tell me, Is it not?

When He from His lofty throne
　　Stooped to do and die,
Everything was fully done:
　　Hearken to His cry,—

Weary, weary, burdened one,
　　Wherefore toil you so?
Cease your doing, all was done
　　Long, long ago.

Till to Jesus' work you cling
　　By a simple faith,
Doing is a deadly thing,
　　Doing ends in death.

Cast your deadly doing down,
　　Down at Jesus' feet,
Stand in Him, in Him alone,
　　Gloriously complete."

"We are left face to face with a creed which tells us that God has created us without the power to keep the commandments,—that He does not require us to keep them; yet at the same time that we are infinitely guilty in His eyes for not keeping them, and that we justly deserve to be tortured for ever and ever, to suffer, as we once heard an amiable clergyman express it, 'to suffer the utmost pain which Omnipotence can inflict, and the creature can endure, without annihilation.' " [3]

III

The prophets have often been men of one formula. They pass through a phase of doubt and despair, and suddenly the heavens open, and in a blinding flash of illumination they discover the clue to the crossword puzzle of life. Thenceforwards, all is plain and clear. In moments of doubt the magic formula is repeated. The one sin for which there is no forgiveness is to cast doubt on the infallibility of the formula.

With Wesley it was otherwise. He accepted, as we shall see, justification by faith; but he was a true child of his century, a century which expected Christianity to prove its case at the Bar of Reason. His temperament was empirical. He could never rest satisfied with a mere formula without continuing to subject it to the test of experiment. And so he was always modifying and transforming his views. To Luther, justification by faith was a doctrine with no round edges. It was as hard and angular as a proposition in Euclid. To Wesley, it was an elastic formula, less a solution than a clue which might guide him to the solution for which he sought.

[3] "Short Studies of Great Subjects," by J. A Froude.

CHAPTER VII

CONVERSION

WESLEY returned to London in a mood of great discouragement. "I went to America," he writes in his Journal, "to convert the Indian, who shall convert me? Who, what, is he that will deliver me from this evil heart of unbelief? I have a fair summer religion. I can talk well; nay, and believe myself while no danger is near; but let death look me in the face and my spirit is troubled."

Shortly after reaching London, Wesley met a young Moravian graduate from Jena, Peter Böhler by name.

"From Böhler," says Mr. Lecky, "he first learned to believe that every man, no matter how moral, how pious, or how orthodox he may be, is in a state of damnation, until by a supernatural and instantaneous process wholly unlike that of human reasoning, the conviction flashes upon his mind that the sacrifice of Christ has been applied to him, and has expiated his sins; that this supernatural and personal conviction or illumination is what is meant by Saving Faith, and that it is inseparably accompanied by an absolute assurance of Salvation, and by a complete domination over sin. It cannot exist where there is not a sense of pardon of all past and of freedom from all present sins. It is impossible that he who had experienced it should be in serious and lasting doubt as to the fact, for its fruits are constant peace—not one uneasy thought."

Wesley, of course, did not accept Böhler's teaching without question. He was an eighteenth century man, and

he required some pretence of an argument based on reason before being convinced. Indeed, had not the Thirty-
nine Articles confirmed Böhler's theory, it is doubtful
whether Böhler would have succeeded.

The Thirty-nine Articles as is well known, represent
an ingenious attempt to split the difference between Rome
and Geneva, between the old Catholic religion and the
black-gowned emissaries of Calvin. The latter were
placated by the article on predestination, which can be
read in almost any sense that one desires, and the Luther-
ans are consoled by the article in which we are told that
"justification by faith" is "a most wholesome doctrine and
very full of comfort."

Article XII adds that good works "done before the
grace of Christ and the inspiration of His spirit are not
pleasant to God for as much as they spring not from
faith . . . yea rather for that they are not done as God
willed and commanded them to be done, we doubt not that
they have the nature of sin."

Wesley was surprised to discover on re-reading these
Articles, how little the official doctrines of the Church
of England differed from those of the doctrine preached
by his Moravian friend.

Wesley and Böhler travelled to Oxford together. Böhler
listened patiently to Wesley's arguments, and remarked
quietly, "My brother, that philosophy of yours must be
purged away."

Wesley was unhappy, and wondered whether he ought
to abandon preaching. Clearly he lacked those emotional
experiences which Böhler had declared to be the essence
of Christianity. He consulted Böhler who replied, "Preach
faith until you have it, and then because you have it you
will preach faith."

So Wesley began to preach the gospel of justification
by faith to congregations composed of people who very

sensibly had omitted to read the Articles of the Church of England, and who therefore did not recognise in Wesley's theme the doctrines of Anglicanism. Wesley tried, as all religious innovators have tried, to persuade them that this was no new thing that he preached. But they were not convinced, and one by one the pulpits of London were closed to him.

II

John and Charles Wesley passed through an experience which it is usual to describe as conversion, within a few days of each other. Charles was the first to attain "a full, complete assurance of salvation." A few days later, on May 24th, 1738, John Wesley passed through a similar experience. Here is the classic extract from his Journal:

"In the evening I went very unwillingly to a society in Aldersgate Street where one was reading Luther's preface to the Epistle to the Romans. About a quarter before nine, while he was describing the change which God works in the heart through faith in Christ, I felt my heart strangely warmed. I felt I did trust in Christ, Christ alone for my salvation; and an assurance was given me that he had taken away my sins, even mine, and saved me from the law of sin and death."

John Wesley walked back to see his brother, and greeted him with the words, "I believe."

Whatever importance we may assign to this phenomenon of conversion, one thing, at least, is clear. Charles Wesley's tongue had been loosened by the experience through which he had passed. When John came into his room and described his own conversion, the two brothers sang together a hymn in which the soul of evangelical experience finds lyrical expression:

"O how shall I the goodness tell,
 Father, which Thou to me hast showed?
That I, a child of wrath and hell,
 I should be called a child of God,
Should know, should feel my sins forgiven,
Blest with this antepast of heaven."

The Oxford don, precise, distrustful of enthusiasm, suspicious of emotion, was suddenly transformed into a flaming evangelist. Together the brothers sang the message which for the next forty years they were to deliver in all the darkest by-ways of submerged England.

"Outcasts of men, to you I call,
 Harlots, and publicans, and thieves!
He spreads His arms to embrace you all,
 Sinners alone, His grace receives;
 . . . . . .
He calls you now, invites you home;
Come, O my guilty brethren, come."

"This hymn," writes Mr. Rattenbury, "was probably sung to the old Twenty-third psalm tune, and the singing of it was the overture to the Evangelical Revival; it was the prelude of a New England."

III

Much ink has been spilled in the attempt to decide the exact importance of Wesley's conversion. The older school of Methodist orthodoxy, of whom Tyerman is the most representative example, have exaggerated the critical importance of the experience through which John Wesley passed in Aldersgate Street.

Dr. Maximin Piette, a Belgian priest, and the author of a brilliant and profound study of John Wesley, tends to err in the opposite direction. Tyerman was influenced by the orthodox Methodist doctrines in his exaggeration, but Dr. Piette may be equally liable to depreciate an experience, the validity of which, as a good Catholic, he could not admit without considerable reservation.

"The famous conversion," writes Dr. Piette, "which was destined to play such an important rôle in the doctrinal life of Methodism, played a very modest rôle in the life of the Founder of Methodism and of his companions. . . . Had he not recorded the incident in his Journal, it is probable that Wesley would have entirely forgotten it. . . . All those authors who speak so freely of the Great Conversion of 1738, and who have done their best to paint Wesley the undergraduate of 1725 as a great sinner, ought, none the less, to have recognised that after Wesley's entry into Holy Orders, there was no further excuse for treating him as a grand sinner. They would have done much better to have antedated Wesley's real conversion by fourteen years before the date fixed by the official Wesleyan legend." [2]

Dr. Piette is right in so far as it is absurd to use the same word indiscriminately for the sudden change of life and habit which has marked the conversion of sinners into saints, and for the much less important change through which Wesley passed in 1738.

It was, of course, natural that Wesley should at first exaggerate the significance of his recent experience. He startled his old friend Mr. Hutton by announcing that he had never been a Christian at all until the Wednesday of the preceding week. Mrs. Hutton, with feminine shrewdness replied, "Well then, you have been a great hypocrite." Indeed, as Canon Overton remarks, "if John Wesley was not a good Christian in Georgia, God help the millions who profess to call themselves Christians."

[4] "La Réaction de Wesley dans l'Évolution du Protestantisme."

At that time, of course, Wesley made the great mistake of treating an emotional state as an indispensable test of Christianity, but it was characteristic of his essential sanity that he soon learned to distrust doctrines which were built up on the evidence of an emotional state. Even within three weeks of his conversion, his references to that event show a great reserve. He was preaching at St. Mary's, Oxford, and he was careful to state that "the assurance" which accompanies faith is perhaps not given "at all times nor with the same fullness of persuasion." In other words, a man might be saved, without experiencing that emotional experience which, according to the Moravians, was the hall-mark of the converted soul. Wesley in his old age looked back with tolerant amusement on the exaggerations of his youth. "When fifty years ago," he wrote, "my brother Charles and I in the simplicity of our hearts taught the people that unless they knew their sins forgiven, they were under the wrath and curse of God, I wonder they did not stone us. We preach assurance, a common privilege of the children of God, but we do not enjoin it under pain of damnation on all who enjoy it not."

Tyerman is puzzled by the changes of spiritual temperature revealed in Wesley's Journal. Tyerman believed that either you were or you were not converted. There is no room for doubt and self-questioning. Either you were in a state of misery because you were not converted, or you were in a state of radiant self-confidence because you were. So he was depressed and puzzled to discover Wesley writing a year after his conversion: "My friends affirm that I am mad because I said I was not a Christian a year ago. I affirm I am not a Christian now . . . I have not any love of God. I do not love either the Father or the Son."

That, however, was the last outbreak. "Thenceforth,"

writes Canon Overton, "during the whole of his long
life, hardly a shadow of a doubt about his spiritual state
crosses his mind. Clouds and darkness constantly swept
over his outward life, but there was always perpetual and
unclouded sunshine within."

The chief contrast between the pre-conversion and the
post-conversion Journals is in the fact, that the former
contain too many and the latter practically no references
to his own emotion. Wesley was always very interested
in the religious experiences of others and was indeed too
ready to accept at their face value, the spiritual autobiog-
raphies of his numerous converts. But of his own emotions and of his own spiritual experiences we read very
little in his Journal for the last fifty years of his life.

What brought about this change? The moody, depressed
and ineffective Wesley who landed in England from
Georgia, weighed down by the sense of failure, was transformed within a few weeks into an Evangelist full of
confidence and hope.

"The priest," as Dr. Cadman remarks, "is merged in
the prophet." The long period of anxious self-questioning
is at an end, or almost at an end.

This is true enough, and to this extent, at least, 1738
is an important date in Wesley's life, but to represent
Wesley's life as divided into two sharply contrasted portions by his experience in Aldersgate Street is absurd.
There is no such sharp breach of continuity.

His conversion was precipitated, as we have seen, by his
long conversations with Böhler, and by the Moravian and
Lutheran doctrines which Böhler preached. But it is curious that the distinctive doctrines which are supposed to
have precipitated Wesley's conversion should have been
those which, in later years, he was most anxious to revise.

Only three years after Peter Böhler, Moravian, had

precipitated Wesley's conversion, we find in his Journal the following drastic criticisms on Martin Luther's comments on the Epistle to the Galatians. Martin Luther, he complains, is "quite shallow in his remarks on many passages, and muddy and confused almost, on all." He is "deeply tinctured with mysticism throughout, and hence often dangerously wrong. . . . How does he decry reason, right or wrong, as an irreconcilable enemy to the gospel of Christ! . . . Again, how blasphemously does he speak of good works and of the law of God—constantly coupling the law with sin, death, hell, or the devil; and teaching that Christ delivers us from them all alike. Whereas it can no more be proved by Scripture that Christ delivers us from the law of God than that He delivers us from holiness or from heaven. Here (I apprehend) is the real spring of the grand error of the Moravians. They follow Luther, for better, for worse. . . . After reading Luther's miserable comment upon the text, I thought it my bounden duty openly to warn the congregation against that dangerous treatise."

Mr. Tyerman, again, was anxious to prove that Wesley's conversion purged his soul of sacerdotalism, but it is easy to show that those views which Mr. Tyerman politely dismisses as "High Church nonsense" were unaffected by Wesley's Aldersgate Street experience. It is a Methodist who reminds us that "there is no greater mistake than to suppose that Wesley ceased to be a High Churchman after 1738." Mr. Rattenbury continues, "The popular argument that the Wesley before 1738 and after were two different men, with different views, is a modern Methodist myth which serious investigation proves to be without foundation. . . . The Wesleys in belief, assertion, and practice were always sacramentalists of a comparatively High Church type, and wished their people to be the same."

Wesley did not, of course, believe in transubstantiation, but Charles Wesley's hymn "Victim Divine" undoubtedly teaches the Real Presence:

"We need not now go up to heaven,
    To bring the long-sought Saviour down;
Thou art to all already given,
    Thou dost e'en now Thy banquet crown:
To every faithful soul appear,
And show Thy real presence here!"

This hymn was amongst those that were issued in the collection called "Hymns on the Lord's Supper," which was the joint publication of John and Charles Wesley, and may therefore be taken as expressing the common sentiment of the two brothers. The first edition of this collection, "Hymns on the Lord's Supper," was published in 1745 (eight years after his conversion) and the ninth edition appeared three years before his death.

Bishop Knox and Mr. Kensit found it necessary to warn faithful Protestants against the dangerous sacramentarian doctrines contained in these hymns, and indeed, those ultra-Protestants for whom Bishop Knox and Mr. Kensit speak, have every reason to view with alarm the sacramentarian hymns which Charles Wesley wrote, and of which John Wesley approved.

It would, indeed, be easier to prove the virtual similarity in outlook and in doctrine between Wesley of the Oxford Holy Club and Wesley as an old man, than to show, as Mr. Tyerman tries to show, that Wesley's conversion corresponds to a real break in continuity. No man changed less between youth and age than did Wesley. His Diary [3] at eighty differed little, either in form or in purpose, from the Diary which he kept at Oxford, and its significance can best be appreciated, as Mr. Curnock pointed out, if it

[3] For the difference between Diary and Journal, see Chapter II § 2.

is regarded as the diary of a member of the Oxford Holy Club. "Hitherto we have taken it for granted," writes Mr. Curnock, "that with the voyage to Georgia, the Holy Club ceased to exist. Wesley's last Diary shows that for fifty-six years after the 'Simmonds' sailed, its Rules of Holy Living formed the substratum of Wesley's daily devotional life, and kept him, as originally they made him, the most useful saint in the British Empire."

From which it would seem that it was not his Aldersgate Street conversion, but precisely those habits which he had formed during that Oxford period of his life, the importance of which Mr. Tyerman tried to depreciate, which made Wesley "the most useful saint in the British Empire." [4]

[4] Moreover the minute introspection and meticulous self-scrutiny which Tyerman supposed to be characteristic of Wesley's Oxford ritualistic period, existed to the last. An amusing instance of this habit is to be found on page 261 of this book. Note the legalistic exactness with which Wesley discriminates between the various shades of "inordinate affection."

CHAPTER VIII

LAYING THE FOUNDATIONS

WESLEY had long desired to visit the Moravians in their own home. On June 15th, 1738, he set out, accompanied by Benjamin Ingham, for Germany. In the course of his journey he visited Marienbad where Count Zinzendorf was living as the "Head" of a family of Moravians, most of whom were in training for the mission field.

The relations between Wesley and Zinzendorf were never cordial. Both men were autocrats by temperament, and both were quick to detect and to resent autocracy in others. There is a story, probably apocryphal, that the Count ordered Wesley to work for him in his garden. Wesley obeyed and had no sooner begun to perspire heavily than the Count ordered him to get into his carriage in order to go with him to pay a ceremonial call on another German Count. Wesley asked for time to wash his hands and to put on his coat, but Zinzendorf replied, "You must be simple, my brother." The Count certainly had quaint notions of entertaining his guests. "If the Count," we are told, "wished to afford anyone a pleasure, he took him to the cemetery and spoke to him of those who were interred there."

From Marienbad, Wesley passed on to Herrnhut, the principal Moravian settlement, a quiet, isolated village on the outskirts of Bohemia.

Wesley passed a very happy fortnight at Herrnhut

cross-examining the Moravians on their spiritual experiences.

Wesley had the mind of a scientist rather than of a theologian. His method was empirical and experimental. He was always listing and re-arranging his collection of theological specimens. And so we watch him at Herrenhut, passing from one Moravian to another, filling his note-book with an exact shorthand record of their spiritual experiences, and insensibly modifying his own position in accordance with the new data which he had collected.

Wesley was always busy with his note-book. He collected ideas not only on spiritual problems, but also on problems of organization. There were certain things at Herrnhut which he copied, and which he would have done well not to copy. It was at Herrnhut that he picked up his devastating ideas as to the proper way in which to run a school for children.

In his Journal, he quotes with approval the time-table of the Herrnhut orphan house. The "larger children" rose at five, the "smaller children" at six. The "larger children" worked continuously with a short interval for food and a long interval for prayers until ten o'clock at night. Such was the Herrnhut orphanage. Parents, even the most unattractive, must have been at a premium in Herrnhut.

Not that Wesley approved wholeheartedly of everything which he had seen at Herrnhut. Five days after returning to London, he drafted a letter which was never sent, but which he carefully preserved. This letter proves that Wesley's critical faculty had not been in abeyance. He propounded the following questions:

"Is not the Count all in all among you?

"Do you not magnify your Church too much?

"Do you not use guile and dissimulation in most cases?

"Are you not of a close, dark, reserved temper and behaviour?"

It is a pity that this letter was never sent. Count Zin-zendorf's reply to this catechism would have been well worth reading.

II

During the winter of 1738 and 1739, Wesley was ex-cluded from all but three or four London churches; which was not altogether surprising for few incumbents could be expected to welcome to their pulpits a young man whose chief concern was to prove that the form of Chris-tianity which they themselves had been preaching, and which Wesley had been preaching until quite recently, was not Christianity at all.

Some of his best work was done in Newgate. Charles had begun to visit the condemned prisoners during his brother's absence in Germany. Charles Wesley had been inclined to doubt the probability of a genuine death-bed repentance, "but," he writes, "in the midst of my lan-guid discourse a sudden spirit of faith came upon me, and I promised them all pardon in the name of Jesus Christ, if they would then, as at the last hour, repent and be-lieve the gospel."

The last scenes at Tyburn made a grim impression on Charles Wesley.

"I rose very heavy, and backward to visit them for the last time. At six I prayed and sang with them all together. The ordinary would have read prayers, and preached most miserably. Mr. Sparks and Mr. Broughton were present. I felt my heart full of tender love to the latter. He administered. All the ten received. Then he prayed; and I after him. At half-hour past nine their irons were knocked off and their hands tied. I went in a coach with Sparks, Washington, and a friend of Newington's (N. himself not being permitted). By half-hour past ten we came to Tyburn, waited till eleven; then were brought the children appointed to die. I got upon the cart with Sparks and Broughton; the ordinary endeavoured to follow, when the poor prisoners begged he might not come; and the mob kept him down. I prayed first, then Sparks and Broughton. We had prayed before that our Lord would show there was a power superior to the fear of death. Newington had quite forgot his pain. They were all cheerful; full of comfort, peace and triumph; assuredly persuaded Christ had died for them, and waited to receive them into paradise. Greenaway was impatient to be with Christ. The black had spied me coming out of the coach, and saluted me with his looks. As often as his eyes met mine he smiled with the most composed, delightful countenance I ever saw. Read caught hold of my hand in a transport of joy. Newington seemed perfectly pleased. Hudson declared he was never better, or more at ease, in mind and body. None showed any natural terror of death; no fear or crying or tears. All expressed their desire of our following them to paradise. I never saw such calm triumph, such incredible indifference to dying. We sang several hymns, particularly:

> Behold the Saviour of mankind
> Nailed to the shameful tree!

and the hymn entitled 'Faith in Christ,' which concludes:

> A guilty, weak, and helpless worm,
> Into Thy hands I fall;
> Be Thou my life, my righteousness,
> My Jesus, and my all.

We prayed Him, in earnest faith, to receive their spirits. I could do nothing but rejoice; kissed Newington and Hudson; took leave of each in particular. Mr. Broughton bade them not to be surprised when the cart should draw away. They cheerfully replied they should not; expressed some concern how we should get back to our coach. We left them going to meet their Lord, ready for the Bridegroom. When the cart drew off, not one stirred, or struggled for life, but meekly gave up their spirits. Exactly at twelve they were turned off. I spoke a few suitable words to the crowd, and returned, full of peace and confidence in our friends' happiness. That hour under the gallows was the most blessed hour of my life." [1]

"Not one stirred, or struggled for life." That is the most impressive touch in the whole story. In those days, hanging was a lingering death, and the final agony lasted for an appreciable time.

Religious exaltation is often an anaesthetic in its effect, and it is more than probable than many of the martyrs who suffered in the flames felt no pain, and perhaps the "meekness" with which Charles Wesley's converts "gave up their spirits" was due to the same cause. But whether this anaesthesia can be explained by natural causes or whether it is in itself evidence of a source of supernatural strength and energy available to men in a state of great religious exaltation, is a point on which people will continue to differ.

III

The chief work of the Wesleys at this time was effected through the medium of religious societies, very similar to the group which had met both at Oxford and in Georgia for mutual counsel. Of course, the Wesleys did not invent religious societies. Such societies had existed in the Church of England for more than fifty years.

On May 1st, 1738, Wesley, acting on the advice of

[1] Charles Wesley's Journal.

Peter Böhler, founded a society which was different from the other societies of the period. Like them it was, in theory at least, a Church of England society, but in many respects it was closely modelled on the Moravian system, and a great many of its original members were Moravians.

This Society met every week in a room in Fetter Lane which became the headquarters of the work of the Wesleys.

When Wesley returned from Germany, the Society numbered thirty-two members. The meeting held on New Year's Day was attended by seven Oxford ministers, old friends of the Holy Club, and sixty laymen.

Such was Wesley's work in the winter of 1738-9. If anybody outside the Movement had been asked the name of the most prominent Methodist, he would probably not have replied "John Wesley," but "George Whitefield." George Whitefield had suddenly sprung into fame, and the story of his early career deserves a chapter to itself.

CHAPTER IX

GEORGE WHITEFIELD

GEORGE WHITEFIELD was born on December 16th, 1714, in the Bell Inn, Gloucester, one of the few inns which preserve to this day the old outside galleries.

His grandfather was a clergyman; his father, who kept the Bell Inn, died when George Whitefield was only two years of age. His mother kept on the Inn, and George worked in it as a common tapster from the age of fifteen to seventeen. Then came the turning point of his life.

An old schoolfellow, who had obtained the position of servitor at Pembroke College, Oxford, was paying a visit to the Whitefields. He described how he had paid all his expenses and had saved money. Whitefield's mother turned to George and said, "Will you go to Oxford, George?" And George replied, "With all my heart."

Whitefield entered Pembroke as a servitor, a year after Samuel Johnson had left Pembroke. Servitors have long since disappeared from the universities, but there is a great deal to be said for an institution which enabled a clever young man to keep himself while reading for his degree.

While he was at Oxford, Whitefield got into touch with the Wesleys, and joined the Holy Club.

Whitefield was ordained, and preached his first sermon in 1736. Twelve months later, this youth of twenty-two, with no advantages of birth or breeding, had established a reputation as the greatest and most popular preacher

of the day. His success was instantaneous; within twelve
months he had to drive to his work by post in order to
avoid the troublesome attentions of the crowd.

What manner of man was George Whitefield? He was
no more than twenty-five when he decided that the world
at large would be grateful for a little information on this
point, so he published a pamphlet of seventy-six pages
with the attractive title, "A Short Account of God's Dealings with the Reverend Mr. George Whitefield, B.A., late
of Pembroke College, Oxford; from his infancy to the
time of his entering into Holy Orders."

Whitefield, like others who had enjoyed a bona fide
conversion, was anxious to emphasise the ungodliness of
his youth, but unlike Wesley, he was not content with a
few brief sentences on this theme. He recalls "the early
stirrings of corruption" in his heart, which abundantly
convinced him that he was "conceived and born in sin."
He assures us that he was "froward from my mother's
womb. . . . I was so brutish as to hate instruction. . . .
Often have I joined with others in playing roguish tricks,
but was generally, if not always, *happily detected*. For
this, I have often since, and do now, bless and praise God."
His dramatic talent soon asserted itself. He used frequently to dress up as a parson and read prayers to his
young friends. Even at school, his remarkable powers of
elocution attracted attention, and he was asked to take
a girl's part in some school theatricals.

The autobiographical sketch is perhaps a little disap-
pointing on the subject of God's dealings with the Reverend George Whitefield, B.A., but it is an acute, if unconscious self-revelation. We admire the grit and
enterprise which enabled Whitefield to rise from the position of tapster to that of a graduate of Oxford. There is
no reason to suspect the sincerity of his conversion, or his
conquest of temptations described with more accuracy

than reserve, temptations which at first proved inevitable but which were finally overcome. But the pamphlet as a whole was a blunder even if it did not merit the stern verdict of the Bishop of Exeter.

"Mr. Whitefield's account of God's dealings with him," wrote Dr. Lavington, Bishop of Exeter, "is such a boyish, ludicrous, filthy, nasty, and shameless relation of himself, as quite defiles paper, and is shocking to decency and modesty. 'Tis a perfect jakes of uncleanness."

At sixteen Whitefield was a tapster, a common servitor, eking out his university fees by menial work. At twenty-five he was the most famous preacher in England. Only a saint whose ambitions were completely divorced from this world could have withstood the temptations to which Whitefield was exposed. It is no wonder that his vanity sometimes got the better of his judgment. He was, for instance, somewhat unbalanced by the patronage which he received from the aristocracy. And so when Lady Huntingdon announced to Whitefield that "his lips drooped like the honeycomb and were a well of life," Whitefield was naturally rather pleased. To a severe taste his efforts to repay these aristocratic compliments may seem a little servile, but they were in the manner of the age. He wrote, for instance, a hymn in honour of Lady Huntingdon of which the following verse is a fair sample:

> "Uphold this Star in Thy right hand—
>   Crown her endeavours with success;
> Among the great ones may she stand,
>   A witness to Thy righteousness;
> Till many nobles join Thy train,
> And triumph in the Lamb that's slain."

Whitefield was no scholar. He had little learning, and his mind had never been disciplined by exact study or research. He had read next to nothing, and he passed at one bound from the status of a pupil engaged in picking up stray fragments of knowledge, to the status of preacher, prophet and dogmatist.

"The lessons which he never drew from books," writes Sir James Stephen, "were never taught him by living men. He allowed himself no leisure for social intercourse with his superiors, or with his equals, but underwent the debilitating effects of conversing almost exclusively with those who sat as disciples at his feet. Their homage, and the impetuous tumult of his career, left him but superficially acquainted with himself. Unsuspicious of his own ignorance, and exposed to flattery far more intoxicating than the acclamations of the theatre, he laid the foundations of a new religious system, with less profound thought and a greater penury of religious research than had ever fallen to the lot of a reformer or heresiarch before."

Johnson, who had a great respect for Wesley, would not allow that Whitefield was a great orator. "His popularity," said Johnson, "is chiefly owing to the peculiarity of his manner. He would be followed by crowds were he to wear a nightcap in the pulpit, or were he to preach from a tree."

It is a pity that Boswell did not invite Johnson to define a little more carefully the distinction between oratory and "that peculiarity of manner" which enabled Whitefield to charm the cynical Horace Walpole, to extract a quizzical compliment from Lord Chesterfield, and even to arouse the envy of Garrick. His command over his congregations was absolute. He could make them laugh or weep at will. There is a story of an old general who heard Whitefield describing a blind man stumbling along to the edge of a cliff, prodding with sticks, ever nearing the precipice. Suddenly, the General exclaimed "Good God, he's over," a remarkable tribute to Whitefield's vivid imagery.

Green, the historian, considers that the real secret of his influence lay in "the intense reality of his preaching," in "its earnestness of belief, its deep, tremulous sympathy with the sin and sorrow of mankind." Even Sir James Stephen, whose severe verdict on Whitefield has just been quoted, pays him a fine tribute:

"If ever philanthropy burned in the human heart with a pure and intense flame, embracing the whole family of man in the spirit of universal charity, it was in the heart of George Whitefield. He loved the world that hated him. He had no preferences but in favour of the ignorant, the miserable, and the poor."

The evangelical revival was based on sense and sensibility, on Wesley's distrust of enthusiasm, and on Whitefield's wholehearted exploitation of emotion. Wesley had disciplined his mind and his body from his youth upwards. He never lost his self-control. Whitefield could work up his congregation to frenzy pitch, but only at the expense of self-surrender to the emotions which he produced. He was the captive of the forces which he set in motion. Wesley, on the other hand, remained calm and even critical, when the thousands around him were in the throes of revival fever.

It was the quiet, donnish little man who held captive the common people in his congregation. Whitefield enjoyed an extraordinary popularity among the aristocracy of his time. The ex-tapster became the pet of the aristocracy, but it was the Fellow of Lincoln who gripped and held the common people.

CHAPTER X

THE BEGINNING OF FIELD PREACHING

IN 1736 Wesley invited Whitefield to come to Georgia. On the day that Wesley returned from Georgia, Whitefield set sail. Where Wesley had failed, Whitefield succeeded in winning the goodwill and the affection of the Colony. After a stay of six months, he returned to England to collect money for an orphanage which he had founded in Savannah.

When Whitefield visited London on the way through to Georgia, many churches had been opened to him. His fame as a popular preacher spread rapidly, and for a few weeks he had been lionised. He was, therefore, not prepared for the reception which awaited him on his return from Georgia, for he found that the embargo imposed on the Wesleys applied no less strictly to himself. He was boycotted, not only because of his associations with the Wesleys, but also because the publication of his Journal had produced a very bad impression.

Whitefield left London in disgust, and went down to Bristol, where his reception eighteen months previously had been most friendly. But Bristol proved as stubborn as London. Whitefield, faced by the possibility of being completely excluded from the pulpits, took a step which was destined to have a decisive influence on the evangelical revival. He decided to preach in the open air. He selected Kingswood, four miles from Bristol, as the scene of his first experiment in this novel form of preaching.

Kingswood was a barren track inhabited by men who

had never seen the inside of a church. It had formerly been a royal chase and had been gradually appropriated by the lords whose estates encircled it. The deer had disappeared, the woods had for the most part been cut down, but coal had been discovered, and Kingswood in Wesley's day was inhabited by colliers as lawless as the foresters from whom they were descended, ignorant and brutal, perhaps the most debased specimens of the forgotten dregs of English life.

They had no church, for they belonged to the parish of St. Philip, and the parish church was, at least, three miles away, and far too small to accommodate the colliers, even if they had ever attempted to invade it. Kingswood was an ecclesiastical no-man's land. So long as the colliers remained in their pits, nobody bothered about them. When money and bread were scarce, they emerged, marched on Bristol and spread panic among the shopkeepers.

And it was to these outcasts that Whitefield opened his field preaching campaign on February 17th, 1739. A few score colliers gathered round out of curiosity, and three weeks later his congregations ran into several thousands.

Whitefield deserves the greatest of credit for an attempt which to his contemporaries appeared to be a highly dangerous innovation, though Whitefield could, of course, have quoted plenty of sound, Catholic precedents in his favour. Preaching in the open air [1] had been quite common before and even since the Reformation. "But in the comfortable eighteenth century," says Dr. Hutton, "it seemed unpleasant; to those who remembered Independency and

---

[1] In the Middle Ages the preaching cross helped to mark the site of the open air preaching stations. Among the most famous of these preaching crosses was St. Paul's Cross in St. Paul's Churchyard, London. An open air sermon was annually preached in a little pulpit of stone set in the wall of Magdalen College, Oxford. This annual open air sermon has, recently, been revived. Those who care to pursue the subject further should consult the fifth chaper of "Preaching in Medieval England," by G. R. Owst.

Quakerism and the Scottish Covenanters it seemed illegal; and to those who lived on pew rents it seemed dangerous."

Whitefield was delighted with the success of field preaching and he was anxious to see whether the same method would prove equally effective among the outcasts of London. But it was necessary to make some arrangement to continue his work at Kingswood, and he accordingly wrote to Wesley, for whose organizing ability he had the greatest respect, and asked him to take charge of of his mission among the colliers at Kingswood.

Wesley hesitated. He had plenty to do in London; his brother Charles and his friends did not wish to lose him, and they did their best to dissuade him from accepting Whitefield's invitation. He fell back, as was his custom when perplexed, on sortilege.

"Get thee up into this mountain . . ." replied the oracle, "and die in the mount whether thou goest up, and be gathered unto thy people." (Deut. xxxii, 49, 50.)

This was discouraging. He opened the Bible again. "And the children of Israel wept for Moses in the plains of Moab thirty days." (Deut. xxxiv. 8.) Worse and worse. Still Wesley persisted. "I will shew him how great things he must suffer for my name's sake." (Acts ix. 16.) "And devout men carried Stephen to his burial, and made great lamentation over him." (Acts viii. 2.)

No wonder that Wesley records that he felt "a little less inclined" to go to Bristol after he had consulted the Scriptures "touching the consequence of removal."

The final decision was left to the lot, and by this means it was determined that Wesley should go to Bristol.

He reached Bristol on March 31st. The following day he heard Whitefield preach. "I could scarce reconcile myself at first to this strange way of preaching in the fields, of which he set me an example on Sunday; having been all my life (till very lately) so tenacious of every point relating to decency and order, that I should have thought the saving of souls almost a sin, if it had not been done in church."

However, there was nothing for it. Whitefield's work among the colliers had to be carried on and at four o'clock next day in the afternoon, the Fellow of Lincoln "submitted to be more vile" and opened his campaign of field preaching, a campaign which was to last over forty years. He chose as his text "The Spirit of the Lord is upon me, because He hath appointed me to preach the Gospel to the poor."

Monday, April 2nd, 1739, was an important date in the life of Wesley. Henceforth, he ceases to fret himself about his soul's salvation, and the long period of self-examination is at an end. John Wesley had found his work, and the world parish which he had chosen for his labours was destined to tax to the utmost his resources of courage, strength and will.

CHAPTER XI

CHURCH AND STATE IN 1740

ENGLAND in 1740 certainly provided the ardent reformer with adequate outlets for his energy. There was plenty to do, indeed, the only difficulty was to know where to begin.

There were of course men of high principles in all ranks of English society when Wesley opened his campaign of field preaching. But the index of an age is not the characters of exceptional individuals, but the general tone of society from the Court downwards.

Let us begin with the Court. The Restoration Court may have been more dissolute, but it was less vulgar than the Hanoverian. The Stuarts were gentlemen, and even in their vices they did not lose a certain air of distinction. George II was a boor. He had no morals and no manners. His wife, Queen Caroline, was a remarkable woman. Walpole paid her the compliment of crediting her with greater political capability than any woman that he had ever met, and that this was no idle compliment is shown by their long, steadfast friendship. But though Queen Caroline did nothing to lower the moral tone of the Court, she certainly did nothing to raise it. She kept the Seventh Commandment, but she alternately connived at and encouraged the infidelities of her husband. She made these the subject of her jests, and succeeded in shocking the Duchess of Marlborough by her outspoken sense of humour, a remarkable achievement.

The Court set the tone, Society followed. Contemporary drama and literature are useful guides in such matters.

Squire Weston may or may not be a faithful portrait of
the eighteenth century, but it is significant that Fielding
never seems to feel that the squire's coarseness of tongue
calls for any particular comment.[1]

Nor does the worthy squire appear to have been in the
least embarrassed by the presence of his daughter Sophy
who is represented as being the incarnation of feminine
purity. A long conversation, too coarse to quote in full,
between the squire and the equally insensitive parson, concludes with a little pleasant banter. "Ask Sophy here—
You have not the worse opinion of a young fellow for
getting a bastard, have you, girl? No, no, the women will
like un the better for 't."

Fielding never hesitated to arrest the action of his
story if he desired to moralise, and the fact that Squire
Weston's table talk drew no comment from the author
is not without significance.

More serious than the prevailing coarseness of tone
was the well-nigh universal passion for gambling which
reached its height during this epoch. "Whist," wrote Walpole to Sir Horace Mann, "has spread a universal opium
over the whole nation. On whatever pretext, and under
whatever circumstances, half a dozen people of fashion
found themselves together, whether for music, or dancing,
or politics, or for drinking the waters or each other's
wine, the box was sure to be rattling and the cards were
being cut and shuffled." [2]

Gambling reached a climax towards the end of the century. Charles James Fox lost a hundred thousand pounds
in one evening, and incurred debts amounting to half a
million pounds before the age of twenty-four. In the
course of his lifetime he lost a million pounds at the gam-
ing tables.

[1] "The History of Tom Jones," by Henry Fielding.
[2] "Early History of Charles James Fox," by Sir George O.
Trevelyan.

Again, there has perhaps been no period in English history when drunkenness was so common in every class of society. The rapid increase in gin drinking was a fact of the greatest importance in the history of the century. "Incomparably more important," so writes the historian Lecky, "than any event in the purely political or military annals of the country." Every sixth shop in London was a gin shop, and the passers-by were invited to enter, and to get drunk for a penny or dead drunk for twopence. Straw was provided free for those who desired to sleep off the effects of their debauch.

Gin drinking threatened to change the character of the nation. The English are naturally a kindly race, but under the influence of gin drinking they were rapidly becoming cruel. Dr. Benson, the Bishop of Gloucester, writing to Bishop Berkeley of Cloune on February 18th, 1752, paints the situation in gloomy colours. "Your Lordship calls this the freest country in Europe. There is indeed freedom of one kind in it . . . a most unbounded licentiousness of all sorts . . . a regard to nothing but diversion and vicious pleasures. . . . Our people are now become, what they never were before, cruel. Those accursed spirituous liquors which, to the shame of the Government, are so easily to be had, and in such quantities drunk, have changed the very nature of our people." [3]

The amusements of the period certainly tended to develop any latent tendencies to cruelty. The hangings at Tyburn provided a spectacle of which the proletariat never tired, a spectacle that had the great advantage of being free. Cock-fighting and bull-baiting were very popular. The bull was sometimes released with fireworks all over its body, or, to the greatest joy of the onlookers, a cat was tied to the bull's tail.

[3] "England and the English in the Eighteenth Century," W. C. Sydney.

Through this period crime continued to increase in spite of savage laws. Crimes of violence predominated. There was every inducement to finish off your victim and thereby to reduce your chances of conviction, a conviction to be followed by the gallows, even if robbery had not been aggravated by murder. Horace Walpole gives us an amusing description of a period when the highwaymen were more than usually active.

"Is it not delightful," he wrote, "not to dare to stir out of one's own castle but armed for battle?" His foreign guests were afraid to come to breakfast with him: "So it is an ill highwayman that blows nobody good. In truth it would be impossible in this region to amass a set of company for dinner to meet them. The Hertfords, Lady Holdernesse, and Lady Mary Coke did dine here Thursday, but were armed as if going to Gibraltar; and Lady Cecilia Johnstone would not venture even from Petersham—for in the town of Richmond they rob even before dusk—to such perfection are all the arts brought! Who would have thought that the war with America would make it impossible to stir from one village to another? Yet so it literally is. The colonies took off all our commodities down to highwaymen. Now being forced to mow and then turn them out like pheasants, the roads are stocked with them, and they are so tame that they come even into our houses."

Neither the criminal nor the criminal code had any respect for the sanctity of human life. In those days, there were no less than a hundred and sixty offences which were expiated on the gallows. Theft from a person of an article one shilling in value, or from a shop of an article five shillings in value, sending threatening letters, illegally cutting down trees, cutting hopbinds or breaking down the banks of a fish-pond were all punishable by death.

Women were liable to be burnt alive for high or petty treason, which included coinage. In 1782, Rebecca Downing was burnt for poisoning her master.

A case is reported of a young married woman of nineteen, whose husband had been captured by the press-gang. She had no means of support and she was starving. She went into a shop, took up a piece of linen from the counter, and then laid it down when she saw that her action had been noticed. For this she was condemned to death, and was hanged with her child at her breast.

II

What of the Church?

Many of the eighteenth century bishops command our respect. Thomas Wilson, who was Bishop of Sodor and Man more than half a century (1697–1755), was beloved and esteemed, not only by his own communion, but also by the Roman Catholics and Dissenters many of whom attended his services.

There is a delightful contemporary sketch of Martin Benson, who was Bishop of Gloucester from 1734 to 1752, quoted by the Reverend C. J. Abbey in his excellent book, "The English Church and its Bishops 1700 to 1800."

"He was from his youth to his latest age the delight of all who knew him. His manner of behaviour was the result of great natural humanity polished by a thorough knowledge of the world, and the most perfect in good breeding, mixed with a dignity which, on occasions that called for it, no one more properly supported. . . . He looked upon all that the world calls important—its pleasures, its riches, its various competitions—with a playful and good-humoured kind of contempt, and could make persons ashamed of their follies by a raillery that never gave pain to any human being."

And there were other eighteenth century bishops, such as Butler of the "Analogy." Thomas Secker and Sherlock who helped to modify a verdict which is, in the main, unfavourable; for the bishops as a whole were sadly out of touch with the problems of their age. They never mixed with the people, seldom preached before popular assemblies, and associated almost exclusively with the upper classes, with the men of letters and learning. From time to time they emerged from their palaces to conduct a ceremonial confirmation tour. But they never troubled themselves with any plans for improving the condition of the people, or tried to establish contact with the neglected hordes who never came inside a church. Bishop Butler, for instance, lived at Bath almost all the time that he was Bishop of Durham.

"Their official work completed, they retired with a thoroughly satisfied conscience to fill up the long remainder of the days in the quiet employments of study or of society, of friendships or of hospitality. The graver and more serious had abundant time for theological reading, and of devoting as much labour as they chose to the work of meeting the arguments of the Deist or the Arian, the Roman Catholic or the Methodist. Those who preferred other studies could follow without blame or compunction their classical, or literary, or scientific, or antiquarian tastes. Some, no doubt, took great interest in various charitable institutions, but with rare exceptions there was sadly little in common between them and the multitude, whose irreligion they deplored, who hung with pangs of awakened conscience upon the impassioned lips of Whitefield. Enthusiasm, which to their minds was synonymous with gross fanaticism, seemed scarcely less formidable to them than infidelity itself. In one sense it was almost more alarming. For unbelief, or what was generally held to be such, was a familiar enemy, against whom the more learned of them were trained, equipped, and prepared. Enthusiasm was a new opponent, or rather it might be the requickening into life of a power which a century before had dashed to the ground crowns and mitres, churches and constitutions.

They knew not what it might be, or how far, if it gained head, it might corrupt all pure and reasonable religion." [4]

The lesser clergy followed the episcopal lead.

Religion was represented as essentially rational. Christianity was justified on prudential grounds. Honesty was the best policy. Christianity paid good dividends both in this world and in the next.

The universal hatred of "enthusiasm" was partly due to a reaction from Puritanism. The sense and meaning of this word have altered since the eighteenth century. "Enthusiasm" is derived from the Greek and literally means "possessed by a god." It was only in the nineteenth century that the word gradually lost its original suggestion of divine inspiration. In Wesley's time it was always used in a hostile sense as a misconceit of inspiration, that is, as a false claim to be inspired. The enthusiast was a man who rejected tradition and the authority of the Church, and who claimed to be the channel for divinely-inspired messages. Translated into eighteenth century terms, the charge on which St. Joan was tried and convicted was the charge of enthusiasm. Under the Puritans, England had suffered from a veritable plague of enthusiasm. Muggletonians, Fifth Monarchy men and Anabaptists overran the land, to be followed by French prophets and prophetesses, many of whom passed into trances, accompanied, like the trances of the modern medium, by physical contortions.

Enthusiasm was often associated with loose morals and indifference to the conventional standards of society. And so when the Puritans were overthrown, and the Muggletonians and Fifth Monarchy men had been sent about their business, men sighed with relief and said, "Enough of enthusiasm. We have seen where the Inner Light and

[4] "The English Church and its Bishops," by the Rev. C. J. Abbey.

the New Light and the New Models lead us. Let us
eschew these false guides, and follow instead the Light of
Reason, logic and common sense."

It is therefore easy to understand Wesley's indignation on being accused of enthusiasm. "To object *enthusiasm,*" he wrote, "to any person or doctrine is but
a decent method of begging the question. It generally
spares the objector the trouble of reasoning, and is a
shorter and easier way of carrying his cause. . . . I believe thinking men mean by *enthusiasm* a sort of religious
madness; a false imagination of being inspired by God;
and by an *enthusiast* one that *fancies* himself under the
influence of the Holy Ghost, when, in fact, he is not. Let
him prove me guilty of this who can."

The hatred for enthusiasm which characterised the
Latitudinarian bishops was not unreasonable. Indeed, the
Latitudinarians have received much less than their due
from historians of the evangelical revival. They did their
best to guide their flock into safe, if unromantic pastures.
The gospel of moral rectitude and probity which they
preached was a gospel which restored good works to
their proper place in the scheme of salvation. They insisted on the importance of probity, and probity was a
commodity for which there was little competition among
the politicians of the early eighteenth century.

Tillotson, Burnet and his school appealed to the common sense of the English people. They insisted on the
supreme obligation of duty. "It was," as Mr. Baring-
Gould has reminded us, "the broad principles of honesty,
probity in religion, as in all else" [5] on which Tillotson
and the Latitudinarians insisted. And if, as is the
case, the Englishman wherever he is placed, carries with

---

[5] "The Evangelical Revival," by S. Baring-Gould.

him the sense of duty, this is due to Tillotsonianism."

It has been the fashion to depreciate the Latitudi-narians, probably because theirs was a humdrum creed and a humdrum ideal. The dust lies deep on their sermons, sermons which were the best-sellers of the eighteenth century, and which were criticised and appraised with loving discernment by the literary pundits of the age. "I should not advise anybody to imitate Tillotson's style," said Johnson thoughtfully, "though I do not know; I should be cautious of censuring anything which has been applauded by so many Suffrages.—South was one of the best, if you accept his peculiarities and his violence. Seed has a very fine style; but he is not very elegant. Sherlock's style too, is very elegant, though he has not made it his principal study. And you may add Smaldridge." *Boswell:* "I like Ogden's sermons on Prayer very much, both for neatness of style and subtlety of reasoning."

This is all rather pathetic. Who precisely are these worthies? South and Seed and Sherlock and Jordan, "and you may add Smaldridge." Even Tillotson is forgotten, great man though he was in his day. He has no background of romance or tragedy or passion to keep fragrant his memory. Cranmer, Latimer, Newman. The imagination reacts at once at the bare mention of their names, but no pulse has ever stirred the quicker for seeing the name of Tillotson on a printed page. "It is," as Mr. Max Beerbohm remarks, "a solemn thought that so little is conveyed to us by names which to the paleo-Georgians conveyed so much. We discern a dim, composite picture of a big man in a big wig, a billowing black gown, with a big congregation beneath him. But we are not anxious to hear what he is saying. We know it is all very elegant. We know it will be printed and be

bound in finely-tooled full calf, and no paleo-Georgian
gentleman's library will be complete without it. Literary
people in those days were comparatively few; but bait-
ing that, one may say that sermons were as much in request as novels are to-day. I wonder, will mankind continue to be capricious. It is a very solemn thought indeed
that no more than a hundred-and-fifty years hence the
novelists of our time, with all their moral and political
and sociological outlook and influence, will perhaps shine
as indistinctly as do those old preachers with all their
elegance now."

CHAPTER XII

THE GENESIS OF THE REVIVAL

WHITEFIELD left Bristol in April 1739, and after spending a few hectic weeks in London, set sail for America. Wesley was left in charge of his work, and he accordingly divided his time for the next two years between Bristol and London.

Whitefield had taken London by storm during the few weeks that he spent in the capital before setting sail. Thousands had flocked to hear him, but there is little evidence that his preaching produced much permanent effect. Very few people seem to have applied for admission to the religious societies in consequence of his missionary efforts. Whitefield always produced a more immediate, but Wesley a far more lasting effect by his preaching. Whitefield was a rhetorician, Wesley an organizer. The latter was not content to evoke a passing mood of penitence. He never struck without following up the blow. He regarded preaching that was not followed up, as worse than useless. The sermon was only valuable because the effect produced could be consolidated by means of a society. His work as a preacher was less strenuous than his constant efforts to keep in personal touch with his converts, his lay preachers, and his class leaders.

Whitefield loved preaching, but Wesley refused to preach in a place at which he had no hope of being able to found a Society.[1] He knew that though it was the ser-

[1] "We stopped an hour at Mullingar. The sovereign (governor) of

mon which might kindle the flame, it was the Society
which kept the fire alive.

At Bristol, Wesley busied himself with laying the
foundations. There was plenty of scope for an organizer.
Chapels had to be financed, and schools had to be founded.
Before long, Wesley's activities began to attract attention. At that time, Butler was Bishop of Bristol.
Butler was a great scholar and a persuasive and skilled
controversialist. Wesley read his great book, "The Analogy of Religion," and considered it "a strong and well-
wrote thesis, but far too deep for their understanding
to whom it is primarily addressed."

Butler was a man of great wisdom and piety. He had
heard of Wesley, and had been much perturbed by the account of the frenzied and hysterical scenes which attended
his preaching. He therefore issued an order prohibiting
Wesley from preaching, in consequence of which Wesley sought and obtained an interview with him.

It was a dramatic encounter. The scholarly Bishop who
had devoted so much of his life to intellectual warfare
with the Deists, was face to face with a man who had
gone into the highways and hedges to discover a congregation, a congregation which had never read the
"Analogy," and which had probably never even heard of
its able author.

The Bishop opened the debate by criticising the doctrine of justification by faith. Wesley had no difficulty
in justifying that doctrine by the articles and homilies
of the Church of England. Wesley clearly won the first
round on points, and the Bishop began to lose patience.
The debate as reported by Wesley continued as follows:

"B. Mr. Wesley, I will deal plainly with you. I once

the town came to the Inn and expressed much desire that I should
preach but I had little hope of doing good by preaching in a place
where I could preach but once." (Journal iii, p. 488.)

thought you and Mr. Whitefield well-meaning men; but I cannot think so now. For I have heard more of you: matters of fact, sir. And Mr. Whitefield says in his Journal: 'There are promises still to be fulfilled in me.' Sir, the pretending to extraordinary revelations and gifts of the Holy Ghost is a horrid thing—a very horrid thing!

W. My lord, for what Mr. Whitefield says, Mr. White-field, and not I, is accountable. I pretend to no extraor-dinary revelations or gifts of the Holy Ghost: none but what every Christian may receive, and ought to expect and pray for. But I do not wonder your lordship has heard facts asserted which, if true, would prove the contrary; nor do I wonder that your lordship believing them true, should alter the opinion you once had of me. A quarter of an hour I spent with your lordship before, and about an hour now; and perhaps you have never conversed one other hour with any one who spake in my favour. But how many with those who spake on the other side? So that your lordship could not but think as you do. But pray, my lord, what are those facts you have heard?

B. I hear you administer the Sacrament in your So-cieties.

W. My lord, I never did yet, and I believe I never shall.

B. I hear, too, that many people fall into fits in your Societies, and that you pray over them.

W. I do so, my lord, when any show by strong cries and tears that their soul is in deep anguish. I frequently pray to God to deliver them from it, and our prayer is often heard in that hour.

B. Very extraordinary indeed! Well, sir, since you ask my advice, I will give it you very freely. You have no business here; you are not commissioned to preach in this diocese. Therefore I advise you to go hence.

W. My lord, my business on earth is to do what

good I can. Wherever, therefore, I think I can do most good, there must I stay, so long as I think so. At present I think I can do most good here; therefore here I stay. As to my preaching here, a dispensation of the gospel is committed to me, and woe is me if I preach not the gospel wherever I am in the habitable world! Your lordship knows, being ordained a priest, by the commission I then received I am a priest of the Church Universal. And being ordained as Fellow of a College, I was not limited to any particular cure, but have an indeterminate commission to preach the word of God in any part of the Church of England. I do not, therefore, conceive that, in preaching here by this commission, I break any human law. When I am convinced I do, then it will be time to ask, 'Shall I obey God or man?' But if I should be convinced in the meanwhile, that I could advance the glory of God and the salvation of souls in any other place more than in Bristol, in that hour, by God's help, I will go hence, which till then I may not do."

It was a pity that the Bishop and Wesley parted on such unfriendly terms. But only a very broadminded bishop could have appreciated Wesley. To the Bishop, Wesley no doubt appeared a very opinionated, self-confident young man. Instead of laying down the law, he should have been ready to accept with humility the rebuke from a venerable father in God. There was, indeed, only one excuse for Wesley, an excuse which the Bishop may be pardoned for overlooking. Had Wesley been a little more deferential to Bishops, the Evangelical Revival might never have taken place.

And so they parted. The Bishop went back to his books with a sigh. He was a great man, and perhaps Wesley's visit had left him vaguely uneasy. He may have found it difficult to concentrate on his beloved

Deists. Who were these colliers of Kinsgwood to whom
the arrogant young man had referred so often . . . were
they in his diocese . . . what parish were they in? . . .
He really must look into the matter.

II

It is idle to deny that both Whitefield and Wesley
had deserved an episcopal rebuke; for episcopal rebuke
must follow the defiance of ecclesiastical order and discipline. They had preached in the fields, they had selected
what they pleased out of the liturgy of their church, they
had invaded the parishes of other men, and had organized societies governed by rules of their own invention within those parishes. And finally, they persisted in
preaching a doctrine of which the Bishops disapproved.

Wesley had only one defence. "I must obey God rather
than man," a defence which, of course, stamped Wesley
as an "enthusiast" in the correct technical sense of the
word. For, as we have seen, an enthusiast is a man who
refuses to submit to the discipline and the authority of
his church on the ground that he cannot disobey the
voice of God revealed in the forum of his soul.

The judicious Samuel Wesley was much perturbed.
A few days before his death he wrote to his mother:
"My brothers design separation. They are already forbidden all the pulpits in London; and to preach in that
diocese is actual schism. In all likelihood it will come
to the same all over England, if the bishops have courage enough. . . . As I told Jack, I am not afraid the
Church should excommunicate him (discipline is at too
low an ebb), but that he should excommunicate the
Church. It is pretty near it."

To a friend who charged him with invading other
men's parishes and meddling with souls that did not be-

long to him, Wesley replied in a letter which contains the famous phrase "I look upon the world as my parish":

"God in scripture commands me according to my power to instruct the ignorant, reform the wicked, confirm the virtuous. Man forbids me to do this in another's parish; that is, in effect to do it at all: seeing I have now no parish of my own, nor probably ever shall. Whom then shall I hear: God or Man? . . . I look upon the world as my parish; thus far, I mean, that, in whatever part of it I am, I judge it meet, right, and my bounden duty to declare unto all that are willing to hear the glad tidings of salvation."

Nothing succeeds like success. Had Wesley failed, his name might, perhaps, be mentioned in a footnote to a History of the English Church as an example of the evil effects of unbalanced egoism. But he did not fail, and his famous phrase has become immortal. A modern Wesleyan, however, who looked upon the world as his circuit would receive shorter shrift from the Methodist Conference than Wesley ever received from the Bench of Bishops, and one shudders to think what would happen to a doctor who announced that he regarded all the world as his practice.

Wesley was a genius, and it is the privilege of genius to make its own rules.

Wesley never understood the parochial system. He attached, perhaps, too much importance to sudden conversion, to the dramatic change from despair to assurance, a change accompanied by unmistakable evidence of God's favour. He was, perhaps, a little too anxious to precipitate conversion, and a little too impatient for immediate results. An itinerant preacher who moves from place to place sows his seed and hopes to reap his harvest within a few brief days. He naturally tends to underestimate the tame and unsensational work of a village priest living among his flock, and slowly winning their respect for a high ideal by the example of his own life. And yet Wesley had seen the results of his father's work among a stubborn and ungrateful people. And he must have heard from his mother of Dr. Annesley's success and great record as a parish priest. With these examples in view, it was indeed strange that Wesley should have stated that he would preach himself and his congregation to sleep if he lived in the same place for a twelve-month. He never appreciated the parish work of men like Walker of Truro, Venn of Huddersfield or Adam of Wintringham. Wesley did not, of course, desire to upset the parochial system. He believed that his work would supplement the work of the Church of England, and he imposed on his Societies restrictions which his more extreme followers considered entirely unnecessary, in order that the itinerant preachers should not clash with the parish priests. In all parishes during his lifetime, and in many parishes for at least a century after Wesley died, the hour of the Methodist services was deliberately fixed to permit Methodists to attend both Church and Chapel. Wesley ordained that the Methodist services should be in his own words "essentially defective, for it seldom has the four great parts of public prayer. If the people put ours in the place of the Church we hurt them that stay with us and ruin them that leave us." Three years before he died, he wrote, "Wherever there is any Church Service, I do not approve of any appointment at the same hour, because I love the Church of England, and would assist, not oppose it, all I can."

In other words, Wesley may have looked upon all the world as his parish, but he did not look upon himself as the parish priest of all the world.

III

Bishop Butler was not the only person at Bath who disapproved of Wesley. Beau Nash, the uncrowned King of Bath, would have agreed with the Bishop that "pretending to extraordinary revelations is a very horrid thing, a very horrid thing." He had heard of Wesley, and he disapproved of him. The rumour went round Bath that the great preacher was coming. Beau Nash frowned and gave his admirers to understand that Wesley would have good reason to regret his impudence if he invaded Beau Nash's territory.

"There was," as Wesley drily remarks, "great expectation at Bath of what a noted man was to do to me there; and I was much entreated not to preach; because no one knew what might happen."

In spite of Beau Nash, Wesley preached to a much larger audience than he had expected, but was interrupted by Beau Nash himself. Wesley tells the story of their encounter in his Journal:

I told them plainly, the Scripture had concluded them all under sin;—high and low, rich and poor, one with another. Many of them seemed a little surprised, and were sinking apace into seriousness, when their champion appeared, and coming close to me, asked by what authority I did these things. I replied, "By the authority of Jesus Christ, conveyed to me by the (now) Archbishop of Canterbury, when he laid hands upon me, and said, 'Take thou authority to preach the Gospel.'" He said, "This is contrary to Act of Parliament: This is a conventicle." I answered, "Sir, the conventicles mentioned in that Act (as the preamble shows) are seditious meetings: But this is not such; here is no shadow of sedition; therefore it is not contrary to the Act." He replied, "I say it is: And beside, your preaching frightens people out of their wits." "Sir, did you ever hear me preach?" "No." "How then can you judge of what you never heard?" "Sir, by common report." "Common report is not enough. Give me leave, Sir, to ask, Is not your name Nash?" "My name is Nash." "Sir, I dare not judge of you by common report: I think it is not enough to judge by." Here he paused awhile, and, having recovered himself, said, "I desire to know what this people comes here for:" On which one replied, "Sir, leave him to me: Let an old woman answer him. You, Mr. Nash, take care of your body; we take care of our souls; and for the food of our souls we come here." He replied not a word, but walked away.

The well-known story of the second encounter between Beau Nash and Wesley is not recorded in Wesley's Journal. They are supposed to have met on a crowded pavement in Bath. Beau Nash glared at Wesley and would not move. "I never make way for a fool," he said. "I always do," replied Wesley quietly as he stepped off into the street.

The story may be true, but it does not ring true. Wesley never spared his friends. He was a ruthless critic, but he criticised to improve. "I dare not judge you by common report: I think it is not enough to judge by." *That* does ring true. It was as near to a stinging retort as Wesley ever permitted himself. No term of abuse ever crossed his lips, and I do not think he would have condescended to have adopted, if only for the purpose of deflecting, a term of abuse hurled at him by an opponent.

Wesley was a great gentleman, and Beau Nash was not without breeding. This anecdote does them both less than justice.

IV

The Bishop's prejudice against Wesley was, as I have shown, largely due to the reports which he had received of extraordinary happenings among Wesley's congregation. There was, indeed, some excuse for the Bishop. Wesley's Journal records a whole succession of these incidents. "At Weavers' Hall, seven or eight persons were constrained to roar aloud while the sword of the spirit was dividing them asunder." People swooned, sunk down on the ground as if dead, groaned, shrieked, and trembled in every limb. A domestic servant remained in a trance-like condition, as if possessed, and was so affected that she did not recover properly for fourteen hours. Her master dismissed her saying, "he would have none in the house who had received the Holy Ghost." This was, of course, very wrong of him, but the "pretending to extraordinary revelations" is not only a "very horrid thing" but also a very inconvenient thing in a domestic servant.

Wesley's published sermons certainly supply no clue to these distressing incidents. His sermons are essentially sober and calm, for no man disliked more intensely, or rebuked more severely, the technique of the hot gospel type of revivalist. Indeed, had people groaned and shrieked during Whitefield's sermons, one would have had far less cause for surprise. But no one was "constrained to roar aloud" when Whitefield preached, a fact which appears to have distressed him. For it was clearly injured vanity which prompted his letter to Wesley in which he voiced his disapproval of those convulsions, while hastening to emphasise the fact that he would have had no difficulty in provoking them, had he so desired. "Honoured Sir," he wrote, "I cannot think it right in you to give so much encouragement to those convulsions which people have been thrown into under your ministry. Were I to do so, how many would cry out every night? I think it is tempting God to require such signs."

The frequency of these scenes was grossly exaggerated by common report, and one is glad to note that they steadily diminished during the course of Wesley's ministry. Charles Wesley had to endure similar interruptions until he hit upon a very simple device for putting an end to these fits. He says:

"Many, no doubt, were, at our first preaching, struck down, both soul and body, into the depth of distress. Their *outward affections* were easy to be imitated. Many counterfeits I have already detected. To-day one who came from the ale-house drunk, was pleased to fall into a fit for my entertainment, and beat himself heartily. I thought it a pity to hinder him; so instead of singing over him, as had been often done, we left him to recover at his leisure. Another, a girl, as she began to cry I ordered her to be carried out. Her convulsion was so violent as to take away the use of her limbs till they laid and left her without the door. Then immediately she found her legs and walked off. Some very unstill sisters, who always took care to stand near me, and tried which could cry loudest, since I had them removed out of my sight have been as quiet as lambs. The first night I preached here half my words were lost through their outcries. Last night, before I began, I gave public notice that whosoever cried so as to drown my voice should, without any man hurting or judging them, be gently carried to the farthest corner of the room. But my porters had no employment the whole night; yet the Lord was with us, mightily convincing of sin and of righteousness."

Wesley's views on these strange happenings varied

from time to time. On the whole, he was inclined to believe that their origin was supernatural, but he was never very dogmatic on this point. "I relate just what I saw," he says. "Some of the circumstances seem to go beyond the ordinary course of nature."

Wesley, of course, was not so foolish as to consider these happenings as evidence of supernatural approval of his evangelical labours. He may have emancipated himself from the attitude of dark suspicion with which the eighteenth century regarded all unusual emotional states, but he was still a child of his century in so far, at least, as he insisted that the nature and value of an emotional state could only be gauged by the subsequent and permanent effects, if any, on a man's character and life.

A notorious sinner shrieking on the floor intrigued Wesley not a little, but it was not the momentary convulsions, however striking, but the subsequent change of life, if any, which really impressed him. Wesley believed in the possibility of sudden conversion, not because he had witnessed a scene such as this, but because he had taken the trouble to follow up his converts and to keep in personal contact with them. His letter to his brother Samuel written at an earlier stage of his ministry expressed very clearly much the same views as those which inclined him at a later date to believe in the supernatural origin of these fits.

"Let any judge of it as they please. But that such a change was then wrought appears not from their shedding tears only, or sighing, or singing psalms, as your poor correspondent did by the woman of Oxford, but from the whole tenor of their life, till then many ways wicked; from that time holy, just, and good.

"Saw you him that was a lion till then and is now a lamb; he that was a drunkard, but now exemplarily sober: the whoremonger that was, that now abhors the very lusts of the flesh? These are my living arguments for what I assert, that God now, as aforetime, gives remission of sins and the gift of the Holy Ghost, which may be called visions."

It is easy to exaggerate the importance and the frequency of these occasional outbreaks and disturbances. One cannot but regret that they occurred, for they damaged Wesley and the Methodist Movement irretrievably in the eyes of the clergy, but they have no real bearing on Wesley's career. They are irrelevant as evidence either for or against the validity of evanglical experience.

Wesley's published sermons do not help us to understand his power over the hearts of men. We are impressed by their plainness, their sincerity and their absence of rhetoric. He made no concessions to his audience, he never vulgarised his message to adapt it to the tastes of the illiterate. And yet, though men of education heard him with pleasure, his preaching produced the most marked effect among the uneducated.

"After preaching the poor people were ready to tread me underfoot, out of pure love and kindness."

"As I was preaching at Pelton, one of the old colliers, not much accustomed to things of this kind, in the middle of the sermon began shouting amain, for mere satisfaction and joy of heart. But their usual token of approbation (which somewhat surprised me at first) was clapping me on the back."

A pleasant picture. The precise little Oxford Don "somewhat surprised" by the affectionate demonstration of the rough colliers.

His grip on his congregations was absolute. There is more than one instance in his Journal of floors subsiding during his sermon, but even the possibility of a further collapse did not bring Wesley's sermon to a conclusion by a lack of hearers. Here is a striking instance.

He was preaching to a congregation many of whom were
sitting on a long wall built of loose stones. In the middle
of his sermon, this wall fell down. "I never saw, heard,
nor read of such a thing before. The whole wall, and
the persons sitting upon it, sunk down together, none
of them screaming out, and very few altering their posture. And not one was hurt at all; but they appeared
sitting at the bottom just as they sat at the top. Nor was
there any interruption either of my speaking or of the
attention of the hearers."

V

The effect of John's sermons was reinforced by Charles
Wesley's hymns. It was a wonderful chance which
brought together in the same movement John Wesley,
with his genius for leadership, and Charles Wesley, with
his genius for poetry. More than 6,000 hymns are at-
tributed to Charles Wesley, and these include many of
the most popular hymns in the English language, such
as "Jesus, Lover of my soul," "Hark, the Herald Angels
sing," "Christ Whose glory fills the sky," "O for a
thousand tongues to sing."

John Wesley did not write many original hymns, but
he had a genius for translation, and his translations
from the German owe at least as much to the translator
as to their original author.

Before 1737, the Church of England had no hymn
book. The psalms, metrically rendered by Tate and Brady,
were sung in Church, but there were no hymn books.

After the Restoration, it was the Non-Conformists
who revived hymnody. The first hymn book of the Con-
gregationalists appeared in 1696, and among its contribu-
tors were Doddridge and Dr. Watts, who share with

Charles Wesley the glory of being the greatest hymn writers in the English language.

The first hymn book for the Anglican communion was a hymn book drawn up by John Wesley in 1737 for his parishioners in Georgia. "Consequently," writes Mr. Sydney Dimond, "the congregational singing, which the Wesleys had learned from the Moravians, appealed to the people with all the attractiveness of complete novelty. The hymns stimulated curiosity and helped to create the attitude of wonder, surprise and astonishment among those by whom they were heard for the first time. . . . The fact that the whole congregation could take part in singing made the hymn a means for the expression of the violent emotions aroused by the revival experiences; and at the same time the emotion was intensified by its expression. Thus it is that 'the hymn is especially valuable for both suggestion and auto-suggestion.' While singing lustily in rhythmic phrases the ideas and sentiments which the Wesleys desired to instil into him, each member of the congregation suggested them to himself in the technical meaning of that phrase. And at the same time he was passing on the suggestion to his neighbour. 'The whole audience thus acts upon each individual in the audience and so acts and reacts upon itself, thus spreading the desired suggestion by geometrical progression.' Consider, for example, the revival value of these verses sung by a large congregation:

> 'For you and for me
> He prayed on the tree:
> The prayer is accepted, the sinner is free.
>
> That sinner am I,
> Who on Jesus rely,
> And come for the pardon God cannot deny.'

"The dramatic passage from the second to the first person identifies the poet with the audience, and by a perfect combination of suggestion and auto-suggestion the hymn conveyed from one individual to another an immediate and vital experience." [2]

Mr. Rattenbury draws attention to the power of movement which Charles Wesley's hymns possess. "They march, they dance, they fly. . . . Who but a Charles Wesley would have thought of setting the solemn theme of the Crucifixion to a jig? And yet,

> 'O Jesus, my hope,
>   For me offered up,
> Who with clamour pursued Thee to Calvary's top,'

is the very metre Wesley loved to use for his most exuberant hymns."

Charles Wesley said that he did not see why the devil should have all the best tunes. He therefore borrowed some of the most popular tunes of the day, and married them to hymns of his own composing. In order to convert sailors whom he heard singing "Nancy Dawson," a musical hall song of the day, Charles Wesley immediately wrote a hymn to the tune of "Nancy Dawson."

VI

John Wesley was by no means an indulgent critic of his brother's writings. He pointed out their defects with his customary "openness." Of an earlier collection of Charles's verses, he wrote, "Some are bad, some are mean, and some are most excellently good."

"His least praise was his talent for poetry." Thus wrote John Wesley in the Minutes of Conference which recorded Charles Wesley's death. The laconic phrase must,

[2] "Psychology of the Methodist Revival," by Sydney G. Dimond.

however, be taken as a compliment to Charles Wesley's piety rather than a criticism of his poetic genius.

John Wesley's considered judgment on his brother's hymns may be found in his famous preface to the Methodist Hymn Book:

"As but a small part of these hymns is of my own composing, I do not think it inconsistent with modesty to declare, that I am persuaded no such hymn-book as this has yet been published in the English language. . . . May I be permitted to add a few words with regard to the *poetry?* Then I will speak to those who are judges thereof, with all freedom and unreserve. To these I may say, without offence, 1. In these hymns there is no doggerel; no botches; nothing put in to patch up the rhyme; no feeble expletives. 2. Here is nothing turgid or bombast, on the one hand, or low and creeping, on the other. 3. Here are no *cant* expressions; no words without meaning. Those who impute this to us know not what they say. We talk common sense, both in prose and verse, and use no word but in a fixed and determinate sense. 4. Here are, allow me to say, both the purity, the strength, and the elegance of the English language; and, at the same time, the utmost simplicity and plainness, suited to every capacity. Lastly, I desire men of taste to judge, (these are the only competent judges,) whether there be not in some of the following hymns the true spirit of poetry, such as cannot be acquired by art and labour, but must be the gift of nature. By labour a man may become a tolerable imitator of Spenser, Shakespeare, or Milton; and may heap together pretty compound epithets, as 'pale-eyed,' ('meek-eyed,' and the like; but unless he be *born* a poet, he will never attain the genuine spirit of poetry."

"There is to-day," writes Mr. Rattenbury, "a growing tendency to admit that this is not only a sound judgment of poetry, but a very moderate estimate of his brother's genius."

As this book is the Life of John, and not of Charles Wesley, I must resist the temptation to criticise the hymns as literature.

I resist the more readily because it would be difficult to add anything of value to Mr. Rattenbury's admirable chapter on the hymns in his book, "Wesley's Legacy to the World."

Charles Wesley's hymns range from the simplicity of his hymns for children to the mysticism and the splendid imagery of "Wrestling Jacob."

Mr. Brash has compared the hymn which opens:

> "Gentle Jesus, meek and mild,
> Look upon a little child,
> Pity my simplicity,
> Suffer me to come to Thee.
>
> Fain I would to Thee be brought;
> Gracious Lord, forbid it not;
> In the kingdom of Thy grace,
> Give a little child a place."

to William Blake's "Little Lamb, who made thee?" a comparison which the most ardent admirers of Blake need not resent.[3]

Or again, consider the opening verses of Charles Wesley's greatest hymn, "Wrestling Jacob."

> "Come, O thou Traveller unknown,
>   Whom still I hold, but cannot see!
> My company before is gone,
>   And I am left alone with thee;
> With thee all night I mean to stay,
> And wrestle till the break of day.
>
> I need not tell thee who I am,
>   My misery and sin declare;
> Thyself hast called me by my name,
>   Look on thy hands and read it there;
> But who I ask thee, who art Thou?
> Tell me Thy name, and tell me now.

[3] "Methodism," by W. Bardsley Brash.

In vain thou strugglest to get free,
I never will unloose my hold!
Art thou the Man that died for me?
The secret of thy love unfold;
Wrestling, I will not let thee go,
Till I thy name, thy nature know."

Mr. W. J. Corthorpe in his "History of English
Poetry" describes Charles Wesley as the "most admirable
devotional lyric poet in the English language," on which
Mr. Rattenbury comments: "The time will come when
some of Charles Wesley's hymns will not only be cata-
logued at the head of the sub-class 'devotional' but will
take a high place, without qualification, among English
lyrics. Nothing but absurd prejudices against 'hymns'
could exclude 'Wrestling Jacob' from our anthologies.
There are few English lyrics to compare with it, not only
in its splendid ascension of emotional feeling, gathering
strength in its flight, till it reaches its overwhelming
climax, but also in its felicity of phrase and the rich and
suggestive beauty of its expressive and allusive imagery."

CHAPTER XIII

THE BIRTH PAINS OF METHODISM

METHODISM was cradled in controversy, and would probably never have survived had not John Wesley taken a firm stand on two great issues. Had Wesley surrendered to the doctrine of stillness as preached by the Moravians or to the doctrine of election as preached by the Calvinists, Methodism would, in all human probability, have died with its founder.

The first crisis was precipitated by Whitefield's departure for America on August 18th, 1739. Charles and John Wesley exchanged places. Charles went to Bristol and John returned to London to find the Fetter Lane Society in a critical condition.

Molther, a Moravian pastor from Jena, had made many converts to the engaging doctrine of stillness. Those who had not received the gift of faith were urged to do nothing, to possess their souls in quietness, and not to attempt to force the hand of God by making use of the means of grace, such as the Sacraments.

Wesley argued at length both with Molther and Spangenberg, but to no avail. The Moravians in the Fetter Lane Society disliked the aggressive tactics of the Wesleys. Their missionary enterprise offended them, for they held that the spiritual élite did not need to be hounded into salvation. They should just sit quiet waiting "in stillness" until they received the gift of faith. Again, they resented the fact that the Wesleys had insensibly assumed the leadership of the Fetter Lane Society. They accused the Wesleys of arrogance and of egoism. Wesley's efforts to heal the breach were of no avail. The Meetings of the Society, as he complained, were ruined by "a harsh, dry, heavy, stupid spirit."

Meanwhile, Wesley was losing ground in the Society. In the middle of July, 1740, he was informed that he could no longer preach in the Fetter Lane room. On the following Sunday, Wesley attended the Love Feast of the Fetter Lane Society, and read a paper in which he summarised the points at issue between him and the Moravians. He concluded with these words: "I have borne with you long, hoping you would turn. But as I find you more and more confirmed in the error of your ways, nothing now remains but that I should give you up to God. You that are of the same judgment, follow me."

It was just as well that these remarks were made at a *Love* Feast. Otherwise, one feels, they might have given offence.

Eighteen or nineteen members withdrew with John Wesley and fortunately there was another Society waiting to receive them. Towards the end of 1739, Wesley had been asked to meet a little group of religious people weekly in prayer. He thus formed the first of those united Societies which were to be the units of the Methodist organization.

The weather that winter had been unusually cold, and Wesley, who had been preaching in the open air, gratefully accepted the suggestion of two gentlemen, then unknown to him, that he should preach in a disused empty building, called the Foundery, near Moorfields.

This building had been used for casting cannon for the Government, and had been partially wrecked by an accidental explosion. Wesley eventually bought the Foundery for £115 and raised by loans and subscriptions another £700 which was required to transform the structure into a Meeting House.

The Foundery stood on Windmill Hill near Finsbury Square. The chapel, when complete, accommodated 1,500 people. The men were divided from the women, as was the custom of the Primitive Church. Wesley tells us that none were suffered to call any place their own, but the firstcomer sat down first. They had no pews, and all the benches for rich and poor were of the same construction.

The Foundery was the cradle of London Methodism, and it was here that Wesley began to preach in 1739. Above the chapel, apartments were fitted up for Wesley's use, and it was in these apartments that his mother lived for the last years of her life, and it was there that she died.

The Foundery was the headquarters of Methodism until the City Road Chapel was opened in 1778.

II

The breach with the Moravians was far less serious in its consequences than the breach with Whitefield. Whitefield was a Calvinist, and the controversy between Whitefield and Wesley was destined to split Methodism into two camps.

Calvinism is one of the unsolved problems of history. It is the duty of the historian to discover the root principles which have induced intelligent men to yield passionate loyalty to creeds which later ages have rejected, but this duty is nowhere more difficult than in the case of Calvinism. One is, of course, tempted to represent Calvinism in the most favourable light if only to placate the modern fashion of universal toleration. The religious historian, whatever may be his theme, from the Spanish Inquisition to the philosophy of Calvin, is sure to be told that he lacks historical imagination if he records a hostile verdict against any institution, however vile, or against any superstition, however stupid. He will be told that his facts are correct, but that he lacks sympathy with the past, and that he has no sense of atmosphere.

One can argue about facts, but not about atmosphere. The "atmosphere" line of defence for the indefensible was thoroughly exploited by Wesley's Moravian opponents. Wesley, who believed in logic and reason, and who enjoyed the stately progress of debate from premiss to conclusion expressed his impatient contempt for opponents who retreated behind a mist of verbiage.

"I do not admire the manner wherein they treat their opponents. I cannot reconcile it either to love, humility, or sincerity. Is utter contempt, or settled disdain, consistent with love or humility? And can it consist with sincerity to deny any charge which they know in their conscience is true? To say those quotations are unjust which are literally copies from their own books? To affirm their doctrines are misrepresented, when their own sense is given to their own words? To cry, "Poor man! He is quite dark! He is utterly blind! He knows nothing of our doctrines!" though they cannot point out one mistake this blind man has made, or confute one assertion he has advanced!"

III

The historian of religious movements should divide the beliefs which he attempts to criticise into three classes. First, there are the beliefs which he himself considers to be true. Secondly, there are the beliefs which he rejects, but which are defended by argument which compel, if not agreement, at least respect. Thirdly, there are beliefs which seem to him both absurd and mischievous. Toler-

ance has its dangers and temptations no less than intolerance. To condone what is demonstrably evil is as bad as
to condemn what is good.

Calvinism as a philosophy is absurd and contradictory,
and its ultimate effects on conduct are bound to be mischievous. I say "ultimate" for these effects may take some
time to appear.

The universe is fundamentally rational. Grapes do
not grow on bramble bushes. An immoral philosophy will
ultimately produce an immoral effect. The first prophets
of a false philosophy may be unaffected, for their lives
are still influenced by the traditions which they have inherited from the philosophy which they reject. Materialism is a case in point. A moral machine is a contradiction in terms, and according to materialists we are all ma-
chines governed by forces over which we have no control.
The ultimate outcome of such a creed must be the breakdown of all moral restraint, a conclusion which the Victorian materialist repudiated with lively indignation.
"Consider Darwin and Tyndall," urged the Victorian ag-
nostics, "these men are not influenced by the hope of
heaven or the fear of hell, but they do not take chorus girls
down to Brighton for the week-end." Of course not, partly
because they would never have survived the excruciating
boredom of a week-end in such society, and partly because they were living on the inherited capital of Christian tradition. The Victorian materialist was not consistent. He might poke fun at Gadarene swine, but the
enthusiasm with which he set out to prove Christianity
a myth was no greater than his anxiety to preserve the
moral code which was based on that myth. Men are, in
the main, more rational than the rationalists, and it is
vain to expect them to retain the restrictions while re-
jecting the consolations of supernatural religion. It is,
indeed, difficult to understand the mental attitude of those

"who cannot have the faith and will not have the fun."

A code which is based on a creed will not long survive the rejection of that creed. Russia, for instance, has formally rejected, not only Christianity, but also that "bourgeois morality" which derives its sanction from Christianity. Let a Bolshevist, writing in an official Bolshevist paper, describe the result:

"Our young people," writes Madame Smidovich in "Pravda," [1] "have certain principles in affairs of love. All those principles are governed by the belief that the nearer you approach to extreme, and, as it were, animal primitiveness, the more communistic you are. . . . Every student, man or girl, considers it as axiomatic that in affairs of love they should impose the least possible restraint on themselves."

Madame Smidovich, so Mr. Fülöp-Miller assures us in his brilliant and impassioned study of Bolshevism, "quotes cases which she declares to be typical: for example, one day two sixteen-year-old fathers appeared before the amazed officials of the Foundling Hospital with a 'collective child' . . . In this heavy sexual atmosphere suicides abound."

So with Calvinism which must ultimately lead to antinomianism. Froude's defence is based on a fallacy:

"I am going to ask you to consider how it came to pass that if Calvinism is indeed the hard and unreasonable creed which modern enlightenment declares it to be, it has possessed such singular attractions in past times for some of the greatest men that ever lived. And how—being, as we are told, fatal to morality, because it denies free will—the first symptom of its operation, wherever it established itself, was to obliterate the distinction between sins and crimes, and to make the moral law the rule of life for States as well as persons. I shall ask you, again, why, if it be a creed of in-

[1] Quoted by René Fülöp-Miller in "The Mind and Face of Bolshevism," page 200.

tellectual servitude, it was able to inspire and sustain the bravest efforts ever made by man to break the yoke of unjust authority." [2]

The answer to Froude's problem is quite simple. William the Silent and Cromwell are no more the products of Calvinism than Darwin, Tyndall and Huxley are the products of materialism. All these men were great in spite of, rather than because of the creeds which they held. Calvinism is Theism plus determinism. Materialism is atheism plus determinism. Both creeds deny free will and make man a machine, thereby reducing morality to a farce. The ultimate (but not immediate) result of any creed based on the denial of free will must be the replacement of moral endeavor by fatalistic despair.

IV

"I do not think," writes a distinguished critic, "that you are quite fair to the philosophy underlying Calvinism. No one would suggest that Deism is absurd, and Calvinism is Deism plus religious emotion, reverence and fear." Perhaps, but Calvinism is also Deism plus the belief in eternal punishment. Calvinism is not absurd simply because Calvin denied free will; for the freedom of the will is not a self-evident proposition. Calvinism is absurd because Calvin tried to reconcile determinism with the existence of an all-loving God who dealt out in arbitrary fashion infinite rewards and infinite penalties.

Superficial criticism of a creed is usually easy to rebut. A clever Catholic can make rings round the average Protestant who embarks on criticism of Catholic doctrines such as Papal infallibility or the nature of Indulgences, doctrines which at first sight appear difficult to

[2] "Short Studies on Great Subjects," by J. C. Froude. Vol. ii, pp. 5–6.

defend. But in the case of Calvinism, it is the first facile criticism which remains unanswered.

Wesley summed up Calvinism in less than fifty words. "The sum of all is this: one in twenty (suppose) of mankind are elected; nineteen in twenty are reprobated. The elect shall be saved, do what they will; the reprobate shall be damned, do what they can. Reader, believe this or be damned. Witness my hand."

Try to sum up Catholicism, Buddhism or Theosophy in five hundred words, and you will find your task beyond your powers. But Wesley's fifty-word summary of Calvinism does full justice to the fundamental tenets of Calvinism, even though there may be secondary aspects of Calvin's teaching which merit praise.

If you study the apologetics of most creeds you will learn something. You may not be convinced, but you will understand how wise men have found it possible to accept a creed which your reason rejects. But if you read through Calvin's Institutes from end to end, as the present writer has done, you will be no nearer understanding the paradox of his mind or the fascination of his creed than when you turned the first page. The wall of an asylum separates you, and if Calvin is outside that wall, your place is the padded cell.

It is impossible to caricature Calvinism. "We believe, though it is incomprehensible, that it is just to damn such as do not deserve it." Thus Beza, Calvin's great lieutenant. No vulgar misrepresentation of Beza's views could be more damaging than his own simple credo.

Or again, consider Calvin's reply to those who argue that man must be free to repent, seeing that God offers His grace to sinners. God would not mock the sinner with false hopes had He decreed his eternal damnation. "God speaketh to them," Calvin replied, "that they may be the deafer; He gives light to them that they may be the blinder; He offers instruction to them that they may be more ignorant; and uses the remedy that they may *not* be healed."

To represent your own creed in the worst possible light is an effective method for silencing the opposition. There is nothing left to be said.

v

John Wesley had wrestled with the nightmare of Calvinism during his undergraduate days. He was much helped by his mother's letters, lucid, well reasoned and admirably expressed. He read them and was convinced. But even without their aid, it was humanly certain that Wesley would never have become a Calvinist. He had too overpowering a conviction of the universal love of God.

Whitefield, during his first visit to America, came under the influence of Jonathan Edwards, that a great apostle of Calvinism, and it was as a convinced Calvinist that Whitefield returned to England. Wesley was one of the least controversial of men, and he did his best to avoid this dangerous topic. He was, however, forced against his will to define his own position. An ardent predestinarian accused him of not daring to preach the whole truth, and based his attack on the fact that Wesley never referred to the doctrine of predestination in his sermons.

Wesley could no longer avoid the challenge.

On April 29th, 1739, he preached his great sermon on Free Grace, a sermon which was a vigorous attack on Calvinism and contains one trenchant passage:

"This is the blasphemy clearly contained in *the horrible decree* of predestination! And here I fix my feet. On this I join issue with every assertor of it. You represent God as worse than the devil; more false, more cruel, more unjust. But you say you will prove it by Scripture? Hold!

What will you prove by Scripture? That God is worse
than the devil? It cannot be. Whatever that Scripture
proves, it never can prove this; whatever its true meaning be, this cannot be its true meaning. . . . It cannot
mean, whatever it mean besides, that the God of truth
is a liar. Let it mean what it will, it cannot mean that
the Judge of all the world is unjust. No scripture can
mean that God is not love, or that his mercy is not over all
his works; that is, whatever it prove beside, no scripture
can prove predestination."

This passage is interesting, not only for the views which
it expresses, but also for the light which it throws on
Wesley's mental processes. "No scripture can mean that
God is not love." In other words Scripture must be in-
terpreted by personal experience. The final touchstone of
truth is the inner witness. The keynote to Wesley's religious experience was the discovery that God is love,
and anything which contradicted that discovery must be
false. To make personal experience the touchstone of
dogma comes perilously near that enthusiasm which Wesley condemned. But in one sense, at least, most religious
people are enthusiasts. They may take their official belief
from the Church, but the beliefs which give reality to
their inner life are based on personal experience.

Whitefield, who was just on the point of sailing for
America, begged Wesley not to publish his sermon. Wesley cast lots and the Oracle replied "Preach and print."
He therefore published the sermon, and added to the sermon his brother's hymn of universal redemption. Charles
had summed up the absurdity of Calvinism in a memorable epigram:

> "To damn for falling short,
> Of what they could not do,
> For not believing the report
> Of that which was not true."

But men are seldom converted by epigrams or irony. You must touch their hearts. The most decisive factor in the campaign against Calvinism was neither John Wesley's sermon, nor Charles Wesley's epigram, but Charles Wesley's hymns.

The theme of those hymns was the universal love of God.

> "Father, whose *everlasting love*
>   Thy only Son for *sinners* gave,
> Whose grace to all did freely move,
>   And sent Him down the *world* to save:
> Help us Thy mercy to extol,
>   Immense, unfathomed, unconfined;
> To praise the Lamb who died *for all,*
>   The *general* Saviour of mankind." [3]

It was the gospel of the universal love of God which destroyed Calvinism. The words "universal," "every man," "for all" recur and recur, and are sometimes printed in italics to emphasise the central doctrine of the hymns. The hymn which was affixed to John Wesley's sermon includes these verses:

> *"For every man He tasted death,*
>   *He suffer'd once for all;*
> He calls as many souls as breathe,
>   And all *may* hear the call.
>
> A power to choose, a will to obey,
>   Freely His grace *restores;*
> We all *may* find the living way,
>   And call the Saviour ours.
>
> Thou canst not mock the sons of men;
>   Invite us to draw nigh,
> Offer Thy grace to all, and then
>   Thy grace to most deny."

[3] "Poetical Works." Vol. iii, p. 36.

Whitefield appears to have been less incensed by John Wesley's sermons than by Charles Wesley's hymns. A copy of John Wesley's sermon reached him in America. He was much perturbed, and wrote at once to Wesley:

"I find your sermon has had its expected success; it has set the nation a disputing. You will have enough to do now to answer pamphlets. Two I have already seen. O that you would be more cautious in casting lots! O that you would not be rash and precipitate! If you go on thus, honoured sir, how can I concur with you? It is impossible. I must speak what I know. This I write out of the fulness of my heart. About spring, you may expect to see, ever, ever yours in Christ."

Wesley's sermon still rankled. Three days later he wrote again:

"Dear Brother Wesley,—What mean you by disputing in all your letters? May God give you to know yourself; and then you will not plead for *absolute perfection* or call the doctrine of *election* a 'doctrine of devils.' My dear brother, take heed. See you are in Christ a new creature. Beware of a false peace. Strive to enter in at the strait gate; and give all diligence to make your calling and election sure. Remember you are but a babe in Christ, if so much. Be humble; talk little; think and pray much. Let God teach you; and He will lead you into all truth. I love you heartily. I pray you may be kept from error, both in principle and practice. Salute all the brethren. If you must dispute, stay till you are master of the subject; other wise you will hurt the cause you would defend. Study to adorn the gospel of our Lord in all things; and forget not to pray for your affectionate friend and servant,

GEORGE WHITEFIELD."

This last letter reveals the muddle-headedness which characterises Calvinistic controversy. "Strive to enter in at the strait gate." Why strive? As if striving could alter God's eternal decree. "Give all diligence to make your calling and election sure." But there are no degrees of certainty in the matter of election. A man either is or is not elected. The question was settled once and for all long before he was born. So why worry?

The excellent advice, "Be humble; talk little; think and pray much," provokes a smile, for few men talked more and thought less than Whitefield. There is more thought, more close reasoning in a page of Wesley's Sermons than in a volume of Whitefield's.

Whitefield, on his return to England, lost no time in replying to Wesley. He published his reply, and being anxious to show that the Calvinists wrote better poetry and hymns than Charles Wesley, he affixed to his reply the hymn by the great Dissenter, Dr. Watts:

"Behold the potter and the clay,
He forms his vessels as he please;
Such is our God, and such are we,
The subjects of his high decrees.

Doth not the workman's pow'r extend
O'er all the mass, which part to choose,
And mould it for a nobler end,
And which to leave for viler use?

May not the sov'reign Lord on high
Dispense His favours as He will;
Choose some to life, while others die,
And yet be just and gracious still?

What, if to make His terror known,
He lets His patience long endure,
Suff'ring vile rebels to go on,
And seal their own destruction sure?

Shall man reply against the Lord,
And call his Maker's way unjust,
The thunder of whose dreadful word
Can crush a thousand worlds to dust?"

Hymns by Isaac Watts
in our Hymnal.
3 – 17 – 19 – 22 – 63 – 82 –
89 – 142 – 148 – 172 – 227 –
284 – 424 – 479 – 513 –
528 – 633 –

Dotology 618

A fine hymn, more suitable however for a mosque than a church. Fatalism, as such, is not ridiculous. The philosophy which steels a man to seek no favour from the indifferent gods is neither ignoble nor absurd. Fatalism is only absurd when grafted on to Christianity. Dr. Watts's sombre hymn achieves grandeur and escapes absurdity because the God he worships is, in reality, not the Christian God of Love, but the eastern potentate

"The thunder of whose dreadful word
Can crush a thousand worlds to dust."

There is, indeed, a striking resemblance between the "potter and the clay" theme of Dr. Watts's hymn and the well-known lines from "Omar Khayyam."

"After a momentary silence spake
Some Vessel of a more ungainly Make;
    'They sneer at me for leaning all awry:
What! did the Hand then of the Potter shake?'

.   .   .   .

'Why,' said another, 'Some there are who tell
Of one who threatens he will toss to Hell
    The luckless Pots he marr'd in making—Pish!
He's a Good Fellow, and 't will all be well.' "

Omar only differs from Dr. Watts, in that Omar rebels and Dr. Watts submits to the decree of the Supreme Potter. Calvin's fatalism is the fatalism of an abject slave, Omar's of a slave who remains the Captain of his Soul.

"Oh, Thou, who didst with pitfall and with gin
Beset the Road I was to wander in,
    Thou wilt not with Predestined Evil round
Enmesh, and then impute my Fall to Sin!

Oh, Thou, who Man of baser Earth didst make,
And ev'n with Paradise devise the Snake:

For all the Sin wherewith the Face of Man
Is blacken'd—Man's forgiveness give—and take!"

There is more real religion in the revolt of Omar than
in the submission of Dr. Watts.

VI

Wesley believed in hitting the ball, not the man. He
was seldom stung into making a personal retort. He made
no allusions, direct or indirect, in his sermons to Whitefield or any other Calvinist. The Calvinists, on the other
hand, seemed determined to turn an academic discussion
on doctrine into a personal duel. Many years later, Wesley
wrote as follows:

"Mr. Whitefield first wrote a treatise against me by name.
He sent it to my brother, who endorsed it with these words,
'Put up again thy sword into its place.' It slept awhile; but
after a time, he published it. I made no reply. Soon after,
Mr. Whitefield preached against my brother and me by name.
This he did constantly, both in Moorfields, and in all other
public places. We never returned railing for railing, but
spoke honourably of him, at all times, and in all places. . . .
It was not merely the difference of doctrine that caused the
division. It was rather Mr. Whitefield's *manner* wherein he
maintained his doctrine, and treated us in every place."

Whitefield's partisans did their best to envenom the
wound. Whitefield's letter, reproduced on a previous
page, was printed without Whitefield's permission. This
letter contained a depreciative reference to the fact that
Wesley had decided to appeal to the Lot to decide
whether he should publish his Sermon or no. Thirty-
seven years later, during another great Calvinistic controversy, Rowland Hill taunted Wesley with having "cast
lots for a creed." This was, of course, a gross misrepresentation, but Wesley was sensitive to this particular

taunt. Copies of Whitefield's letter were distributed at the doors of the Foundery just before Wesley was due to preach. Wesley acted wtih characteristic promptitude.

"1741. February 1, Sunday. Having procured one of the copies, I related, after preaching, the naked fact to the congregation, and told them 'I will do just what I believe Mr. Whitefield would, were he here himself.' Upon which I tore it in pieces before them all. Every one who had received it, did the same. So that, in two minutes, there was not a whole copy left. Ah! poor Ahithophel!"

Fortunately, the breach between Wesley and Whitefield did not last long. They agreed to differ, and though their disagreement inevitably created a division which endures to this day, for the Calvinistic Methodists trace their descent to Whitefield, their founder, the friendship between Wesley and Whitefield was re-established and endured till Whitefield's death, nearly thirty years later. This was greatly to the credit of both men.

Whitefield died on December 30th, 1770, in America. In accordance with his dying wishes, John Wesley was invited by the executors to preach the funeral sermon at the chapel in Tottenham Court Road.

"If it be inquired," John Wesley said, "what was the foundation of this integrity, or of his [Whitefield's] sincerity, courage, patience, and every other valuable and amiable quality, it is easy to give the answer. . . . It was the love of God shed abroad in his heart by the Holy Ghost, which was given unto him, filling his soul with tender, disinterested love to every child of man. From this source arose that torrent of eloquence, which frequently bore down all before it from this, that astonishing force of persuasion, which the most hardened sinners could not resist. This it was, which often made his head as waters, and his eyes as a fountain of tears. This it was, which enabled him to pour out his soul in prayer, in a manner peculiar to himself, with such fulness and ease united together, with such strength and variety both of sentiment and expression." [4]

VII

After Whitefield's death the controversy broke out again. Wesley's potted summary of Calvinism, which we have quoted on a previous page, greatly enraged the Calvinists. Toplady, who edited the Calvinistic Gospel Magazine, was a young man at the time, Wesley's junior by little short of fifty years. His scurrilous attack on John Wesley would have been unjustifiable had he been engaged in controversy with a man of his own age and standing. The venomous invective with which he pursued and continued to pursue for years one of the most revered figures of his day had a great effect in discrediting the cause of which he had proved himself so violent a champion.

"Wesley," he writes, "is guilty of Satanic shamelessness," of "acting the ignoble part of a lurking, sly assassin," of "uniting the sophistry of a Jesuit with the authority of a pope," and of sinking the discussion "to the level of an oyster woman."

Toplady appears to have modelled his controversial style on Calvin. But though he did his best, he never attained the superb heights of invective which distinguished the writings of the great Genevese. There is nothing, for instance, in Toplady's Gospel Magazine quite so trenchant as this:

"The villainous cur, though refuted by obvious argument did but wipe his nozzle and say 'There is no harm done here. Let us go on.' "

Calvin's attitude to the villainous cur would have been

[4] "The Life of George Whitefield," L. Tyerman. Vol. ii, page 67.

more urbane if he had felt more confident that the cur had been refuted. But his peevish and fretful style is the outward witness of a mind that is not at peace with itself.

Indignation is, of course, ridiculous in a Calvinist; for the Calvinist is entitled to pity, but not to abuse his opponents. Their blindness to truth is a misfortune for which they are not responsible, and their persistence in error is part of God's eternal and inscrutable decree.

Wesley treated Toplady's attack with contemptuous silence. His Christianity and his breeding were never more notably displayed than in this controversy. In a brief preface to his sermon on Free Grace, he writes, "Whereas a pamphlet entitled 'Free Grace Indeed' has been published against this Sermon; this is to inform the publisher, that I cannot answer his tract till he appears to be more in earnest. For I dare not speak of 'the deep things of God' in the spirit of a prize-fighter or a stage-player."

In this controversy it was the prize-fighter who took the count. Wesley's controversial technique was an admirable advertisement for the Sermon on the Mount.

CHAPTER XIV

THE MASTER BUILDER

YOUNG men, with Napoleonic ambitions, anxious
to discover the secret of organizing and con-
trolling vast undertakings, should study Henry
Ford's Autobiography and Wesley's Journal.

Methodism, as an organized Society, may be said to date
from the foundation of the Fetter Lane Society in 1738.
Ten years passed, and Methodist Societies had already
spread over England, Wales and Ireland. At the Conference in 1748 Methodism was divided into nine great
geographical divisions, each of which contained several
flourishing Methodist Societies, the main divisions being
London, Bristol, Ireland, Wales, Staffordshire, Cheshire,
Yorkshire and Newcastle. Each main division was further
sub-divided into sub-divisions, and in many of these sub-
divisions there were more than one Society. Ireland, for
instance, had the following sub-divisions: Dublin, Philips-
town, Tullamore, Tyrrell's Pass, Ballybay and Athlone.
This result was achieved in spite of the persistent ill-will
of magistrates and the clergy, and in spite of frequent
attacks by the mob. In less than ten years, Wesley had
covered the face of England, Ireland and Wales with his
Societies. He ruled over these scattered Societies like an
autocrat. His decisions were seldom disputed, and never
disputed with success.

Even to-day, with all the modern advantages of quick
communications, it would be almost impossible for one
man to control societies distributed over three kingdoms.

In the eighteenth century the problem of control was infinitely more difficult. For all practical purposes, Dublin was further from London in the eighteenth century than New York is to-day. Wesley crossed the Irish Channel no less than fifty times at first from Chester, then from Parkgate and finally, as the Dee silted up, from Liverpool. Again and again, he was delayed by calms and by unfavourable winds, and he spent longer on the journey between London and Dublin than a modern traveller would spend on the journey between London and Bombay.

Wesley must have failed, had he not possessed unlimited energy, a genius for administration, and the power to impose his will on the vast scattered organization. He built up his organization on autocratic lines. He was never a democrat and never pretended to be a democrat, and in this he resembled the founders of all great religious movements, Mahomet, Calvin, Loyola, and in our own time, General Booth.

It is said that Wesley had very little originality. His organization was built up on ideas borrowed from other societies. This may be true, and the details of Methodist organization may not have been original, but surely the result was original. The architect does not "invent" his bricks, but his work as a whole may be original though every detail in that work is borrowed.

Wesley had one sure sign of genius, the power to recognise at a glance the things that were worth imitating, adapting or borrowing. Few men have been quicker at picking up anything good which happened to be lying around, and few men have shown less conscience in adapting or borrowing the work of other men.

I think it is George Moore who remarks that the great artists have never scrupled to borrow a good idea if they could thereby improve their own creations. Joy in the thing created is the hall-mark of the great artist, pride

in being able to claim full credit for the thing created
is the distinguishing mark of the second rate. A dangerous, but amusing doctrine. If plagiarism be the hall-
mark of literary genius, Wesley is sure of a place among
the Immortals, for no man borrowed more freely, and
no man derived more enjoyment from bowdlerising, revising and adapting the work of other men. In 1735, he
published without permission, several poems from Dr.
Young's "Night Thoughts" which he included in an
anthology of his own. An indignant publisher drew his
attention to the law of copyright, and compromised for
a sum of fifty pounds. Even this experience, which provoked Wesley's righteous indignation, did not cure him
of his love for touching up other men's work. Here is an
entry, twenty years later, from his Journal:

"In the latter part of the month I took some pains in
reading over Dr. Young's 'Night Thoughts,' leaving out
the indifferent lines, correcting many of the rest, and explaining the hard words in order to make that noble work
more useful to all, and more intelligible to ordinary
readers."

But though Wesley was shameless in the liberties which
he took with the works of other men, he was most incensed
if other writers ventured to tamper with his own and his
brother's hymns. In the famous preface to his Hymn
Book he writes:

"Many gentlemen have done my brother and me
(though without naming us) the honour to reprint many
of our hymns. Now they are perfectly welcome so to do,
provided they print them just as they are. But I desire
they would not attempt to mend them; for they really are
not able. None of them is able to mend either the sense
or the verse. Therefore I must beg of them one of these
two favours: either to let them stand just as they are,
to take them for better for worse; or to add the true

reading in the margin, or at the bottom of the page; that we may no longer be accountable either for the nonsense or for the doggerel of other men."

And such is the power of honourable indignation, that no single writer on Wesley appears to have been struck by the humorous aspect of this indignant protest.

II

Wesley was not only quick to adopt what was good; he was always equally ready to discard what was bad. Few religious leaders have shown more readiness to be guided by experience. Wesley was a pragmatist. He treated theories, not as answers to problems, answers in which he could rest, but as instruments with which to hammer out the desired result. He was prepared to sacrifice any theory which cramped his evangelical activities. His prejudices against extemporary prayer were the first to be shed. He disliked field preaching, but he was converted by the test of practical results. "What marvel," he writes, "that the devil does not love field preaching. Neither do I; I love a commodious room, a soft cushion, a handsome pulpit. But where is my zeal if I do not trample all this under foot in order to save souls?"

Wesley not only loved a commodious room and a soft cushion, he also loved discipline and order and disliked irregularities. Every step on the road to schism cost him a pang. He did not like extemporary prayer, he did not like field preaching, he did not like appointing lay preachers, and he did not like ordaining Dr. Coke. In all these cases, his sense of vocation triumphed over his ecclesiastical prejudices.

"All this" he was prepared "to trample under foot in order to save souls."

Ordinary people, perhaps, are not called upon to crit-

icise their Church or to decide when loyalty to the Church
is inconsistent with loyalty to God. "My Church right or
wrong" is the good working motto for the average Christian. It is, however, the privilege of religious genius to
decide between these conflicting loyalties. "The sabbath
was made for man, not man for the sabbath" is a sentiment which cannot fail to shock the institutionalist, just
as it will please the pragmatist, but Jesus, though He out-
raged the institutionalists of His day, loved the ceremonial
of the Temple, and revered and practised the religion of
His fathers. And it is a Roman Catholic, not a Methodist,
who draws a striking parallel between the early evolution of Christianity and the early evolution of Methodism:

"He never hints at the idea that His followers are destined to break away from Israel: nor did they ever do so
by any definite act of separation. During His life they
were in the Jewish Church as the Wesleyans were once
in the Church of England—a school of pietists, whose aim
was to purify, not to abandon, their Church." [1]

III

Many years before Wesley opened his campaign, new
life had been brought into the Church of England by the
"Religious Societies." Wesley no doubt hoped that the
Methodist Societies would be equally successful in reviving the spirit of religion within the Church of England.

Wesley had been much impressed by the Life of
Ignatius Loyola, "surely one of the greatest men," he
observes, "ever engaged in the support of so bad a cause."
The Counter-Reformation may well have seemed "a bad

---

[1] "Christianity at the Cross-Roads," by George Tyrrell, page 75.

cause" to Wesley, but he can hardly fail to have been impressed by the services which the Jesuits rendered to the Church of Rome, and no doubt he hoped that the Order which he had founded, for it was as an Order that he regarded the Methodists, might prove equally effective in reviving the Church of England.

"Wesley," writes Canon Overton, "dearly loved the Church of England, and when he varied from her at all in practice—(in doctrine he never knowingly varied from her)—it was because he thought he was justified in so doing by the customs of primitive times." [2]

Wesley had no difficulty in discovering a primitive precedent for the origin of his own societies. These societies arose, as we have seen, from the natural desire of the new converts to be united more closely for mutual help and encouragement. Wesley points out that those to whom the apostles preached were mostly Jews or heathens. "But as soon as any of them were so convinced of the truth, as to forsake sin and seek the gospel of salvation, they immediately joined them together, took an account of their names, advised them to watch over each other, and met these 'catechumens' (as they were then called), apart from the great congregation; that they might instruct, rebuke, exhort, and pray with them, and for them according to their several necessities."

The Love Feasts corresponded to the *Agapae* and the Watch Nights to the *Vigiliae* of the Early Church, and the visitors to the sick to the ancient deacons, "for what," asks Wesley, "was Phoebe the Deaconess but such a visitor to the sick?"

It is again easy to quote primitive precedent for the distinctive features of the Quarterly Meetings. At these Meetings, Wesley distributed tickets, which he compares to the commendatory letters mentioned by the apostles,

[2] "John Wesley" by J. H. Overton, page 125.

to members whom he wished to retain in the Societies. "These supplied us with a quiet and inoffensive method of removing any disorderly member. He has no new ticket at the quarterly visitation (for so often the tickets are changed), and hereby it is immediately known that he is no longer of the community."

These tickets were much prized. Methodists often left instructions that their tickets should be buried with them, but more often they were handed down from father to son, and a series of tickets proving a long connexion with the Methodist Societies was treasured no less than a certificate of *limpieza* issued by the Spanish Inquisition to those who could prove an uninterrupted descent from faithful Catholics who had never been penanced for heresy.

IV

I will spare the reader a detailed account of the Methodist Constitution, but a brief sketch is necessary in order to appreciate Wesley's administrative genius.

The original Fetter Lane Society was divided into "bands." Each "band" consisted of not fewer than five, nor more than ten persons, who met weekly to "confess their faults one to another and to pray for one another that they may be healed."

It is important to distinguish between the "bands" and the classes, a distinction which is not always made very clear in Methodist writings. Long after the class meetings had become an integral part of Methodism, the "bands" remained a distinct institution. They consituted an inner ring, an exclusive order of very devout Methodists. They were the Ironsides on whom Wesley relied in a crisis. He made the members of the "bands" his counsellors, and he was accustomed to bring difficult cases before them for consideration.

In 1744, the Methodists were arranged in the following groups, "United Societies," "Bands," "Select Societies," and "Penitents."

The United Societies was the largest and least select group, for it merely consisted of "awakened persons." The Bands were more select, and "the Select Societies" as its name implies, were really extremely exclusive. Finally, there were the Penitents, who had made "shipwreck of their faith."

But whereas the "bands" were composed of the elect, every member of a Methodist Society normally belonged to a class, and the Class Meeting is an instance of Wesley's quickness to recognise the latent tactical possibilities of every suggestion which was brought before him.

February 15th, 1742, is an important date in the history of Methodism. On that day, a Meeting was held in Bristol to discuss the best method of liquidating the debt on the Meeting House. A certain Captain Foy, one of the many sea-going captains in the Society of Bristol, suggested that every member of the Society should contribute a penny a week. It was objected that many of the members were too poor to afford a weekly contribution. "True," replied Captain Foy, "then put ten or twelve of them to me. Let each of these give what they can weekly and I will supply what is wanting."

The captain's proposal was accepted. It was agreed to divide the Bristol Society into "classes" and to appoint in each class a "leader" to collect the weekly contributions and to hand them over to the stewards. Wesley appointed the leaders, and assigned to each of them a class of about twelve members.

The penny collection for the relief of the poor, was

already in existence, and as Mr. Simon points out, "The novel feature of the captain's suggestion is its recognition of the principle that, in the Methodist Society, the richer members should make up the deficiency in a common fund which arises from the inability of the poorer members to contribute to it. That principle still governs the whole system of Methodist finance."

Wesley was quick to discover that Captain Foy's plan had other virtues besides solving the financial problem at Bristol. Shortly after the captain's scheme had been adopted, one of the class leaders reported to Wesley that he had discovered a member of his class, on whom he had called for a contribution, "in drink." It flashed across Wesley's mind that there was yet another rôle for the class leader. He could watch over the souls of his brethren, while extracting pennies from their pockets. He could encourage the faint-hearted, admonish the backsliders, and report the impenitents to Wesley.

Wesley determined to try out this new experiment, not only in Bristol, but in London. It was becoming increasingly difficult for Wesley to keep in touch with the two thousand members of his London Society, scattered as they were between Westminster and Wapping. He realised that the reputation of Methodism depended on effective control, for Methodism was on trial, and the jury consisted of a hostile and prejudiced public only too ready to exploit the shortcomings of individual Methodists as an argument against Methodism in general.

Wesley, himself, was no longer able to support the entire pastoral care of the Societies. It was a stroke of genius to transform the class leaders into a lay pastorate. The experiment proved as successful in London as it had proved in Bristol, and thenceforwards the class leaders became an integral part of the Methodist constitution.

Before long, the class leaders discovered that it was

well-nigh impossible to pay twelve weekly visits to the twelve members of their class. Difficulties often arose because masters or mistresses, relatives or parents hostile to the Methodists prevented the invasion of their households by the class leaders. It was therefore decided that class members should meet together for an hour twice a week. The class leaders were expected to present a report every three months to Wesley on the spiritual condition of the class members appointed to their care.

Wesley's journeys during the course of the next forty years were undertaken in order to meet his class leaders, receive their reports, and to give them personal advice.

It is not difficult to understand the success of the class meetings. Man is a social animal. Those who have never lacked friends will not find it easy to realise the loneliness of our great cities, and the Methodists deserved to succeed because they put into practice the Christian ideal of brotherliness. They sought out the friendless and befriended them. The class meeting was, in effect, a club, a Travellers' Club whose members met twice a week to compare notes, and to exchange experiences in their spiritual progress towards the New Jerusalem. Lonely folk for whom nobody cared, were invited, nay urged, to talk about their souls. Can one wonder that the class meeting succeeded, for it exploited the most universal, and the most human of failings—vanity.

Consider a concrete case—Jane Smith. Jane is a maid-of-all-work. She is on the go for fifteen hours a day, and provided that she does her work in this world, neither her master nor her mistress very much cares what happens to her in the next. Of course, Jane has been to church, but it would be idle to pretend that the portly gentleman in the flowing gown, who reads a weekly sermon on the errors of the Deists, or on the folly of enthusiasm, is interested in Jane as an individual. Then one day, Jane meets a Methodist, and is persuaded to accompany her to the Foundery and is drawn into the orbit of the Methodist Society. Jane's heart, like Wesley's in Aldersgate Street, is strangely warmed, not perhaps by the doctrines which the Methodists preached, but by the glow of that friendship which the Methodists practised.

v

If Methodism owes much of its success to the class meetings, it owes its very existence to the institution of the lay preacher.

John Cennick, whose hymns "Children of the Heavenly King" and "Thou Dear Redeemer dying Lamb" are still popular favourites, was the first lay preacher. He was a master at the Kingswood school, and he spoke and preached in public with Wesley's approval as early as 1739. Wesley, however, seems to have felt that his position as a teacher differentiated his case from that of other laymen. Wesley certainly did not regard Cennick as a precedent for appointing other lay preachers.

Early in 1740, Wesley heard that a certain Thomas Maxfield, one of his converts, had been preaching before the Foundery Society. He was much alarmed, and hurried to London, where he was met by his mother on his arrival. "John," she said, "take heed what you do with reference to that young man, for he is as surely called to preach as you are." Wesley was much impressed. He knew that his mother's devotion to the Church of England equalled his own, and her view therefore, carried additional weight. He listened to Maxfield's preaching and exclaimed, "It is the Lord's doing. Let Him do what seemeth good." Within the year, twenty lay preachers had been appointed.

There would have been fewer lay preachers, had all bishops been ready to help Wesley as the good Dr. Barnard, Bishop of Londonderry. A little later Maxfield was ordained by Dr. Barnard, who said to him, "Sir, I ordain you to assist that good man, Mr. Wesley, that he may not work himself to death."

VI

The growth of Methodism rendered it necessary to provide a systematic arrangement of circuits and to appoint a preacher for each. Every lay preacher had to begin as a "local" before he was permitted to be an "itinerant." The preacher who superintended the whole of a circuit was called "the Superintendent."

The temporal affairs of these Societies were managed by Stewards.

The officers of the Societies were the Ministers, Assistants, Stewards, Leaders of the Bands, Leaders of the Classes, Visitors of the Sick, Schoolmasters, and Housekeepers.

Wesley soon realised that it was necessary to provide a governing body for the scattered Societies. He intended, during his lifetime to control any governing body he might find it necessary to create, and unless some such organization was called into existence, the Societies, as Wesley foresaw, could hardly survive his death.

The Annual Conference, which is still the supreme governing body of Methodism, first met on June 25th, 1744.

At this Conference, it was decided to invite from time to time such lay preachers as the Conference should decide to summons. This decision politely disguised the fact that it was Wesley, rather than the Conference, who decided which lay preachers should be invited to attend.

"The Conference," as Wesley wrote to an unruly sub-ordinate, "while I live is 'the preachers whom I invite to confer with me.' "

A characteristic utterance—with which we can fittingly bring to a close this sketch of Wesley, the Master Builder, and of the organization over which he held benevolent and autocratic sway.

CHAPTER XV

WESLEY'S GENERALSHIP

WESLEY kept in personal touch with his preachers and with his class leaders, partly by his unending journeys, and partly by correspondence. "His short, sharp letters," writes Mr. Eayrs, "ring like officers' orders."

His intuition and his memory were seldom at fault. He knew exactly what his subordinates were worth, the work for which they were most, and the work for which they were least suited. "Abstain from controversy," he writes to one of his lay preachers, "indeed you have not a talent for it. You have an honest heart, but not a clear head."

Wesley never wasted a word. He had a simple, direct way of putting people right, which must have been exasperating for the victim but which makes his letters very amusing reading. There are, of course, many ways of telling people disagreeable truths, and Wesley seldom chose the gentlest. This was partly due to his early upbringing. He had been taught by his brothers and sisters to give hard blows without malice, and to receive hard blows without resentment.

Wesley, unlike many people who criticise freely and who preen themselves on their bluff candour, did not resent being criticised himself. In his description of Grace Murray, his last love, he mentions among her virtues that she was in the habit "of telling me with all faithfulness and freedom if she thought anything amiss in my con-

duct." Wesley, indeed, seldom resented honest criticism.
Whitefield's letters to Wesley have been quoted on a
previous page. Wesley was a distinguished Fellow of his
college, and many years the senior of the ex-servitor who
addressed him with such patronising impertinence. "Be
humble; talk little; think and pray much." Wesley showed
no signs of resenting this ill-timed advice.

"If anyone will convince me of my errors," he once
wrote to an opponent, "I will heartily thank him." This,
of course, reads like a conventional controversial gambit,
but Wesley meant what he said. Indeed, he complained
bitterly when people did not take him at his word.
"Neither you nor John Jones have ever sent me your
remarks upon that tract in the late volume of Sermons.
You are not kind. Why will you not do all you can to make
me wiser than I am?"

John Wesley had a passion for "openness." He confessed that he hated keeping a secret, and he was certainly
incapable of keeping secret the views which he had
formed about the shortcomings of his friends. But he
expected his friends to be equally "open" with him. He
was always overjoyed if he discovered somebody who
displayed the same "absolute openness and unreserve" in
their dealings with him, which he habitually used in his
relations to his fellow men. Characteristic is his letter to
the Reverend Henry Venn:

"Having at length a few hours to spare, I sit down to
answer your last, which was particularly acceptable to me,
because it was wrote with so great openness. I shall write
with the same. And herein you and I are just fit to converse together; because we both like to speak blunt and
plain, without going a great way round about. I shall
likewise take this opportunity of explaining myself on

some other heads. I want you to understand me inside and out. Then I say, Sic sum: Si placeo, utere."

His plain, blunt, literary style was the result of his ruthless exploitation of time. To every moment of the day, from 4 A. M. when he rose until 10 P. M. when he retired, its appropriate task was allotted. The man who never wasted a minute could not afford to waste a word. Inevitably he developed the habit of coming to the point at once, and of telling his mind "flat and plain without any preface or ceremony." The following letter to a friend rings true:

"I bless God that you are not disgusted at the great plainness with which I wrote. Indeed I know not but it might be termed roughness; which was owing partly to the pressure of mind I then felt, and partly to my being straitened for time; otherwise I might have found softer expressions. I am thankful likewise for your openness; which obliges me to be open and unreserved, and to say all I mean, and that in the most simple manner, on each of the articles that lie before us."

Few people would be believed if they urged being "straitened for time" as an excuse for "roughness." But a man who makes a habit of rising at 4. A. M. may well be believed when he pleads that he has no leisure for "courtly phrases."

His abrupt style of course sometimes gave offence. Judged, however, by literary rather than by social standards, it is precisely this curtness which is the great merit of his style.

"It would be difficult," writes Leslie Stephen, "to find any letters more direct, forcible and pithy in expression. He goes straight to the mark without one superfluous flourish. He writes as a man confined within the narrow limits of time and space, whose thoughts are so well in hand that he can say everything needful within those limits. The compression gives emphasis and never causes confusion."

A young man learning to write could have had no better tutor than Wesley. Pope, I think, said that in writing the greatest art is the art to blot, to dispense, that is, with every redundancy, to aim at "the utmost simplicity and plainness."

Here is an excellent example of emphasis due to compression. Francis Wolfe had been appointed second preacher in the Bristol circuit. Six weeks passed, and Francis Wolfe failed to put in an appearance. Wesley wrote him a letter consisting of exactly thirteen words: "Franky, are you out of your wits? Why are you not at Bristol?"

We may be sure that "Franky" wasted as little time in getting to Bristol, as Wesley had wasted words sending him there.

The famous letter which he wrote to George Shadford is another example of masterly compression.

"Dear George,—The time is arrived for you to embark for America. You must go down to Bristol, where you will meet with Thomas Rankin, Captain Webb and his wife.

"I let you loose, George, on the great continent of America. Publish your message in the open face of the sun, and do all the good you can."

Wesley was in command of an army of nearly seven hundred local preachers. Some of them were men of breeding and education, but many, indeed the majority, were not. Wesley was alive to the peculiar temptations of the preacher's life, temptations which are especially dangerous to men whose gifts of rhetoric has promoted them from obscurity to comparative prominence in their own circle.

Wesley could not endure the easy vanity of the popular preacher. He did not try to soften his rebuke to one who had been corrupted by applause.

"I think you tasted of the powers of the world to come thirteen or fourteen years ago, and was then simple of heart, and willing to spend and be spent for Christ. But not long after, not being sufficiently on your guard, you suffered loss by being applauded. This revived and increased your natural vanity; which was the harder to be checked, because of your constitutional stubbornness;— two deadly enemies which have lain in wait for you many years, and have given you many deep, if not mortal, wounds."

His advice on the art of preaching was always to the point. "I hope you have now got quit of your queer, arch expressions in preaching, and that you speak as plain and dull as one of us."

And again,

"Scream no more, at the peril of your soul. God now warns you by me, whom He has set over you. Speak as earnestly as you can, but do not scream. Speak with all your heart but with a moderate voice. It was said of our Lord, 'He shall not *cry*': the word properly means, He shall not *scream*. Herein be a follower of me, as I am of Christ. I often speak loud; often vehemently; but I never scream; I never strain myself; I dare not; I know it would be a sin against God and my own soul."

Wesley was alive to the dangers not only of formalism, but of informalism in religion. The letter killeth. Perhaps, but the spirit doth not always make alive. Formalism may lead to deadness, but informalism often leads to ranting. Towards the end of his long life he wrote, "I find more profit in sermons on either good tempers, or good works, than in what are vulgarly called Gospel sermons. That term has now become a mere cant word: I wish none of our society would use it. It has no determinate meaning. Let but a pert, self-sufficient animal, that has neither sense nor grace, bawl out something about Christ, or his blood, or justification by faith, and his hearers cry out, 'What a fine Gospel sermon!' Surely the Methodists have not so learned Christ!"

II

Few religious leaders have been served with more wholehearted devotion by his disciples than was Wesley. Even those whose faults he criticised with such merciless candour loved and revered him. They recognised that his reproofs were prompted by his disinterested passion for salvation. They knew that though his words might be rough, his heart was "most wonderfully kind." The phrases with which he gave expression in his anxiety for their souls were not the routine formulae of the case-hardened evangelist. They rang true. He loved his friends; even the terseness of his literary style does not hide his affection. Because he was an evangelist, he could not refrain from rebuking them for the good of their souls, and because he loved them, he dreaded lest those rebukes might imperil the affectionate ties with which they were linked.

"Lift up your hearts to God or you will be angry with me" is a phrase which is repeated twice in a letter which Wesley wrote at the age of eighty-three. He could still spare the time and the energy to write a long letter full of tender rebuke and patient pleading. This letter must be quoted in full:

"Dear ———, You know I love you. Ever since I knew you I have neglected no way of showing it that was in my

power. And you know I esteem you for your zeal and
activity, for your love of discipline, and for your gifts
which God has given you; particularly quickness of apprehension and readiness of utterance; especially in prayer.

"Therefore I am jealous over you, lest you should lose
any of the things you have gained, and not receive a full
reward. And the more so because I fear you are wanting
in other respects. And who will venture to tell you so?
You will scarce know how to bear it from me, unless you
lift up your heart to God. If you do this, I may venture
to tell you what I fear without any further preface. I
fear you think of yourself more highly than you ought
to think. Do not you think too highly of your understanding? Of your gifts, particularly in preaching? as if
you were the very best preacher in the Connexion? of
your own importance? as if the work of God, here or
there, depended wholly or mainly on you? and of your
popularity? which I have found to my surprise far less,
even in L——, than I expected.

"May not this be much owing to the want of brotherly
love? With what measure you mete, men will measure to
you again. I fear there is something unloving in your
spirit; something not only of roughness but of harshness,
yea, of sourness! Are you not also extremely open to
prejudice, and not easy to be cured of it? so that whenever you are prejudiced you commence bitter, implacable,
unmerciful? If so, that people are prejudiced against you
is both the natural and judicial consequence.

"I am afraid lest your want of love to your neighbours
should spring from want of love to God; from want of
thankfulness. I have sometimes heard you speak in a
manner that made me tremble; indeed in terms that not
only a weak Christian but even a serious Deist would
scruple to use.

"I fear you greatly want evenness of temper. Are you

not generally too high or too low? Are not all your passions too lively, your anger in particular? Is it not too soon raised? And is it not too impetuous, causing you to be violent, boisterous, bearing down all before you?

"Now lift up your heart to God, or you will be angry at me. But I must go a little farther. I fear you are greatly wanting in the government of your tongue. You are not exact in relating facts. I have observed it myself. You are apt to amplify; to enlarge a little beyond the truth. You cannot imagine, if others observe this, how it will affect your reputation.

"But I fear you are more wanting in another respect: that you give a loose to your tongue when you are angry; that your language then is not only sharp, but coarse and ill-bred. If this be so, the people will not bear it. They will not take it either from you or me."

During the war, the Germans coined an expressive nickname for a military type which exists in other armies than the German. "Bicyclists" was the name they gave to officers who pedalled down their subordinates while preserving a broad respectful back to their superiors.

Wesley was no "bicyclist." He was as "open" and outspoken to cabinet ministers as to lay preachers. Here, for instance, are a few extracts from his letter to Lord Dartmouth, Colonial Secretary during the American crisis:

"I can truly say, I neither fear nor desire anything from your Lordship. To speak a rough truth, I do not desire any intercourse with any persons of quality in England. I mean, for my own sake. They do me no good; and I fear, I can be none to them. If it be desired, I will readily leave all those to the care of my fellow-labourers. I will article with them so to do, rather than this shall be any bone of contention.

"Were I not afraid of giving your Lordship pain, I

would speak yet still further. Methinks you desire I
should; that is, to tell you, once for all, every thought that
rises in my heart. I will then. At present I do not want
you; but I really think you want me. For, have you a
person in all England who speaks to your Lordship so
plain and downright as I do? who considers not the Peer,
but the man? not the Earl, but the immortal spirit? who
rarely commends, but often blames, and perhaps would do
it oftener if you desired it? who is jealous over you with
a godly jealousy, lest you should be less a Christian by
being a nobleman? lest, after having made a fair advance
towards heaven, you should

'Measure back your steps to earth again.'

O my Lord, is not such a person as this needful for you
in the highest degree? If you have any such, I have no
more to say, but that I pray God to bless him to your
soul. If you have not, despise not even the assistance which
it may please God to give you by,

My Lord,
Your Lordship's ready servant.
JOHN WESLEY.

III

Wesley believed in unity of command, the unity, of
course, being John Wesley. It would be idle to deny that
he was an autocrat. True he asked for, and often took
advice, just as a general will consult his staff officers,
Wesley, like a general, reserved the power of acting or
not acting on advice which had been given to him.

Wesley did not disdain advice, but he was too clear-
headed to pretend that he believed in democratic control.
"If by absolute power," he remarked with disarming

simplicity, "you mean power which I exercise without any coadjutor, it is certainly true, but I see no objection to it."

Earlier in his life, of course, he shared control with Charles, but Charles married and was no longer free to travel as he had been before. The control passed more and more to John. "It appears to me," wrote Whitehead, "that after the first difference with his brother who disputed his intended marriage, John made up his mind not to suffer either a superior or an equal in these respects. From that time he seemed determined to be *aut Caesar aut nullus.*"

The letters which John Wesley wrote during 1753 confirm this view.

On October 20th, he writes to his brother as follows:

"I give you a dilemma. Take one side or the other. Either act really in connexion with me, or never pretend to it. Rather disclaim it; and openly avow you do and will not.

"By acting in connexion with me, I mean, take counsel with me once or twice a year, as to the places where you will labour. Hear my advice before you fix; whether you take it or not.

"At present you are so far from this, that I do not even know when and where you intend to go. So far are you from following any advice of mine; nay, even from asking it. And yet I may say, without vanity, that I am a better judge of this matter than either Lady Huntingdon, Sally Jones, or any other: Nay, than your own heart; that is, will.

"I wish you all peace, zeal, and love."

A letter written a few days later was endorsed by Charles with the words, "Brother, October 31, 1753, trying to bring me under his yoke."

On one occasion when Charles Wesley threatened to

leave the Conference if laymen were allowed to join in
the discussions John turned to his neighbour and said,
"Give my brother his hat."

The breach between the brothers was only temporary.
The old, affectionate relations were soon restored, but
after 1753 Charles was more wrapped up in his family,
and less and less inclined to challenge John's undisputed
control over the Societies.

John Wesley intended that Methodism after his death
should be governed by the Annual Conference of preachers, but during his lifetime, the Conference was an ad-
visory, but not a legislative body, consisting as it did of
"those preachers whom I invite to confer with me."

Some years before he died, he defined the scope of Conference in a letter to a dissatisfied preacher :

"You seem likewise to have quite a wrong idea of a
Conference. For above six years after my return to England, there was no such thing. I then desired some of my
preachers to meet me, in order to advise, not control me.
And you may observe, they had no power at all, but what
I exercised through them. I chose to exercise the power
which God had given me in this manner, both to avoid
ostentation, and gently to habituate the people to obey
them when I should be taken from their head. But as
long as I remain with them, the fundamental rule of
Methodism remains inviolate. As long as any preacher
joins with me, he is to be directed by me in his work."

Few men disputed this claim, and none disputed it
twice. Wesley's supremacy was absolute, and extended
even to the most trivial details of daily life. "Dear
Tommy" is informed that Mr. Wesley requires that he
should go to bed at about "a quarter after nine." The
preachers in Ireland were warned not to fall into the
dirty habit of the country, and given precise instructions
as to personal cleanliness. Wesley, not only rose at 4 in

the morning, which was trying enough, but he expected
his preachers to avoid "intemperance in sleep." "Knowing no reason why we should make God's Day the shortest of the seven, I desired Joseph Thomson to preach
at 5."

His word was law, not only with his preachers, but
with his congregation. He decided that tea was unwhole-
some, and his people were commanded to abstain from this
dangerous beverage. "Many tell me to my face," he writes,
"that I can persuade the people to do anything." Having,
therefore, prevented his people from drinking tea, he determined to replace the lack of tea by prescriptions of his
own compounding. "I thought," he says, "of a kind of
desperate experiment. I will prepare and give them physic
myself." Wesley wrote a book on medicine. He distrusted
doctors, and was never happier than when prescribing for
his friends.

He provided, not only for their souls and bodies, but
also for their minds. He edited a Christian Library, "a
complete library for those that fear God" to borrow his
description, and for this purpose, he edited and con-
densed and abridged an enormous number of books. Wesley made great sums of money by his writings, all of
which he gave away. It is difficult to decide whether his
enormous circulation is a tribute to his literary gifts or
to the power of imposing his will, even to the extent of
making people buy his books. "You remember the rule
of Conference," he writes to a preacher, "that every
assistant should take my books into his own hands, as
having better opportunities of dispersing them than any
private person can possibly have. I desire you would do
this without delay. The *Primitive Physic* should be in
every family. So should the *Christian Pattern* if possible."

No wonder Wesley was a best-seller.

Wesley was an autocrat, but he was a disinterested autocrat. No importance should be attached to his own statement that "he feared and shunned, rather than desired authority of any kind . . . Only when God lays that burden upon me, I bear it for His sake and the people's sake." This remark should be treated as the equivalent of a formal plea of "not guilty"; for all autocrats profess to dread authority, and to be inspired only by a high sense of public duty. This particular plea is of no value unless supported by evidence. In Wesley's case the evidence is not lacking.

Wesley was free from that obstinate self-confidence which is too often associated with autocracy. He was the most easily influenced of men.

Wesley was always revising and modifying his views and doctrines, so much so that his Calvinistic adversaries accused him of being "the veriest weathercock that ever was; he has not wit enough to be fixed in anything, but is tossed to and fro continually."

In the week that preceded his Aldersgate Street conversion, Wesley appears in the rôle of a very humble disciple. And who is the great teacher at whose feet he sits? Peter Böhler, a young Moravian, many years his junior, distinguished neither for learning nor for great judgment.

No great religious leader has been less of a doctrinaire. No founder of a great religious movement has been more open to conviction.

"I have no more right," he writes, "to object to a man for holding a different opinion from mine than I have to differ with a man because he wears a wig and I wear my own hair; but if he takes his wig off and shakes the powder in my eyes, I shall consider it my duty to get quit of him as soon as possible."

And even when angry people took off their wigs and shook the powder in Wesley's eyes, he showed the most remarkable forbearance. Witness the following incident recorded in his Journal.

"Thursday. 19. June, 1740.

"In the evening Mr. Acourt complained that Mr. Nowers had hindered his going into our society. Mr. Nowers answered, 'It was by Mr. C. Wesley's order.' 'What,' said Mr. Acourt, 'do you refuse admitting a person into your society only because he differs from you in opinion?' I answered, 'No; but what opinion do you mean?' He said, 'That of election. I hold a certain number is elected from eternity. And these must and shall be saved. And the rest of mankind must and shall be damned. And many of your society hold the same.' I replied, 'I never asked whether they hold it or no. Only let them not trouble others by disputing about it.' He said 'Nay, but I will dispute about it.' 'What, wherever you come?' 'Yes, wherever I come.' 'Why, then, would you come among us, who you know are of another mind?' 'Because you are all wrong, and I am resolved to set you right.' 'I fear your coming with this view would neither profit you nor us.' He concluded, 'Then I will go and tell all the world that you and your brother are false prophets. And I tell you, in one fortnight you will all be in confusion.'

"Fr. 20. I mentioned this to our society, and, without entering into the controversy, besought all of them who were weak in the faith not to 'receive one another to doubtful disputations,' but simply to follow after holiness, and the things that make for peace."

Wesley's anxiety to retain complete control of the Societies was inspired by well-founded alarm lest intolerance and bigotry should ruin his great work. He retained the rôle of a dictator to protect the spirit of liberty and charity within the Societies.

IV

Who cast the first stone? Who was the first pharisee to accuse Wesley of restless ambition? John Hampson. And who was John Hampson? A Methodist preacher who never forgave Wesley for excluding him from the Legal Hundred. It was the Legal Hundred which constituted the Methodist Preachers' Conference. Hamson himself was an ambitious man, and as Wesley refused to gratify his ambitions, he left the Methodist connexion in a huff.

The ambitious man is usually anxious to secure the flattering and respectful verdict of his contemporaries and of posterity. There was only one verdict which interested Wesley, and that was the verdict of God. A man can, of course, be very holy, and yet not indifferent to the praise of his fellow men. It is not uncommon for religious people to be consumed with self-pity when they reflect on the inadequate recognition which their work receives. Few men have bothered less about recognition than John Wesley. He resented unjust attacks on Methodism, but he dismissed personal attacks on himself with quiet contempt. Even his sternest critics admired and admitted his unruffled peace of mind, a characteristic which, as Alexander Knox remarks, "is inconsistent with that restless ambition with which he was charged."

No man was less moved by the appeal, "Think what people will say," as Charles Wesley discovered when he tried to dissuade his brother from marrying one who had been a common servant. Jackson, in his "Life of Charles Wesley," relates an interesting anecdote which illustrates John Wesley's indifference to his reputation.

He had promised to take Charles's daughter Sarah, of

whom he was very fond, to Canterbury. Just then, Charles Wesley arrived with the news that Mrs. John Wesley was circulating scandalous rumours about her husband, supported by the evidence of letters which she had deliberately mutilated.

"My dear father," wrote Sarah in describing the incident, "to whom the reputation of my uncle was far dearer than his own, saw the importance of immediate refutation, and set off at once to see my uncle to induce him to postpone his journey.

"When he returned, he said—'My brother is indeed an extraordinary man. I placed before him the importance of the character of a ministry, the evil consequences which might result from his indifference to it; and urged him by every relative and public motive to answer for himself, and stop the publication. His reply was—'Brother, when I devoted to God my ease, my time, my life, did I except my reputation? No. Tell Sally I will take her to Canterbury to-morrow.'"

"The difference between the two men," remarks Mr. Rattenbury, "could hardly be better illustrated than by this incident—the one quite indifferent to scandal, the other more conventional, and moved by the feelings that influence most normal persons. John was careless about reputation, Charles careful. Both men had sublimated, to use a good psycho-analysis label, their natural characteristics, but John's superiority to reputation at a lower level means pride, and Charles's respect of it at a lower level means vanity."

V

John Wesley sincerely believed that he could best serve the cause of God and the people by retaining autocratic control over Methodism. Undoubtedly, he was right.

But though he was in sole control, he was always ready to delegate responsibility. He welcomed the institution of the class leader, and the class meeting, because the class leaders relieved him of much of his pastoral work. He did not seek power or authority for its own sake. He was always alert to discover men who could be trusted with responsibility, for he was overworked, and he often felt the strain of his appalling labours.

"What if fifty of the preachers disjoined themselves?" he wrote to a rebellious Methodist, "what should I lose thereby? Only a great deal of labour and care, which I do not seek; but endure because no one else either can or will."

Those who have studied his Journals and his letters will not feel disposed to dispute the absolute sincerity and unadorned truth of this assertion.

VI

"No founder of a monastic order," writes Southey, "ever more entirely possessed the respect as well as the love and the admiration of his disciples."

Autocrats may be admired and respected, but they are seldom loved unless their subordinates believe in their disinterested sincerity. Wesley was beloved because those who served him believed that he had their interests at heart, and knew that his whole life was based on the two great commandments, "Thou shalt love the Lord thy God with all thy heart and with all thy strength," and "Thou shalt love thy neighbour as thyself."

It is difficult in writing of Wesley not to overdo trite analogies from war, for Wesley was a great general, and many of his methods were military. His attitude towards his subordinates was certainly in the best traditions of the great generals. "We think," as Mr. Eayrs remarks, "of Napoleon, whose formula, 'We were at Toulon together,' covered a multitude of sins"; for few who had been at Toulon with Napoleon appealed in vain for his help. We think of Lord Haig, and of his unresting and untiring campaign for the men who had fought under him in France.

The men who enlisted under Wesley faced hardship and hatred, the brutality of mobs and the petty tyranny of squire and parson. These things Wesley did not forget. Nor was he mindful only of those who had been steadfast to the end, the tried and trusted brothers-in-arms. There were some who fell by the way, and even for these he cherished compassionate memories. Such was William Shent, a Leeds barber, who had been one of Wesley's preachers, but who had been expelled from the Leeds Society for immorality.

I cannot conclude this chapter better than by quoting in full the letter, which in its indignation and in its chivalry is characteristic of the writer, a letter which makes it easy to understand the love with which Wesley was regarded.

"I have a few questions, which I desire may be proposed to the society at Keighley.

"Who was the occasion of the Methodist preachers first setting foot in Leeds? William Shent.

"Who received John Nelson into his house at his first coming thither? William Shent.

"Who was it that invited me, and received me when I came? William Shent.

"Who was it that stood by me when I preached in the street, with stones flying on every side? William Shent.

"Who was it that bore the storm of persecution for the whole town, and stemmed it at the peril of his own life? William Shent.

"Whose word did God bless for many years in an eminent manner? William Shent's.

"By whom were many children now in Paradise begotten in the Lord, and many now alive? William Shent.

"Who is he that is ready now to be broken up and turned into the street? William Shent.

"And does nobody care for this? William Shent fell into sin, and was publicly expelled the society; but must he be also starved? Must he with his grey hairs and all his children be without a place to lay his head? Can you suffer this? Oh, tell it not in Gath! Where is gratitude? Where is compassion? Where is Christianity? Where is humanity? Where is concern for the cause of God? Who is a wise man among you? Who is concerned for the Gospel? Who has put on bowels of mercy? Let him arise and exert himself in this matter. You here all arise as one man, and roll away the reproach. Let us set him on his feet once more. It may save both him and his family. But what we do, let it be done quickly.

"I am, dear brethren, you affectionate brother.
JOHN WESLEY."

CHAPTER XVI

THE OPPOSITION

"THREE things," writes a medieval author, "all have the same sort on most of us when they get the upper hand; a water-floor, a wasting fire, and the common multitude of small folk."

Certainly the "common multitude of small folk" showed little mercy to the founders of Methodism.

Here is an extract from James Jones's record of the Wednesbury Riots:

"The mob had been gathering all Monday night, and on Tuesday morning they began their work. They assaulted, one after another, all the houses of those who were called Methodists. They first broke all their windows, suffering neither glass, lead, nor frames to remain therein. Then they made their way in; and all the tables, chairs, chests of drawers, with whatever was not easily removable, they dashed in pieces, particularly shop goods, and furniture of every kind. What they could not well break, as feather-beds, they cut in pieces and strewed about the room. William Sitch's wife was lying-in, but that was all one; they pulled away her bed too, and cut it in pieces. . . . All this time none offered to resist them. Indeed, most part, both men and women, fled for their lives; only the children stayed, not knowing whither to go.

"Wearing apparel, and things that were of value or easily saleable, they carried away, every man loading himself with as much as he could well carry of whatever he liked best.

"Some of the gentlemen who had set the mob to work, or threatened to turn away collier or miner out of their service that did not come and do his part, now drew up a paper for those of the Society to sign, importing that they would never invite or receive any Methodist preacher more. On this condition they told them they would stop the mob at once; otherwise they must take what followed.

"This they offered to several, but they declared, one and all, 'We have already lost all our goods, and nothing more can follow but the loss of our lives, which we will lose too rather than wrong our consciences."

For sheer malignity, the women seem to have surpassed the men. Here is John Nelson's description of his homecoming:

"When I got home I found my wife much better, though never likely to recover her former strength, owing to the persecution she met with at Wakefield when Mr. Larwood was mobbed there. After they had abused him, she, with some women, set out for Birstall. A mob followed them into the fields. When they overtook them she turned about and spake to them; upon which all the men returned without touching them; but the women followed them till they came to a gate, where they stopped them; they damned her, saying, "You are Nelson's wife, and here you shall die." They saw she was big with child, yet beat her on the body so cruelly that they killed the child in her womb; and she went home and miscarried directly. This treatment she had reason to remember to her life's end; but God more than made it up to her by filling her with peace and love."

Wesley's lay preachers were remarkable men. One seldom hears of a quitter among them. Well might Wesley ask, "I pray, for what pay could we procure men to do this service? to be always ready to go to prison or to death?"

II

Left to themselves, the mob would perhaps never have troubled about the Methodists. The riots were too often instigated by an unholy alliance between the parson and the squire. The parson resented the invasion of his parish by irregular preachers, and the squire disliked the Methodists, because it is the habit of English squires to distrust religious and political innovations. The squirearchy suspected that the doctrines of the Methodists tended to obliterate social distinctions. "I asked a little gentleman at St. Just," writes Wesley, "what objection there was to Edward Greenfield. He said, 'Why the man is well enough in other things; but his impudence the gentlemen cannot bear. Why, sir, he says he knows his sins are forgiven!'"

The impudence of the Methodists spread dismay in exalted quarters. The Duchess of Buckingham, having been invited by Lady Huntingdon to hear Whitefield preach, replied as follows:

"I thank your ladyship for the information concerning the Methodist preachers. Their doctrines are most repulsive, and strongly tinctured with impertinence and disrespect towards their superiors, in perpetually endeavouring to level all ranks, and do away with all distinctions. It is monstrous to be told that you have a heart as sinful as the common wretches that crawl on the earth. This is highly offensive and insulting; and I cannot but wonder that your ladyship should relish any sentiments so much at variance with high rank and good breeding."

Once it was generally realised that the Methodists might be mobbed with impunity, the new sport became as popular as bear-baiting. Indeed, much of the trouble with which Wesley and his preachers had to contend was due to nothing more malicious than the brutal horseplay so common in a brutal period. Sometimes the mob just wanted a fight. If a Methodist was handy all the better.

Neither the squire nor the parson would be likely to make a fuss if some stray Methodist had his bones broken.

The hostility to the Methodists was increased by a foolish rumour which associated Wesley with the Young Pretender, a rumour which gained wide credence at the time when the country was in a fervour of patriotism.

In 1743, English and French troops had fought against each other in the Battle of Dettingen. In the south of England a French invasion was expected from day to day. The Young Pretender was believed to be planning an invasion, supported by the French. It was realised that its success would result, not only in the overthrow of the dynasty, but also of the national religion.

The whole of England was suffering from an acute attack of spy fever, and moreover of a particularly virulent type, for it was complicated by religious loyalties. In the forties of the eighteenth century, it was enough to hint that a passing stranger was a popish emissary to raise the town against him.

There was much about the Methodists which excited suspicion. They met at night, and they met in private. Very suspicious in war time; for it is obvious that a secret society in war-time can have only one object, treachery. The Methodist class meeting was said to be modelled on the Roman confessional. The lay preachers were restless men. They appeared suddenly in a place, remained for a few days—doubtless collecting information for the enemy—and then silently stole away.

Again, it was asserted that these preachers were required to make regular reports to a smooth, secretive, little man in the background, a man like . . . like . . . yes, of course, like Loyola, the General of the Jesuits. The Methodists reminded people of a brotherhood or an Order. A Roman Order. Moreover, there was proof positive that in '44, when an invasion was hourly expected,

Wesley had been seen with the Young Pretender in France. There was no doubt about this. So and So had it from a lady of quality, whose cousin was in the Admiralty.

All this will seem silly only to those who have forgotten the Russian rumour during the Great War.

The Roman Catholics had been ordered by Royal Proclamation to leave London. Wesley resolved to remain, even though it happened to be most inconvenient. He did not wish to give any colour to the rumour that he was a Catholic in secret, and as such, affected by the Proclamation.

Charles Wesley had been even more inconvenienced. He had been haled before a magistrate and charged with favouring the Pretender. The evidence against him was damning. It was said that at an open air service he had prayed that "the Lord would call home His banished." The witness to this damning fact failed to put in an appearance, and the magistrate told Wesley that he might go. But Charles was not content to leave the question undecided. "This is not sufficient," he said. "It is no trifling matter. Even my life is concerned in this charge." Nor would he leave until the magistrate assured him definitely that his loyalty was not in doubt.

Both the Wesleys were staunch Tories, whose personal loyalty to the King was as strong as their patriotism.

The suggestion that Wesley was a papist in disguise was revived a few years later by Bishop Lavington whose scurrilous tract "The Enthusiasm of Methodists and Papists compared" was probably intended to exploit this particular calumny. Lavington hoped to discredit the Methodists by pointing out the sinister resemblance of "the wild and pernicious enthusiasm of some of the most eminent saints in the Popish communion" and the enthusiasm of "the Methodists in our own country." He proceeds to draw a damning comparison between Wesley and St. Francis of Assisi, never realising that some readers might draw from this comparison a conclusion very different from the Bishop's.

Here is a specimen fo the Bishop's controversial style:

"Another bait to catch admirers, and very common among enthusiasts, is a restless impatience and insatiable thirst of travelling and undertaking dangerous voyages for the conversion of infidels. Accordingly our itinerant Methodists are fond of expressing their zeal on this account. . . . But all this only shows the natural, unsettled humour, the rapid motion, of enthusiastic heads. And we may assure them that the zealous impatience of Popish fanatics are, by all accounts, greatly superior . . . 'Tis almost incredible what miseries were endured by St. Francis, in his heroic voyage to convert the Sultan of Egypt, in that of St. Anthony to convert the Moors, and of St. Ignatius to convert the Turks."

It did not occur to Bishop Lavington that an equally damning comparison might be drawn between Wesley and St. Paul, for St. Paul, like St. Francis and like Wesley, had "an insatiable thirst for travelling and undertaking dangerous voyages for the conversion of infidels." Indeed, the whole passage might be read as an attack on Christianity rather than on Methodism.

III

The magistrates, rather than the mob, were responsible for the persecution of the Methodists. Where the magistrates did their duty, the Methodists had little to fear. Had all J. Ps. behaved like Mr. George Stovin of Crowle, the Methodists would have been left in peace. Here is the story, as recorded in the Journal:

"Wed. 9. I rode over to a neighbouring town to wait upon a Justice of Peace a man of candour and understanding; before whom (I was informed) their angry neighbours had carried a whole wagon-load of these new heretics. But when he asked what they had done there was a deep silence; for that was a point their conductors had forgot. At length one said, 'Why they pretended to be better than other people; and besides, they prayed from morning to night.' Mr. Stovin asked, 'But have they done nothing besides?' 'Yes, sir,' said an old man: 'an't please your worship, they have *convarted* my wife. Till she went among them, she had such a tongue! And now she is as quiet as a lamb.' 'Carry them back, carry them back,' replied the Justice, 'and let them convert all the scolds in the town.' "

The Foundery in the early days was often assailed by the mob, but in London these assaults were stopped, for Sir John Ganson, the Chairman of the Middlesex magistrates, informed Wesley that he would receive full protection if he applied for it. "Sir, I and the other Middlesex magistrates," he said, "have *orders from above* to do you justice whenever you apply to us."

"Henry Moore throws a pleasant light on these 'orders from above.' John Wesley told him that one of the members of the original Society of Methodists at Oxford had become a Quaker, and had settled at Kew. Being a man of considerable property and of exemplary behaviour, he was much respected, and had permission to walk in the royal gardens. There he frequently met George II, who was accustomed to talk freely with him. On one occasion, knowing that he had been at Oxford, George II asked him if he knew the Wesleys. 'They make a great noise in the nation,' he said. The Quaker replied, 'I know them well, King George; and thou mayest be assured that thou hast not two better men in thy dominions, nor men that love thee better than John and Charles Wesley.' He then gave the King an account of their principles and conduct, with which he seemed much pleased. When the question of the riots came before the Council the King declared that no man in his dominions should be persecuted on account of religion while he sat on the throne. This declaration was made known, and by the vigorous action of the Middlesex magistrates the persecution of the Methodists by mobs in process of time ceased in London." [1]

Had the magistrates in other parts of the country modelled themselves on the Middlesex magistrates, the riots would have soon come to an end. But this was far from being the case. "Do what you will to them," was the advice given by the magistrate at Otley, "so you break no bones." "But may a man," Wesley drily comments, "cut his neighbour's throat without breaking his bones?"

In Cornwall, a Methodist applied for justice to the worshipful and Reverend Dr. Borlasse against a rioter who had broken open his house and stolen his goods. "Thou conceited fellow," was the answer, "art thou too turned religious? They may burn thy house if they will; thou shalt have no justice."

In many places, the clergy, so far from discouraging the mob, played a leading rôle in inciting it. A certain Reverend George White, for instance, issued a proclamation and mobilised his troops by means of a subtle appeal:

"Notice is hereby given, if any man be mindful to enlist into His Majesty's Service, under the command of the Rev. Mr. George White, Commander-in-Chief, John Bannister, Lieut.-General of his Majesty's forces for the defence of the Church of England, and the support of the manufactory in and about Colne, both which are now in danger, &c., &c., let them now repair to the Drum-head at the Cross, when each man shall have a pint of ale in advance, and other proper encouragements."

[1] "John Wesley and the Methodist Societies," by J. S. Simon, D.D.

It was clever of Mr. White to suggest that trade and the Church of England stood or fell together, and the "pint of ale *in advance*" was certainly a masterstroke.

IV

Wesley replied with great effect to Bishop Lavington and remained unruffled by Episcopal thunders. It was a curate, not a Bishop, who inflicted the deepest wound.

Wesley had arrived at Epworth in June 1742, and Mr. Romley, the curate, to whom Samuel Wesley had shown the greatest kindness,[2] refused to allow the son of his old benefactor "to assist him by preaching or reading prayers."

That same evening John Wesley preached in the church-yard, standing on his father's tombstone.

"Accordingly at six I came, and found such a congregation as I believe Epworth never saw before. I stood near the east end of the church, upon my father's tomb-stone, and cried, 'The kingdom of heaven is not meat and drink; but righteousness, and peace, and joy in the Holy Ghost.'"

A moving scene, one of the most dramatic in the history of the Church. For a whole week, Wesley preached from the same spot. "There were few places," writes Southey, "where his teaching was attended with greater or more permanent results." No wonder, for the popular mind was captured by the picture of John Wesley delivering from his father's tombstone the message which he had been forbidden to deliver in his father's church.

"Nothing," writes Canon Overton, has tended more to encourage the popular idea that Wesley was 'turned out of the Church.' If he might not preach in the church of which his father had been rector, and himself curate,

[2] See Moore's "Life of Wesley," Vol. i, page 549.

where might he preach? The argument is not logical;
for exclusion from a building and exclusion from a
society are different things. But simple people do not
discriminate; and the Church owes a deep grudge to Mr.
Romley, who half a year later completed the disastrous
work which he had begun by repelling Wesley from the
Holy Communion."

"There could not have been," writes Wesley in his
Journal, "so fit a place under heaven where this should
befall me first as my father's house, the place of my
nativity, and the very place, where, 'according to the
straitest sect of our religion,' I had so long 'lived a
Pharisee.' It was also fit in the highest degree, that he
who repelled me from that very table where I had myself
so often distributed the Bread of Life, should be one who
owed all in this world to the tender love which my father
had shown to his, as well as personally to himself."

Five years later, Wesley "had once more the comfort
of receiving the Lord's Supper at Epworth," for Mr.
Romley had left, and his tragic blunder was not repeated
by his successor, Mr. Hay.

V

It is a sad story, but in order to understand the attitude
of the clergy, we must try to forget all that we know of
Wesley. For us he is one of the greatest figures of the
eighteenth century; to his fellow priests he was merely
an irregular preacher with no respect for ecclesiastical
decencies. The Methodists revived in a new form the
old rivalry between the parish priests and the preaching
friars. Like the friars, the Methodists cut right across
the routine of parish life. The clergy would have found
it easier to forgive them had they described themselves
as Dissenters, but it was difficult to tolerate men who

claimed to be members of the national Church, but who showed no deference to their ecclesiastical superiors, and who apparently owed no allegiance excepting to a wandering presbyter from Lincoln College, Oxford.

Moreover, in spite of Wesley's advice, the itinerant preachers often criticised in no unmeasured terms the shortcomings of the clergy whose parishes they invaded.

There is a significant sentence—or rather a significant word—in a letter which John Wesley wrote many years later to his brother. "Some obedience I always paid to the bishops."

A modern bishop might, perhaps, be reasonably satisfied with "some obedience," but in Wesley's day there were no advanced Anglo-Catholics to teach bishops their place, and Wesley presented a problem which was both new and most unwelcome.

We need hardly be surprised that the bishops preferred that people should take their chance of hell under their own parish priests, rather than go to heaven under an irregular preacher. Some generals would prefer to lose a battle in accordance with, rather than to win a battle in defiance of King's Regulations. It is a common failing to transfer to an institution the loyalty which should be reserved for the object for which that institution was founded; to forget that the Church was created to save souls, not souls to save the Church.

In justice to the bishops, we must not forget the alarm with which John Wesley's elder brother, Samuel, regarded his irregularities. "I am not afraid," he wrote, "the Church should excommunicate him (discipline is at too low an ebb), but that he should excommunicate the Church. It is pretty near it."

"Now if a good man," as Canon Overton justly remarks, "who loved John Wesley dearly, and must have known his real goodness, could be so strongly opposed to his irregular proceedings, is it not more than probable that many other good men, who knew and cared nothing about him personally, opposed him simply because they thought he was wrong, and not because they were hostile to spiritual religion?"

Moreover much of this clerical opposition was perfunctory, and melted away after personal contact with the Wesleys. Here is a pleasant story of a certain Mr. Cordeux:

Mr. Cordeux had warned his congregation against "hearing that vagabond Wesley." Shortly afterwards, Wesley entered the church and Mr. Cordeux, observing a strange clergyman in the congregation, invited him to preach. After the service he asked his clerk who the stranger was. "Sir," replied the clerk, "it is that vagabond Wesley, against whom you warned us." "Aye, indeed," was the reply, "we are trapped this time; but never mind, we have had a good sermon."

The Dean heard of the matter, and threatened to complain to the Archbishop. Accordingly, Mr. Cordeux took an early opportunity of telling the Archbishop himself that he had allowed Mr. Wesley to preach. "And you did right," replied the primate. Some years later, Wesley accepted a second invitation from Mr. Cordeux to preach in his pulpit.

Clerical opposition gradually died away. In 1785, Charles Wesley in a letter to his brother pointed out that the bishops had left them alone to do just as they pleased for fifty years. "At present, some of them are quite friendly towards us, particularly towards you. The churches are all open to us, and never could there be less pretence for a separation."

It is not surprising that Wesley should have been faced with opposition. Trade unions, whether of bishops, generals or physicians, invariably close their ranks against unauthorised practitioners. But it was strange that the opposition should have died away, and that all pulpits should have been opened to Wesley during the closing years of his life. For though the Church of his baptism was never dearer to John Wesley than in the closing years of his life, his actions towards the end tended more and more towards schism.

We may deplore, but we can understand and perhaps even forgive much of the hostility with which John Wesley was faced in the early years of his career, but we should allow the Church of England due credit for its tolerant and affectionate attitude towards John Wesley in the closing years of his life. A free-lance, such as Wesley, would have received and would still receive short shrift in the Roman Catholic Church.

CHAPTER XVII

PERILOUS DAYS

JOHN WESLEY would have made an ideal infantry officer, well, perhaps not ideal, for even King's Regulations would not have prevented Wesley completing his famous series of tracts [1] by "A word to a Field Marshal" or "A calm address to the War Office."

But Wesley had, at least, two qualities which are highly esteemed in the army. He was cool and courageous in moments of peril, and he was scrupulously neat in his personal appearance. "Wesley is a lean elderly man," wrote Horace Walpole in 1766, "freshly coloured, his hair smoothly combed, but into a soupçon of curls at the ends. Wondrous clean." In describing attacks by the mob, he often records with indignation the fact that some speck of mud had attached itself to his clothes or to his person. And he appears to have been far more depressed by such outrages than by the perils through which he had passed.

A mob is far more alarming than an army. Soldiers need not, and frequently do not hate their enemies. It is their business to kill and be killed, and they do what they have to do under orders. But the very spirit of evil seems incarnate in the senseless fury and unmotived hatred of a mob. It takes a stouter heart to face a hostile crowd than to remain calm under a heavy bombardment.

Wesley never lost his self-possession. He says in his

[1] This series includes "A word to a Freeholder," "A word to a Drunkard," "A word to a Streetwalker."

211

Journal that he made it a rule "confirmed by long experience, always to look a mob in the face." He saved his life more than once by acting on this rule.

Wesley was, perhaps, never in greater danger than in Falmouth in the summer of 1745. The whole country was in a state of the greatest excitement. The Pretender was marching south from Scotland, and the ridiculous rumour that Wesley was an emissary of the Pretender had reached Cornwall.

Wesley was calling on an invalid and the house which he had entered was beset on all sides by the rabble, who "roared with all their throats, 'Bring out the Canorum, Where is the Canorum?' (an unmeaning word which the Cornish generally use instead of Methodist)."

They forced open the outer door and filled the passage. Only a thin partition separated them from the room in which Wesley awaited their attack. At that moment he tells us he did not think his life was worth an hour's purchase. He was urged to hide, but he answered, "No. It is best for me to stand just where I am."

Away went the hinges, and the door fell back into the room.

Wesley stepped forward at once into the middle of the mob and said, "Here I am. Which of you has anything to say to me? To which of you have I done any wrong? To you? Or you? Or you?"

A mob sings well in chorus, but is not good at providing solos. The secret of handling a crowd is to disintegrate it into a series of individuals. The personal appeal, the personal retort, the personal question, have an embarrassing effect on individuals who will roar very lustily in chorus, but who prefer to sink their personality into that of the crowd.

"I continued speaking," says Wesley, "till I came, bare-headed as I was (for I purposely left my hat, that they might all see my face)`, into the middle of the street, and then, raising my voice, said, 'Neighbours, countrymen! Do you desire to hear me speak?' They cried vehemently, 'Yes, yes. He shall speak. He shall. Nobody shall hinder him.' . . . I never saw before," adds Wesley "no, not at Walsall itself, the hand of God so plainly shown as here . . . here, although the hands of perhaps some hundreds of people were lifted up to strike or throw, yet they were one and all stopped in the mid-way; so that not a man touched me with one of his fingers; neither was anything thrown from first to last; so that I had not even a speck of dirt on my clothes."

Note the crowning mercy, "not even a speck of dirt on my clothes."

Wesley never showed the least sign of being rattled. On one occasion, when he was just about to preach, an excited friend rushed into the room and warned him that the house was surrounded and that the mob proposed to burn it down. "Then our only way is to make use of it while it is still standing," Wesley replied quietly, and proceeded to expound the tenth chapter of St. Matthew.

He was a master of mob psychology. He knew that a mob must be led and not driven. He knew how to attract its attention, and how to coax it into respect. Here is a typical scene:

An open street. A curious, hostile crowd watching Wesley who is just about to preach. Suddenly, he whips off his hat, and in clear, easy accents addresses them. "Friends, let every man do as he pleases, but it is my manner when I speak of the things of God, or when another does, to uncover my head."

Let every man do as he pleases. A master touch. No wonder that every head was bared.

An English crowd admires pluck and respects breeding. Wesley had both. There was an air of distinction about the little man which had a devastating effect on the wildest of mob leaders. None could resist him once he came into personal contact with them. Here are three characteristic entries from his Journal:

"Finding the uproar increase, I went into the midst, and brought the head of the mob up with me to the desk. I received but one blow on the side of the head; after which we reasoned the case, till he grew milder and milder, and at length undertook to quiet his companions."

"The cry of one and all was 'Bring out the minister; we will have the minister.' I desired one to take their captain by the hand and bring him into the house. After a few sentences interchanged between us the lion was become a lamb. I desired him to go and bring one or two more the most angry of his companions. He brought in two, who were ready to swallow the ground with rage; but in two minutes they were as calm as he."

"Perceiving the violence of the rabble still increasing, I walked down into the thickest of them, and took the captain of the mob by the hand. He immediately said, 'Sir, I will see you safe home. Sir, no man shall touch you. Gentlemen, stand off; give back. I will knock the first man down that touches him."

An amusing instance of Wesley's personal magnetism occurred in Cornwall. To understand what follows, the reader should know that the practice of pressing men to serve in the army had been made free use of by local magistrates in order to get rid of the Methodists. Of course, in order to press a man for service, there had to be some pretence that the man was incapable of earning his own living and that he was likely to become a charge on the parish. To press for service the Fellow of a college and an Anglican priest was, of course, an outrage against the law.

A certain Mr. B., however, carried away by his furious
rage against the Methodists, attempted to break up a meeting at which Wesley was preaching, and actually had
the audacity to seize Wesley himself; but the story had
better be told in Wesley's own words:

"Upon this Mr. B. lost all patience, and cried out with
all his might, 'Seize him, seize him! I say, seize the
preacher for his Majesty's service.' But no one stirring,
he rode up and struck several of his attendants, cursing
them bitterly for not doing as they were bid. Perceiving
still that they would not move, he leaped off his horse,
swore he would do it himself, and caught hold of my
cassock, crying, 'I take you to serve his Majesty.' A servant taking his horse, he took me by the arm, and we
walked arm-in-arm for about three quarters of a mile.
He entertained me all the time with the 'wickedness of
the fellows belonging to the society.' When he was taking
breath I said, 'Sir, be they what they will, I apprehend
it will not justify you in seizing me in this manner, and
violently carrying me away, as you said, to serve his
Majesty.' He replied, *I seize you! And violently carry
you away!* No, sir; no. Nothing like it. I asked you to go
with me to my house, and you said you was willing; and
if so, you are welcome; and if not, you are welcome to
go where you please.' I answered, 'Sir, I know not if it
would be safe for me to go back through this rabble.'
'Sir,' said he, 'I will go with you myself.' He then called
for his horse, and another for me, and rode back with
me to the place from whence he took me."

The epic story of those early struggles is often relieved, as in the above passage, by humour, sometimes
conscious, sometimes unconscious. Once, an over-zealous
leader of a mob followed Wesley into a house, and discovered that he could not get out again, and that he was
a target for the stones which the mob were pouring in

through the windows. He was hit on the forehead, and the blood spurted out like a stream. "We shall be killed," he cried out, "what shall I do, what shall I do?" Wesley advised him to pray to God, and he adds drily in telling the story, "He took my advice, and began praying which he had never done since he was born."

II

It was in Staffordshire in the towns of Darleston, Wednesbury and Walsall that the Methodists were called upon to endure their fiercest opposition. Wesley himself nearly lost his life in Wednesbury on the night of October 20th, 1743.

For some time past, the influence of the local magistrates and clergy had been steadily exerted against the Methodists. A document, for instance, was signed by two Justices of the Peace, J. Lane and W. Persehouse.

"Whereas we, His Majesty's Justices of the Peace for the said county of Stafford, have received information that several disorderly persons, styling themselves Methodist preachers, go about raising routs and riots, to the great damage of His Majesty's liege people and against the peace of our Sovereign Lord the King: These are, in His Majesty's name, to command you and every one of you, within your respective districts, to make diligent search after the said Methodist preachers, and to bring him or them before some of us, his said Majesty's Justices of the Peace, to be examined concerning their unlawful doings."

Wesley decided that he ought to go to Wednesbury and investigate matters for himself. On reaching Wednesbury, he preached at mid-day in the middle of the town without being molested, but in the afternoon, the mob surrounded the house in which he was staying.

Wesley, following his usual custom, went out to the

mob, and standing on a chair, asked them what they wanted. "We want you to go with us to the Justice," they replied. "That I will," said Wesley, "with all my heart." Wesley then spoke a few words, "which God applied," with the happy result that they cried out, "The gentleman is an honest gentleman, and we will spill our blood in his defence."

None the less, they insisted that he should accompany them to the Justice. One or two ran on ahead to convey the glad news to Mr. Lane that they were bringing Mr. Wesley "before his Worship." Mr. Lane was not at all grateful. When he signed the Proclamation we have quoted, he had expected to catch a minnow, not a trout. He had hoped, no doubt, to have the pleasure of bully-ragging some uneducated local preacher, but he was not prepared to cope with a Fellow of Lincoln. So he slunk off to bed, and when the main body of the mob arrived, his son was sent out to parley with them.

Mr. Lane junior asked what was the matter. One replied, "Why, an't please you, they sing psalms all day; nay, and make folks rise at five in the morning. And what would your Worship advise us to do?" "To go home," said Mr. Lane, "and be quiet."

But the mob were out to make a night of it, and as Mr. Lane had failed them, they decided to bring Wesley before Mr. Persehouse, the other signatory to the Proclamation. "But Mr. Persehouse, likewise, sent word that he was in bed."

The honest mob had done their best to carry out the wishes of eminent J. Ps. and had got no thanks for their pains. They decided to go home, but they had not gone far when they met a mob from Walsall, and a free fight for the possession of the prisoner terminated in a victory for the invaders.

The second mob seized Wesley and dragged him

through the streets of the town. When he asked leave
to speak and to state his case, they cried out, "No, no!
knock his brains out; down with him; kill him at once."

A "lusty man" did his best to carry these instructions
into effect. He struck at Wesley several times with a
large oaken stick, "with which, if he had struck me once
on the back of my head," writes Wesley, "it would have
saved him all farther trouble. But every time the blow was
turned aside, I know not how."

Another turbulent rascal forced his way through the
press, raised his arm to strike and "on a sudden let it
drop, and only stroked my head, saying, 'What soft hair
he has!' "

Once again, Wesley's magnetic power over men had
saved him. The captain of the mob, a prize-fighter, said,
"Sir, I will spend my life for you: follow me, and not
one soul here shall touch a hair of your head."

The prize-fighter and a few of his friends rescued
Wesley and conveyed him back to his lodgings, "having
lost only a flap of my waistcoat, and a little skin from
off my hand."

The next day he met his brother Charles. "My brother
came delivered out of the mouth of the lion. He *looked*
like a soldier of Christ; his clothes were torn to tatters.
. . . But his work is not finished."

The prize-fighter who saved Wesley joined the Methodist Societies. Charles Wesley asked him what he thought
of his brother. "Think of him!" he replied, "That he is
a mon of God; and God was on his side, when so many
of us could not kill one mon."

III

Charles Wesley was as courageous as his brother, and
survived perils no less great. Witness the story of the
Devizes riots.

In February 1747, Charles Wesley rode into the Devizes as it was then called. The curate strongly objected to the Methodists. He had displayed remarkable energy, had instituted a house to house canvass, and had thoroughly alarmed the householders by the sad tale of blasphemies which Charles Wesley was alleged to have uttered at Oxford.

A mob headed by "the chief gentleman of the town" and the zealous curate "dancing for joy" surrounded the house in which Charles was staying and besieged it till nightfall. Charles Wesley slept that night in a house which was owned by a friendly Baptist. Next morning he walked quietly to the house of a friend and began to preach. He knew that the mob was still searching for him, but none the less, he ordered all the doors to be thrown open to admit any worshippers who cared to attend. Mark the courage of the man. He had no defence excepting his faith.

Before long, the mob discovered him. They brought a fire-engine with them, and soon a stream of water was pouring into the house. Charles retired into an upper room. The mob invaded the house, seized one man, threw him into a horse-pond and broke his back. The constable then read the Riot Act, and the mob dispersed after a siege of three hours. But the truce did not last long. Once more, the house in which Charles Wesley was staying, was besieged. The mob began to take the tiles off the roof. "Mr. Wesley!" called a little girl, "creep under the bed. They will kill you. They are pulling down the house." Once again, a constable put in an appearance, and tried to extract a promise from Charles that he would leave the Devizes and never return to preach again. Charles replied that he refused to surrender the rights which he enjoyed as an Englishman to visit any part of the kingdom that he desired. The constable pleaded

meekly that he would be quite content if Mr. Wesley
would undertake not to return in the immediate future
to Devizes. "I cannot come now," replied Charles, "because I must return to London a week hence; but observe I make no promise of not preaching here when the
door is opened, and don't you say that I do."

The constable left them to parley with the mob. He
spoke smooth words, and doubtless credited Charles Wesley with all manner of pacific sentiments. He was well-
meaning, but it was clear that he could not hold the mob
in check for long. One of Charles's friends suggested
that they should take advantage of this momentary lull
to escape by a back door.

Charles was tempted. After all, why not take the
simplest path to safety? He would betray no trust by
retreating. For two long days, he had been beset and besieged, and his whole being cried out for peace.

Yet he hesitated. He had an instinctive prejudice
against back doors. There was no real reason why he
should not creep quietly away . . . and yet . . .

He picked up his Bible, opened it at random and
chanced on this verse: "Jesus said unto her 'if thou
would'st believe, thou shalt see the glory of the Lord.'"

He had got his answer. For him no easy issue out
of his adversities. Did he believe that God has power
over wind and wave, but also over the violence of human
storms? If so he must be prepared to prove his faith by
a gesture gallant, if irrational. His only extravagances
were those of faith, but these were glorious ones. He
threw open the door and went forth "as easy as Luther
to the Council."

"If thou should'st believe." The rabble greeted him
with a volley of oaths, but they fell back as he approached.
Between two rows of hostile faces Charles and his gallant

friends advanced at an easy, even pace. No man laid hands on them.

As they rode out of Devizes, they sang the battle-song which Charles had written for times such as these.

> "Thine arm hath safely brought us
>   A way no more expected,
> Than when Thy sheep
> Passed through the deep
>   By crystal walls protected.
>
> Thy glory was our rearward,
>   Thine Hand our lives did cover;
> And we, even we
> Have passed the sea,
>   And marched triumphant over."

CHAPTER XVIII

THE DAY'S ROUND

WESLEY was on the road for more than forty years, during which time he travelled a quarter of a million miles, preached more than forty thousand sermons, crossed the Irish Channel fifty times, and wrote more than two hundred books.

During these forty years, Wesley averaged twenty miles of travelling per day. Sometimes he rode as much as a hundred miles within the twenty-four hours.

Such is the bare, bleak statistical record of the most active and crowded life ever lived by mortal man.

But statistics are unsatisfying. You must read the Journal before you can form a just impression of Wesley's career. You must visualise the rough English roads along which Wesley travelled. The cumulative effect of his own life story as told in his Journal cannot be conveyed by any statement of miles travelled and sermons preached.

I open the Journal at random. Here is his diary entry for June 23rd, 1787. Wesley was then eighty-four years of age, and it is worth remarking that his hour of rising (4.30 A. M.) was an unusual lapse. For the previous five days, he had risen at his usual hour of 4. A. M. Here is the record:

Saturday 23.

4.30 Prayed, sermon; 8 tea, conversed, sermon; 2.30 dinner, conversed, sermon; 4.30 tea, conversed; 6 Matt. xiii. 33; 7 at Mr. Smythe's, sermon; 8 supper, conversed, prayer, on business; 9.45.

"Money never stays with me," wrote Wesley, "it would burn if it did," but the man who was spendthrift of money was a miser of minutes. Once upon a time, he wasted five whole minutes. It was long before he could forget those "five minutes lost for ever."

From 4. A. M. when he rose (and continued to rise until a few months before his death) until 10 P. M., his usual hour for retiring, he husbanded each minute as it passed, and invested it to the utmost advantage.

"History, philosophy, poetry," he tells us, "I read on horseback having other employments at other times."

When he was sixty-three, his friends gave him a carriage and pair. He nailed up one side of his coach and built in shelves which were filled with books, and a board which could be let down to serve as a desk. "Who besides Wesley ever turned the saddle at the open road and the changing English skies into a permanent study?"

"Few men travelled more than Wesley," writes Mr. Curnock. "He knew the highways and byways, the great houses and gardens, the churches and schools, and, we may add, the new industries which were marking the advent of a new age. A man of affairs, the care of all the societies fell upon him, often involving laborious correspondence. His innumerable tours hummed with business. His chaise was a study, an office, a book-shop, a library, also a private chapel in which at stated hours, he fulfilled the devotional duties of the Holy Club. Yet, notwithstanding these distractions, he read ancient and modern literature as he might have done in the seclusion of a college or country parsonage. The notices of books scattered throughout his Journal show how thoroughly he digested the books he read. Their character and variety may be judged from the Catalogue compiled by Mr. F. M. Jackson and published in vol iv. of the 'W. H. S. Proceedings.'"

II

Here is a day in Wesley's life. Out of bed at 4. A. M. The first hour is spent in private devotion. Then he preaches to a few hundred ardent Methodists who know that he is leaving them and who do not resent rising at 5. A. M. in order to see and hear the last of their great leader.

The sermon over, Wesley mounts his horse, and off he rides. And as he rides, he reads; not light stuff to beguile a journey, but good, solid fare. He is short-sighted and Belisarius's Life of Sixtus V is a heavy book, so he throws the reins over the horse's neck and holds the book up close to his eyes.

Wesley's views on the technique of horsemanship had, at least, the saving merit of originality. The secret of good horsemanship, so he tells us, is to leave everything to the horse. "In this journey, as well as in many others, I observed a mistake that almost universally prevails; and I desire all travellers to take good notice of it, which may save them from trouble and danger. Near thirty years ago, I was thinking, 'How is it that no horse ever stumbles while I am reading?' No account can possibly be given but this: because then I throw the reins on his neck. I then set myself to observe; and I aver that, in riding above a hundred thousand miles, I scarce ever remember any horse (except two, that would fall head over heels any way) to fall, or make a considerable stumble, while I rode *with a slack rein*. To fancy, therefore, that a tight rein prevents stumbling is a capital blunder. I have repeated the trial more frequently than most men in the kingdom can do. A slack rein will prevent stumbling, if anything will. But in some horses nothing can."

Truth to tell, Wesley often found himself "left behind in an instant" to quote his own graphic phrase, by horses who failed to respond to the negative guidance of a slack rein. But on the whole, he was lucky. By a process of natural selection, he eventually found himself astride the kind of horse which does not object to being treated as a study chair.

And so the horse jogs along and the tacit co-operation between an absent-minded scholar and an unusually intelligent beast finally lands Wesley early in the forenoon at the next village where he intends to preach.

Then again, he takes the road. Twenty dusty miles separate him from his resting place for the night. But the miles slip by easily, for he is deep in Priestley's Treatise on Electricity. The shadows lengthen, the sun sinks. Wesley can no longer read, and for the first time he notices a slight touch of weariness. It is good to reach the little Inn where he proposes to pass the night. But before he sups, there is one urgent duty to perform. Again and again he enjoins on his preachers to be merciful of their beasts. The Minutes of Conference dispose that every one "shall see with his own eyes his horse rubbed, fed and bedded," and we may be sure that he practised what he preached.

Wesley once preached a sermon in which he promised animals their fair share of the general deliverance, and prophesied that at the Last Day, they would enjoy a state of exalted happiness. We may be sure that Wesley was thinking of those uncomplaining beasts who, with unstumbling tread, had carried him so many thousand miles along the muddy road of eighteenth century England. Wesley would have sympathised with Pope's simple Indian:

"Who thinks accompanied to that equal sky
His faithful dog shall bear him company."

After supper, there is still much work to do. There are class leaders to meet, policy to be discussed, and perhaps quarrelsome people to pacify. Or there may be yet a third sermon to be preached.

And then at long last Wesley is left alone. Out comes his note-book and pencil. He jots down his Journal record for the day, and then perhaps makes a few notes on the books he has been reading, comments pungent and critical, or friendly and appreciative as the case may be. Or perhaps he writes a chapter of one of the books which he is preparing for the press.

And so—finally—to bed.

III

Such was the day's round, but we have still to account for his literary output. The sermons he preached, the societies he founded and maintained, the quarter million miles which he travelled, would have kept any normal man fully occupied from dawn till sunset. But, incredible as it appears, Wesley found time in addition, to write no fewer than two hundred and thirty-three original works —some of them very original by the way.

The Wesley Bibliography runs to four hundred and seventeen works, but the list is swollen by Wesley's incurable habit of editing and revising and sometimes mutilating the works of other men.

Two hundred and thirty-three original works. There are few men who could produce such a formidable array of volumes with the aid of secretaries and dictaphones, even if they had nothing else to do. But Wesley wrote all his books with his own hand. Few subjects escaped his pen. He wrote several histories (England, Rome, etc.), a book on logic, and a treatise on primitive physic just to put the doctors in their place. He compiled Hebrew,

Greek and French grammars, and an excellent English dictionary.

In addition to his original works, he edited a magazine, and abridged and revised many scores of books by other writers. His literary style is best described in his own words:

"What is it that constitutes a good style? Perspicuity, purity, propriety, strength, and easiness joined together. . . . As for me, I never think of my style at all, but just set down the words that come first . . . Clearness, in particular, is necessary for you and me, because we are to instruct people of the lowest understanding. We should constantly use the most common, little, easy words (so they are pure and proper) which our language affords. When I had been a member of the University about ten years, I wrote and talked much as you do now. But when I talked to plain people in the castle or the town I observed they gaped and stared. This quickly obliged me to alter my style, and adopt the language of those I spoke to. And yet there is a dignity in this simplicity, which is not disagreable to those of the highest rank."

Wesley consistently applied these principles, not only to his own writings, but to the revision of books by other men. In the extracts which he published from other writers, he ruthlessly excised every redundant word or phrase. "One of his followers," remarks Dr. Legge, "has wondered that he never abridged St. John's Gospel."

Did Wesley ever rest? At the end of his long life, he certainly took a short holiday in Holland, but his normal conception of a rest was to work at about twice the pressure of ordinary folk. "I now rested a week at Bristol," he wrote, "preaching only morning and evening."

"I do not know," writes Mr. Augustine Birrell, "whether I am likely to have among my readers any one who has ever contested an English or Scottish county

in a Parliamentary election since household suffrage. If
I have, that tired soul will know how severe is the strain
of its three weeks, and how impossible it seems at the
end of the first week that you should be able to keep it
going for another fortnight, and how when the last night
arrived you felt that had the strife been accidentally pro-
longed another seven days you must have perished by
the wayside. Well, John Wesley contested the three kingdoms in the cause of Christ during a campaign which
lasted fifty years."

The late Mr. W. T. Stead paid a tribute to Wesley's
iron constitution, "to his marvellous body with muscles
of whipcord and bones of steel, with lungs of leather
and the heart of a lion." Mr. Stead seems to have forgotten that "the lungs of leather" had been affected by
consumption. It was indeed the lion heart rather than
the leather lungs which kept Wesley working at full
speed until a few days before his death at the age of
eighty-eight.

Here, for instance, is the actual record of a week's
campaign, a week which would have proved too strenuous
for many a young man in perfect health. At the time,
Wesley was seventy-four years of age all but a month
and he was suffering from fever and ague.

Friday, May 9th. 1777. Wesley rides fifteen [1] miles
from Osmotherly to Malton, preaches, and hearing that
a friend was ill, started directly after the service and
rode the forty-eight miles to Otley which he reached at
4. A. M., having ridden sixty-three miles in twenty-four
hours.

Saturday, May 10th. After seeing the invalid, he returns to Malton, having ridden between ninety and a

---

[1] I have borrowed the Rev. T. E. Brigden's computation of miles
travelled. See Mr. Brigden's interesting contribution to "A New History of Methodism." Vol. i, page 217.

hundred miles and after an hour's rest rides twenty miles
to Scarborough, which he reaches in the evening. He was
ill, and when he tried to preach, "the flux which I had
for a few days so increased, that at first I could not speak.
Yet the longer I spoke, the stronger I grew. Is not God a
present help?"

Sunday, May 11th. Wesley is shaken by fever and
by a strong fit of ague. He drinks lemonade, perspires,
sleeps for an hour, and after preaching, meets the local
society.

Monday, May 12th. He rides over to Bridlington, and
preaches.

Tuesday, May 13th. Preaches at Beverley in the morning, and in the evening at Hull, having ridden thirty-
six miles.

Wednesday, May 14th. Preaches at Pocklington and
York. (Rides thirty-eight miles.)

Thursday, May 15th. "I would gladly have rested the
next day, feeling my breast much out of order, but
notice having been given of my preaching at Tadcaster,
I set out at nine in the morning. About ten the chaise
broke down. I borrowed a horse; but as he was none
of the easiest, in riding three miles I was so thoroughly
electrified that the pain in my breast was quite cured.
I preached in the evening at York; on Friday took
the diligence; and on Saturday afternoon came to London."

Sunday, May 18th. "Our service at the Foundery began
as usual at four."

And that characteristic touch brings to a close the
record of his week's campaign.

So much for Wesley at the age of seventy-four. Here
is the record of a week's work at the age of eighty-four.

Starting on Sunday at midnight, he travelled 19 hours.
On Tuesday, he rose at 4 A. M., on Wednesday at 2,

on Thursday at 3, and on Friday at 4. He was travelling continuously, and after travelling about 240 miles in eighty hours, went "off with a gentleman to hear a famous musician that plays upon the glasses."

IV

Septuagenarians who are beginning to feel that they are past their prime, should take a daily dose of Wesley's Journal. This should prove an excellent tonic, all the more so because Wesley narrowly escaped death at the age of fifty from a galloping consumption.

His life was saved by an eccentric Quaker physician who prescribed "country air, asses' milk and riding daily"; thus anticipating, as Mr. Curnock points out, the most modern, approved treatment of consumption.

Indeed, Wesley's case is often quoted in medical journals as evidence in support of the belief that riding is beneficial for consumptives.

Wesley himself did not expect to recover, and "to prevent vile panegyrics" he composed the following epitaph:

Here lieth the Body
OF
JOHN WESLEY
A Brand plucked out of the Burning:
Who died of a Consumption in the Fifty-First Year of
his Age,
Not leaving, after his Debts are paid,
Ten Pounds behind him:
Praying,
God be merciful to me, an Unprofitable Servant!

He ordered that this, if any, inscription should be placed on his tombstone.

Eighteen years later he made the following entry in his Journal:

"I can hardly believe that I am this day entered into the sixty-eighth year of my age. How marvellous are the ways of God! How has He kept me even from a child! From ten to thirteen or fourteen, I had little but bread to eat, and not great plenty of that. I believe this was so far from hurting me, that it laid the foundation of lasting health. When I grew up, in consequence of reading Dr. Cheyne, I chose to eat sparingly, and drink water. This was another great means of continuing my health, till I was about seven-and-twenty. I then began spitting of blood, which continued several years. A warm climate cured this. I was afterwards brought to the brink of death by a fever; but it left me healthier than before. Eleven years after I was in the third stage of a consumption; in three months it pleased God to remove this also. Since that time I have known neither pain nor sickness, and am now healthier than I was forty years ago. This hath God wrought!"

CHAPTER XIX

THE HAPPY TRAVELLER

IT would be easy to illustrate the hardships of eighteenth century travel from Wesley's Journal, for it would not be difficult to multiply extracts such as these:

"Our servant came up and said, 'Sir, there is no travelling to-day. Such a quantity of snow has fallen in the night that the roads are quite filled up.' I told him, 'At least we can walk twenty miles a day, with our horses in our hands.' So in the name of God we set out. The northeast wind was piercing as a sword, and had driven the snow into such uneven heaps that the main road was unpassable."

Or again, "We found the roads abundantly worse than they had been the day before, not only because the snows were deeper, which made the causeways in many places unpassable" (and turnpike roads were not known in these parts of England till some years after), "but likewise because the hard frost, succeeding the thaw, had made all the ground like glass. We were often obliged to walk, it being impossible to ride, and our horses several times fell down while we were leading them, but not once while we were riding them, during the whole journey. It was past eight before we got to Gateshead Fell, which appeared a great pathless waste of white. The snow filling up and covering all the roads, we were at a loss how to proceed, when an honest man of Newcastle overtook and guided us safe into the town.

"Many a rough journey I had before, but one like this I never had; between wind, and hail, and rain, and ice, and snow, and driving sleet, and piercing cold. But it is past: those days will return no more, and are, therefore, as though they had never been."

Neither dangers nor difficulties ever prevented Wesley from keeping an appointment to preach.

"I rode from Nottingham to Epworth, and on Monday set out for Grimsby; but at Ferry we were at a full stop, the boatmen telling us we could not pass the Trent: it was as much as our lives were worth to put from shore before the storm abated. We waited an hour; but being afraid it would do much hurt if I should disappoint the congregation at Grimsby, I asked the men if they did not think it possible to get to the other shore. They said they could not tell; but if we would venture our lives they would venture theirs. So we put off, having six men, two women, and three horses in the boat. Many stood looking after us on the river-side, in the middle of which we were, when, in an instant, the side of the boat was under water, and the horses and men rolling one over another. We expected the boat to sink every moment; but I did not doubt of being able to swim ashore. The boatmen were amazed, as well as the rest; but they quickly recovered, and rowed for life. And soon after, our horses leaping overboard lightened the boat, and we all came unhurt to land.

"They wondered what was the matter I did not rise (for I lay along in the bottom of the boat); and I wondered too, till, upon examination, I found that a large iron crow, which the boatmen sometimes used, was (none knew how) run through the string of my boot, which pinned me down that I could not stir; so that, if the boat had sunk, I should have been safe enough from swimming any farther."

So long as Wesley travelled by road, he could form an

approximate guess as to when he would arrive and could turn out his programme accordingly. But nothing was certain if he went by sea. Wesley paid fifty visits to Ireland. To-day if the service to Ireland is suspended for a few hours, a mild sensation is caused. But in the eighteenth century it was normal to hang about for days waiting for a favourable breeze. The traveller dared not leave the docks; for a ship which was waiting for a favourable wind would wait for nothing else.

"*Mon. 13.* I bespoke a cabin in a ship bound for Dublin which only waited for a wind. About ten at night word was brought that she was ready to sail. We went down to the quay immediately, and found she had sailed out a quarter of an hour before, and was then off at sea."

On one occasion, he arrived at Holyhead on February 24th and did not sail until March 8th. Even Wesley's patience was exhausted by this long wait.

"I never knew men make such poor, lame excuses as these captains did for not sailing. It put me in mind of the epigram:

> There are, if rightly I methink,
> Five causes why a man should drink;

which with a little alteration, would just suit them:

> There are, unless my memory fail,
> Five causes why we should not sail:
> The fog is thick; the wind is high;
> It rains; or may do by-and-by;
> Or—any other reason why."

Wesley was slow to complain of hardship or discomfort, but quick to enjoy and appreciate the varied pleasures of the open road. His Journals abound in references to scenery. He was a true child of his century in his admiration for well-planned gardens, stately parks and the more domesticated forms of natural scenery.

"All things contributed to make it a refreshing season: the gently-declining sun, the stillness of the evening, the beauty of the meadows and fields, through which 'The smooth, clear river drew its sinuous train'; the opposite hills and woods, and the earnestness of the people, covering the top of the hill on which we stood; and above all, the day-spring from on high."

Here speaks the eighteenth century. Pope or Gray would have admired a scene such as this, and even old Johnson, most chauvinistic of cockneys, might have grunted a half-hearted approval for "the smooth clear river's sinuous train."

But Wesley was ahead of his age in his genuine passion for wild and rugged scenery. Contrast for instance, his attitude with that of Grimston, a typical eighteenth century traveller. Grimston roundly condemned the famous coast road from Aberavon to Aberystwith, and alludes with contempt to "the uncultivated mountains." "No tree to break the unbroken view, no shrub to beautify the unlimited range of mountains." This recalls a contemporary comparison between Switzerland and Holland. Holland was deemed more beautiful because "there were no mountains to interrupt the view."

Now consider the following passages from Wesley's Journal:

"We took horse at four, and rode through one of the pleasantest countries in the world. When we came to Trecastle we had rode fifty miles in Monmouthshire and Brecknockshire; and I will be bold to say all England does not afford such a line of fifty miles' length, for fields, meadows, woods, brooks, and gently rising mountains, fruitful to the very top. Carmarthenshire, into which we came soon after, has at least as fruitful a soil;

but it is not so pleasant, because it has fewer mountains, though abundance of brooks and rivers."

We do not recapture this note until the Romantic Revival.

Here is another fine passage:

"Taking horse early in the morning, we rode over the rough mountains of Radnorshire and Montgomeryshire into Merionethshire. In the evening, I was surprised with one of the finest prospects, in its kind, that ever I saw in my life. We rode in a green vale, shaded with rows of trees, which made an arbour for several miles. The river laboured along on our left hand, through broken rocks· of every size, shape, and colour. On the other side of the river the mountain rose to an immense height, almost perpendicular: and yet the tall, straight oaks stood, rank above rank, from the bottom to the very top; only here and there, where the mountain was not so steep, were interposed pastures or fields of corn. At a distance, as far as the eye could reach, as it were by way of contrast—

> A mountain huge uprear'd
> Its broad, bare back—

with vast, rugged rocks hanging over its brow, that seemed to nod portending ruin."

There is an element of *odi et amo* in mountain love. All mountains are not beautiful, all hills are not friendly. The true mountaineer will not misunderstand Wesley's references to "horrid mountains" and "dreary mountains."

"Not so pleasant because it has fewer mountains." There speaks the real Wesley, the real mountain lover, there and in his expressed conviction that the God in whom we believe was "a God both of the hills and val-

leys, and nowhere more present than in the mountains
of Cumberland."

II

Wesley, "the Happy Traveller," might have served
Wordsworth as a model for a companion poem to "The
Happy Warrior." "I am content with whatever entertainment I meet with," he writes, "and my companions
are always in good humour. This must be the spirit of
all who take journeys with me. If a dinner ill-dressed or
a hired bed, a poor room or a shower of rain, or a dusty
road would put them out of humour, it lays a burden
upon me greater than all the rest put together."

There speaks the Happy Traveller. He is describing
the misery he felt when accompanied by his grumbling
wife. In a few pregnant words, he sums up his belief
when his wife left him to journey alone. "I leap as broken
from chains."

Wesley had no use for a companion who confessed to
the common infirmities of ordinary mortals. He himself
rode unperturbed through snow and sleet and storm.
"The wind was high and sharp and blew away a few
delicate ones." Such was his contemptuous comment on
the failure of some of his frailer friends.

In "Coryate's Crudities" (published in 1611), you will
find an oration in praise of travel in general. There is a
passage in that oration which sums up in a few inimitable
lines the attitude of the happy traveller that might well
have been placed on the title page of Wesley's Journal.

"Who is so crabbed, austere & angry, whom the humanity, affability, gentleness & placability of our consorts
and companions, that communicate with us in our iorneys
and Innes, will not change? Who is so tender, effeminate,

& cowardly, whom the heat of the sun, cold, snow, raine, hard seats, stony pillows, and such infinite inconveniences of trauels, so many wailayings, & dangers of theues, wil not make more coruagious & valiant? Who is so simple, improvident and incontinent, whom the subtilty of spies, the wonderful cunning of Innkeepers, and the great danger of his life will not stirre up to vigilancy, prudence and temperance?"

CHAPTER XX

WESLEY'S JOURNAL

"JOHN WESLEY'S life," remarked Mrs. Oliphant,[1] "was no life at all in the ordinary sense of the word, but only a mere string of preachings. His Journals are like the note-books of a physician—a curious monotonous, wonderful narrative."

There is some justice in this criticism. Here, for instance, is a typical page of his Journal:

"Tues. 11.—I preached, between one and two, at a village called Millbrook, to a company of plain, serious people; and in the evening, at Wootton Pillinge, where several have already found this word to be 'the power of God unto salvation.'

Wed. 12.—I preached at two in Lidlington, to another company of plain country people. Thence we crossed over to Cople, where is at present the most lively of all the little societies in Bedfordshire.

Thur. 13.—I rode to Bedford, and in the evening spoke with more plainness, I may indeed say roughness, than ever I did before, if haply God might rouse some of these drowsy people.

Fri. 14.—I preached at Luton, and on *Saturday* I returned to London.

Sun. 16.—I strongly inculcated family religion, the grand desideratum among the Methodists. Many were ashamed before God, and at length adopted Joshua's resolution, 'As for me and my house, we will serve the Lord.'

Thur. 27.—I conversed with a young clergyman full of

---

[1] "Historical Sketches of the Reign of George II," by Mrs. Oliphant.

good resolutions. But I judge it impossible they can hold; for he has not the least conception of his own weakness.

Sun. 30.—I preached on the Education of Children, wherein we are so shamefully wanting. Many were now deeply convinced of this. I hope they will not all stifle that conviction.

Dec. 8. Mon.—I went to Canterbury, and on Wednesday the 10th to Dover. At all the seaports we have a multitude of hearers. Is not this a token for good to the nation? Surely mercy 'embraces us on every side.' Will it not likewise go through the land?

Thur. 11.—I preached at Dover, Sandwich, Ramsgate, and Margate; on Friday at Canterbury. I have not seen this society so at unity among themselves for many years.

Sat. 13.—I left them with much satisfaction, and cheerfully returned to London."

If the reader is prepared to plough through page after page of this kind of thing, he will have his reward. "If you want to get into the last century," writes Mr. Augustine Birrell in his excellent introduction to Mr. Eayrs's collection of the Letters of John Wesley, "to feel its pulses throb beneath your finger, be content sometimes to leave the letters of Horace Walpole unturned, resist the drowsy temptation to waste your time over the learned triflers who sleep in the seventeen volumes of Nichols—nay even deny yourself your annual reading of Boswell or your biennial retreat with Sterne, and ride up and down the country with the greatest force of the eighteenth century in England."

Perhaps, and had Wesley been less obsessed by his sense of vocation, his Journal might conceivably have been as interesting to a student of the period as Walpole's Letters or Boswell's Life of Johnson; for Wesley's knowledge of England was far greater than that possessed by either Walpole or Boswell.

"No man lived nearer the centre," continues Mr. Birrell, "than John Wesley, neither Clive nor Pitt, neither

Mansfield nor Johnson. . . . No other man did such a life's work for England."

John Wesley not only knew his subject, he could write. He had a concise and telling literary style, a dry, effective form of wit, and a power of characterisation when he chose to use it. If Wesley had been a little less interested in people's souls, and a little more interested in their human characteristics, he would indeed have given us an unrivalled picture of eighteenth century England.

"The great middle-class of English people," writes Mr. Winchester, "the class full of the most varied, racy, humorous life, Wesley knew, or might have known, better than all the novelists of that century put together. He lived with them for fifty years, was their friend, adviser, father confessor. But you would never guess that he saw the humours of their life."

Mr. Winchester attributes this lack to the fact that Wesley had "very little gift of humour." "He was cheerful—that came of his temperament—and he had a very pretty wit, usually with a satiric edge, and shown best in some mood of criticism or controversy. You expect wit from every man of any eminence in the eighteenth century. But of that sympathetic enjoyment of all the manifold contrasts and incongruities of life which we call humour, I think Wesley had very little. That usually implies a habit of leisurely observation, which he would never indulge. It is a pity, when one thinks what an opportunity he had for the exercise of that fortunate gift."

True. Wesley had more wit than humour, but in this, as in so many other things, Wesley is inconsistent and eludes formal testification. Just as you have neatly pigeonholed him under "Wit," you light on some passage in his Journal or Letters which crosses the borderline between wit and humour. Here are a few examples which the reader may be able to classify, but which the present writer cannot. The wit is obvious, but is there not humour as well as wit in the following passages?

Our first illustration is from "Thoughts on the Consecration of Churches and Burial-Grounds":

"You say, this is consecrated ground, so many feet broad, and so many long. But pray how deep is the consecrated ground?—Deep! What does that signify?—O, a great deal. For if my grave be dug too deep, I may happen to get out of the consecrated ground. And who can tell what unhappy consequences may follow from this?"

He was forbidden on one occasion to visit a young woman in Bedlam. "So we are forbid to go to Newgate for fear of making them wicked; and to Bedlam for fear of driving them mad."

The following is from Wesley's preface to his own English Dictionary:

"N. B. The Author assures you, he thinks this is the best English Dictionary in the world. As incredible as it may appear, I must avow, that this Dictionary is not published to get money. . . . In compliance with the taste of the age, I add, that this little dictionary is not only the shortest and cheapest, but likewise, by many degrees, the most correct which is extant at this day. Many are the mistakes in all the other English Dictionaries which I have yet seen. Whereas, I can truly say, I know of none in this. And I can conceive the reader will believe me; for if I had, I should not have left it there."

Wesley's latent sense of humour suffered, of course, from neglect. He kept it too sternly under control.

"Sat. 31.—An odd circumstance occurred during the morning preaching. It was well only serious persons were present. An ass walked gravely in at the gate, came up to the door of the house, lifted up his head and stood stock-still, in a posture of deep attention. Might not 'the dumb beast reprove' many who have far less decency, and not much more understanding?"

An impressive tribute to Wesley's power over himself and his congregation. Few preachers of to-day could continue to dominate a congregation which included an ass "in a posture of deep attention."

Wesley's sense of humour, such as it was, disappeared completely when he was in love, but many people with an acute sense of humour are incapable of seeing anything funny in their own amours. The records of his own love affairs only prove that his sense of humour was temporarily obscured, and perhaps, the one lasting passion of his life, his love of God, tended to suppress and permanently to obscure that sense of humour which flashes out at rare intervals in his Journal and in his Letters.

"Wesley's sense that he was a man of destiny," writes Mr. Rattenbury, "sometimes obscured his sense of humour. . . . His realization of his tremendous vocation was so great that he always took himself seriously. When a man is overpowered with a conviction of his own importance, even though it be as an instrument only that he feels himself important, such a feeling will open him to the criticism that he lacks a sense of proportion, if not of humour. But it must not be forgotten that history confirms Wesley's own conviction that he was a man plucked by God's hand from the burning for His own great purposes; and that his sense of proportion, however seriously it made him take himself, was perfectly accurate."

II

No man knew England as Wesley knew it, not only her roads and bridle-paths, which certainly no other man had ever explored so thoroughly, but her people, especially the lower-middle and the lower classes. They talked to him freely, not only about their souls, but about their everyday troubles and grievances. They told him what they thought of the parson and the squire, the new taxes and the war. And the common folk who paid the taxes and helped to win the battles of England, allowed Wesley to see what they thought of the great men who controlled the destiny of their country.

The man who knew the English countryside as few men have known it, had no patience with picturesque illusions. His homely penetrating criticisms of that life anticipate the mournful realism of Crabbe.

"Wed. 5.—I rode by Shoreham to Sevenoaks. In the little journeys which I have lately taken, I have thought much on the huge encomiums which have been for many ages bestowed on a *country life*. How have all the learned world cried out—

> O fortunati nimium, sua si bona norint
> Agricolae!

But after all, what a flat contradiction is this to universal experience! See that little house, under the wood, by the river-side! There is rural life in perfection. How happy is the farmer who lives there! Let us take a detail of his happiness. He rises with, or before the sun, calls his servants, looks to his swine and cows, then to his stables and barns. He sees to the ploughing and sowing his ground, in winter or in spring. In summer and autumn he hurries and sweats among his mowers and reapers. And where is his happiness in the meantime? Which of those employments do we envy? Or do we envy the delicate repast that succeeds, which the poet so languishes for?—

> O quando faba, Pythagorae cognata, simulque
> Uncta satis pingui ponentur oluscula lardo!

" 'Oh the happiness of eating beans well greased with fat bacon! Nay, and *cabbage* too!'—Was Horace in his senses when he talked thus, or the servile herd of his imitators? Our eyes and ears may convince us there is not a less happy body of men in all England than the country farmers. In general, their life is supremely dull; and it is usually unhappy too. For of all people in the kingdom, they are most discontented; seldom satisfied either with God or man."

Wesley's England was far more intrigued by theological disputes than the England of to-day.

"The next morning a young gentleman overtook me on the road, and, after a while, asked me if I had seen Whitefield's Journals. I told him I had. 'And what do you think of them?' said he. 'Don't you think they are d—d cant, enthusiasm from end to end? I think so.' I asked him, 'Why do you think so?' He replied, 'Why, he talks so much about joy and stuff, and inward feelings. As I hope to be saved, I cannot tell what to make of it.' "

That young gentleman's modern descendants would hardly have heard of a popular preacher, much less would they have read his sermons.

Here is another extract:

"On Thursday, the 20th May [1742] I set out. The next afternoon I stopped a little at Newport-Pagnell, and then rode on till I overtook a serious man, with whom I immediately fell into conversation. He presently gave me to know what his opinions were, therefore I said nothing to contradict them. But that did not content him. He was quite uneasy to know 'whether I held the doctrines of the decrees as he did;' but I told him over and over: 'We had better keep to practical things, lest we should be angry at one another.' And so we did for two miles, till he caught me unawares, and dragged me into the dis-

pute before I knew where I was. He then grew warmer
and warmer; told me I was rotten at heart, and supposed
I was one of John Wesley's followers. I told him 'No. I
am John Wesley himself.' Upon which

> "Improvisum aspris veluti qui sentibus anguem
>   Pressit—"

he would gladly have run away outright, but being the
better mounted of the two I kept close to his side, and
endeavoured to show him his heart till we came into
the street of Northampton."

"What a picture have we here of a fine May morning
in 1742," writes Mr. Birrell, "the unhappy Calvinist trying to shake off the Arminian Wesley! But he cannot
do it. *John Wesley is the better mounted of the two,* and
so they scamper together into Northampton.

"The England described in the Journal is an England still full of theology. All kinds of queer folk abound;
strange subjects are discussed in odd places. There was
drunkenness and cock-fighting, no doubt, but there were
also Deists, Mystics, Swedenborgians, Antinomians,
Necessitarians, Anabaptists, Quakers, nascent heresies,
and slow-dying delusions. Villages were divided into rival
groups which fiercely argued the nicest points in the
aptest language. Nowadays in his rambles a man is as
likely to encounter a grey badger as a black Calvinist."

Wesley's Journal is indeed, a museum of "nascent
heresies and slow-dying delusions." He is always introducing you to queer people such as the old gentleman who
informed Wesley with much concern that he could have
no place in Heaven without a beard. "Therefore, I beg
you let yours grow immediately." "His long, white beard,"
Wesley remarks, "showed that his present disorder was
of some continuance." And there was the sea captain
who "expressed much love and did not doubt it as I

meant well, but that God would convince me of the great sin in writing books, seeing that men ought to read no book but the Bible."

This was a little hard on the author of 233 original works.

CHAPTER XXI

WESLEY'S LAST LOVE

THE manuscript in which Wesley describes his last love came into the possession of the British Museum in 1829. Its genuineness has never been doubted. In this manuscript, Wesley incorporated Grace Murray's autobiographical sketch of her own early life up to the time when she met and fell in love with Wesley.

The reader who desires a fuller study of this episode in Wesley's life may be recommended to read "John Wesley's Last Love," by Professor J. A. Leger, a brilliant and discriminating study.[1]

Grace Murray (née Norman) was born on January 18th, 1716, and was thus about thirteen years younger than Wesley.

At the age of sixteen, she ran away from home because her parents wished her to marry a young man with whom she was not in love.

"After staying a month with my sister," to quote from her own story as taken down by Wesley, "I went into service, where I was used more like a child than a servant." A very human touch. The fact that Grace Murray had been in service was a sore point.

Two years later she married Alexander Murray, whose father, a member of a good Scotch family, had been con-

---

[1] This book contains a re-print of the British Museum manuscript referred to above.

cerned in the Jacobite rising of 1715, and had forfeited his estates.

Her husband was a sailor, and it was during one of his long absences that Grace first heard Whitefield and Wesley preach. On September 9th, 1748, she was taken by a friend to Moorfields.

"When Mr. W. stood up & look'd round on the Congregation, I fixt my Eyes upon him, & felt an inexpressible Conviction, That he was sent of God."

Her husband on his return was not at all pleased to discover that his wife had been converted. "You are utterly distracted," he said, "and I am determined to send you to the Mad-house." He relented, however, and a little later came back and said, "I cannot bear to put you in a Mad-house. But neither can I bear to see your utter ruin: You have almost ruined yourself already. And if you are resolv'd to go on thus, I will leave you: I will go as far as Ships can sail."

A few months later her husband was lost at sea.

Grace, meanwhile, had impressed Wesley by her talent for evangelistic work. He appointed her a band leader and a visitor to the sick, put her in charge of the orphan house at Newcastle, and finally selected her to be one of the small company of men and women who journeyed with him on his preaching tours throughout England. The men were entertained by one member of the local society, and the women by another member or members.

And so, for ten years, Grace journeyed with Wesley throughout England, Wales and Ireland, her special duty being to meet and to regulate the female classes. Wesley had, therefore, ample opportunity to study her character, and his final decision to make her his wife was not the result of a sudden infatuation, but of a resolution which had been slowly maturing in his mind for many years.

What manner of woman was Grace Murray? Opinions

vary. "Without doubt," wrote Tyerman, "she was talented, talkative, and bewitching; her services, also, as a female itinerant, were popular, and, in a certain sense, successful; but Wesley's opinion of her character and piety were far higher than our own. The woman . . . who so infamously coquetted with the greatest reformer of the age, and with one of his most educated and able helpers,—was not the perfect saint that Wesley pictured her. She was a woman of energy, of dauntless resolution, and of a certain sort of religious zeal, and, later in life, she seems to have been a loving, lovely Christian; but at the period of her dualistic worship, she was uneducated, vain, fickle, selfish, and presuming."

Dr. Rigg, in his book "The Living Wesley" reacts strongly against Mr. Tyerman's unchivalrous indictment: "Grace Murray," he writes, "was a woman not only of singular tact, but of attractive modesty, or perfect propriety, and of deep piety. All we know of her would lead to the conclusion that she would have been not an unworthy helpmeet for John Wesley."

But perhaps the best picture of Grace Murray is the picture which she herself provides in the autobiographical sketch which Wesley took down at her dictation.

Gracy Murray, like all the women that Wesley loved, and unlike the only woman whom he married, was essentially feminine. She was governed, neither by logic nor reason, but by the fleeting mood of the moment. She could run through the whole gamut of religious emotion, from radiant joy to black depression, within the space of a few hours. It would, perhaps, be unfair to describe her as hysterical in the strict medical sense of that term, but she undoubtedly exhibited symptoms which suggest hysteria.

"Often I was so desperate, as not to have a Desire of Salvation, nor to care whether I was sav'd or damn'd.

Sometimes I even wish'd to be in Hell, that I might know the worst. And frequently, in the midst of all this, my Body was so affected that the Bed shook under me: & I felt as if one had begun at the Crown of my Head & flay'd off my Skin, yea, my Flesh & all, to the very Soals of my Feet."

"Often I purposely abstain'd from food, . . . and that for several days together. . . . Another reason of my frequent & long continued fasts was, That I might destroy whatever it was, whereby I had been a Snare to men; that I might never hurt any man more."

This little touch suggests, of course, hysteria.

It is needless to detail her symptoms, loss of memory, violent pains, suicidal desires, hypochondriacal or hysterical fits and paroxysms of horror and despair. They are all set down in great detail in her autobiographical sketch. "Nowhere, indeed," as Dr. Leger remarks, "have the dangers of the theological doctrine of Assurance, so well pointed out in Dr. Workman's masterly introduction to a recent *History of Methodism* (pp. 28–31), been better exemplified than in the anxious, uninterrupted self-examining, brain-racking doubts and fears, maddening distrusts of salvation, which terrfically fill up most of Grace's account of herself."

There are passages in her Autobiography which might have served Pecksniff as a model for his literary style. Among the men who had been attracted to her was a certain John Brydon, whose advances she repulsed.

"While I was at Newcastle John Brydon married, & soon grew quite light & careless. This shock'd me exceedingly: I was afraid his Blood would be upon my Head, because I did not marry him."

Or again her reference to the women who resented her intimacy with Wesley.

"But I did not as yet perceive any resentment toward

them: Only I was griev'd, because they hurt their own Souls."

And yet, in spite of these defects, Grace Murray must have possessed a great charm and fascination. She appears to have been a woman of tact, and the influence which she exercised over the women in her classes was far-reaching in its effect. Had she been purely a hysterical female, we may be sure that Wesley, with his strong common sense would not have tolerated her company for ten years.

In August 1748, ten years after Grace had first heard Wesley preach, she had the honour of nursing him when he fell ill at Newcastle. Wesley, as Dr. Fitchett remarks, was always ready "to propose to the particular face that at the moment was bending over him in his sickness." Sophy nursed him in Georgia, Grace Murray in Newcastle, and Mrs. Vazeille in London. He wanted to marry each of these three nurses in turn, and in the case of Mrs. Vazeille, his wishes—unfortunately—were gratified.

John Wesley's description of his proposal to Grace Murray cannot be bettered:

"In August following, I was taken ill at Newcastle. Grace Murray attended me continually. I observ'd her more narrowly than ever before, both as to her Temper, Sense, and Behaviour. I esteem'd and lov'd her more and more. And, when I was a little recover'd, I told her, sliding into it I know not how, 'If ever I marry, I think you will be the Person.' After some time I spoke to her more directly. She seem'd utterly amaz'd, and said, 'This is too great a Blessing for me: I can't tell how to believe it. This is all I cou'd have wish'd for under Heaven, if I had dar'd to wish for it.' "

But Wesley was not the only Methodist who thought highly of Grace's skill as a nurse. Two years before,

Grace had nursed John Bennet, one of Wesley's lay
helpers. Bennet was an eligible young man, for he was
well-off and well-connected, a gentleman by birth and education. He had corresponded with Grace, and there had
been a certain amount of gossip and talk, but no formal
proposal, still less a formal engagement. Wesley never
thought that the affair with Bennet had gone very deep,
and when he proposed to Grace, he believed that her
heart was free.

He took Grace with him through Yorkshire and Derby-
shire, and finally arrived at Chinly, Bennet's home, on
August 31st. Here Wesley left Grace, and asked Bennet
"to take great care of Mrs. Murray." Bennet took such
good care of "Mrs. Murray" that a few days later she
had promised to become his wife.

Bennet asked her whether there was any contract between her and Wesley. "Partly out of love to him,"
writes Wesley, "partly out of fear of exposing me, she
replied—'There is not.' This was doubtless another false
step. He that standeth, let him take heed lest he fall!"

"Not long after," adds Wesley, "I received a letter
from J. Bennet and another from her. She said, 'She be-
liev'd it was the Will of God.' I was utterly amazed: But
wrote a mild answer to both, supposing they were married already. She replied in so affectionate a manner, that
I thought the whole design was at an end."

Grace and Wesley met again, and Grace persuaded
Wesley that she had been unable to believe in the reality
of his proposal. "Till now all this had seem'd to her as
a Dream, nor could she possibly think, what I propos'd
would ever come to pass."

She accompanied him to Ireland where they spent several months together. "I saw the Work of God," wrote
Wesley, "prosper in her hands. She lightened my burden
more than can be exprest. She examin'd all the Women

in the smaller Societies and the Believers in every place.
. . . Mean time she was to be both a Servant and Friend,
as well as a Fellow-labourer in the Gospel. She provided
everything I wanted."

Before leaving Ireland, Wesley and Grace entered into
a Contract *de praesenti*. "Any contract made *per verba
de praesenti* was, before the time of George II, so far a
valid marriage, that the parties might be *compelled,* in the
spiritual Courts, to celebrate it *in facie Ecclesiae*." [2]

II

Great religious leaders are seldom attractive in the
rôle of Romeo. Romance is apt to be overshadowed by
vocation. "I am not one of those insane lovers," wrote
Calvin, "who when once smitten by the beauty of a woman
embrace her very faults. This is the only beauty which
attracts me—if she be modest, obliging, fastidious, careful, patient, and likely to be attentive to my health."

Compare Whitefield's letter to the parents of the girl
whom he was wooing. He began by explaining that he
wanted a mistress for his orphanage, and then proceeded
to inform the parents of his intended bride, that they
need not be afraid to send him a refusal. "For I bless
God, if I know anything of my own heart, I am free
from that foolish passion the world calls 'love.' "

Wesley's native courtesy would have prevented him
from expressing so unchivalrous a sentiment. Moreover,
he had more than once suffered "from that foolish passion the world calls love." He was deeply in love with
Grace, but weighing the pros and cons of marriage, the
paramount consideration was the effect of marriage on
his life's work. Following his usual custom, he tran-

[2] R. M. Kerr's "Student Blackstone," 103.

scribed a methodical summary of the motives that guided
him in contemplating this momentous step.

"A Dispensation of the Gospel has been committed to
me," he writes, "and I will do nothing which directly or
indirectly tends to hinder my preaching the Gospel."

It is from this angle that he proceeds to examine his
proposed marriage in all its bearings.

First there is the question of expense. "I now clearly
perceive, That my Marriage would bring little expense
if I married one I maintain now, who would afterward
desire nothing more than she had before: And would
cheerfully consent, That our Children (if any) should
be wholly brought up at Kingswood."

Only a man obsessed by a sense of vocation could mention as one of the advantages of matrimony, his intended
wife's cheerful consent to dump such children as might
arrive on a far-distant orphanage.

Then follows a list of Grace Murray's attractions.

"I am persuaded she is in every Capacity an Help meet
for me. First, as a Housekeeper!" A characteristic beginning.

"Grace," we are told, "is remarkably neat in person, in
cloaths,[3] in all things. She is nicely frugal, yet not sordid.
. . . She is a good workwoman, able to do the finest,
ready to do the coarsest Work: Observes my Rules when
I am absent as well as when I am present: And takes
care, that those about her observe them, yet seldom dis-
obliges any of them."

We rub our eyes. Is Wesley providing a housekeeper
with a character or describing his bride-to-be?

As a nurse, Grace is "indefatigably patient, and inex-
pressibly tender. She is quick, skilfull, and understand my
Constitution better than most Physicians."

---

[3] The spelling etc. in the British Museum manuscript has been
preserved in these extracts.

He then pays a glowing tribute to Grace as a companion and as a friend, and lastly as "a Fellow Labourer in the Gospel of Christ (the Light wherin my Wife is to be chiefly consider'd)."

Finally, he adds, "She would remove many Hindrances from others, from Women in particular. She would guard many from inordinate affection for me, to which they would be far less expose'd, both because they would have far less Hope of Success, and because I should converse far more sparingly with them. Perhaps not in private with any Young Women at all; at least not with any Member of our own Societies."

So much for the advantages. With similar thoroughness Wesley proceeds to consider the objections which might be urged against his marriage.

Grace is low-born. "Her parents were poor, labouring people."

"This weighs nothing with me;" answers Wesley, "as it does not prevent either her Grace or Gifts. Besides, whoever I marry, I believe it will not be a Gentlewoman; I despair of finding any such, so qualified."

The second objection "Because she was my Servant. I answer, 'I therefore like her the better. . . . By living so long with her under one Roof, I am as secure against being deceived in her, as I can well be against being deceived in any one. Indeed I should scruple marrying any Woman, who had not done so for some time.' "

"A Third Reason is, 'She has travell'd with me Six Months.' With regard to this, I grant some would probably say, 'She was my Mistress, before she was my Wife.' And let them say this: It would hurt just as much as a thousand things they have said before. But let them know withall I should never marry any Woman, till I had Proof that she both cou'd and wou'd travel with me."

Wesley then proceeds to discuss in detail Grace's re-

lations to John Bennet, and concludes with justice that
he had the prior claim.

III

Wesley and Grace left Ireland and returned to Bristol
together. It was at Bristol, that Grace heard some idle
gossip about Wesley and a certain Molly Francis. In a
sudden fit of jealousy, she wrote to Bennet. Next day
she repented and confessed what she had done to Wesley. It was too late. Bennet's passion had revived and
he wrote her an ardent letter.

Meanwhile, Grace had discovered that her proposed
marriage with Wesley was highly unpopular in Methodist circles. She discussed the problem with an intimate
acquaintance who replied: "Sister M, never think of it.
I know you thro'ly. It will never do. The People here
would never suffer you. And your Spirit would not bear
their Behaviour. You have not Humility enough, or
Meekness, or Patience: You would be miserable all your
Life. And that would make him miserable too. So that,
instead of strengthening, you would weaken his Hands.
If you love yourself, or if you love him, never think of it
more."

Wesley and Grace set out for the North and arrived at
Epworth, where an interview took place between Wesley
and Bennet. Wesley decided that Bennet ought to marry
Grace Murray without further delay, and next day he
wrote to Grace telling her that he did not think that it was
right that they should meet again. She ran to Wesley in
"an agony of tears," and Wesley would probably have
been moved by these tears had not John Bennet appeared
and claimed Grace as his right.

On September 6th, Grace convinced Wesley that she
was determined to marry him. Wesley sat down and wrote

a long letter to Bennet in which he reviewed the whole
case. One of the Rules of a Helper was "Take no steps
towards marriage without first consulting with your
brethren." It was therefore necessary for Wesley to satisfy John Bennet and to obtain his brother's consent to
his proposed marriage.

Unfortunately, the letter which Wesley sent to Bennet
was never delivered, but a copy reached Charles Wesley
safely in Bristol.

IV

Charles was thunderstruck. "The thought of my *marrying* at all," writes Wesley, "but especially of my marrying
a *Servant,* and one so *low-born,* appear'd above measure
shocking to him. Thence he infer'd, That it wou'd appear
so to all Mankind: and consequently, that it would break
up all our Societies, and put a stop to the whole Work of
God."

He rushed off to meet his brother at Whitehaven. "I
was not at all surpriz'd when I saw him," remarks John
Wesley. "He urg'd, 'All our Preachers would leave us,
all our Societies disperse,' if I married so mean a woman."

John heard his brother patiently, and suggested that
the whole question might be referred to Mr. Perronet for
his decision. To this, Charles readily consented.

To do Charles justice, the social aspects of John's intended marriage weighed less with him, than his conviction that his brother had lost his moral balance under
the influence of a passing infatuation, and was about to
commit a sin against John Bennet. In a letter to Grace
Murray he says, "The case thus appears to me, You promised J. B. to marry him—since which, you engage yourself to another. . . . And who is that other? One of

such importance that his doing so dishonest an action would destroy both himself, and me, and the whole work of God."

In other words, he was convinced that his brother was about to marry a woman who had been promised to another, only to discover when too late that he had persuaded John Bennet to marry his brother's betrothed. The fact is, of course, that whatever informal understanding may have existed between Bennet and Grace Murray before Wesley came on the scene, the only engagement into which Grace Murray entered, was her engagement to marry Wesley.

Next morning Charles left his brother without giving him any warning, and rode straight to the village of Hindley near Newcastle where Grace was staying. He was at the end of his strength. Exhausted by the tumult of emotions through which he had passed, and by his rapid journeyings, he burst into the room where Grace was, and gasped out, "Grace Murray, you have broken my heart," and fell in a faint at her feet.

Grace Murray could never resist persuasion. Her vacillating relations with Wesley and Bennet were due, not to coquetterie, but to the fact that her mind was always swayed by the mood and by the man of the moment. Her ambitions, perhaps, inclined to Wesley, and her affections to Bennet, and here was Mr. Charles, whom she revered only second to his brother John, in a faint on the floor. It was too distressing. Charles recovered, and overwhelmed her with reproaches. She had promised to marry one man, and then engaged herself to another, and "one of such importance that his doing so dishonest an action would destroy both himself . . . and the whole work of God."

It was all terribly confusing. Grace tried to col-

lect her thoughts, while Charles addressed her in a steady
stream of reproaches. . . . What was that he was saying? . . . "My brother John agrees with me" . . .
(Charles had persuaded himself that John had seen the
light of reason) "He is of my mind in this matter." "Oh
no . . . Oh no . . . Oh no" . . . pleaded Grace. But
Charles beat down her weak, feeble protests. Surely he
knew his brother best. He had just come from John. She
could take it from him that John desired nothing more
than that she should do her duty and marry John Bennet.

Charles left her in an exhausted condition, but success
had worked like a tonic, and there was no fainting when
he ran into John Bennet in Newcastle.

No marriage-broker ever worked harder than Charles
to make a match. But John Bennet was not enthusiastic.
He had been played with too long. He was sick and tired
of the whole affair.

Charles wheedled, Charles coaxed, Charles wrestled,
until John Bennet from sheer weariness gave a reluctant
consent. Grace was then hustled into his presence. She fell
at his feet and begged his forgiveness. "To satisfy her
entirely, as to any scruple which might remain with regard to me," writes John Wesley, "One was brought in, to
assure her, 'I had given her up, and would have nothing
more to say to her. Only I had order'd him to procure
some place among the Country Societies where she might
live privately.' Upon this, one cried out, 'Good God! What
will the world say? He is tired of her, and so thrusts his
Wh— into a Corner. Sister M., will you consent to this!'
She answer'd, 'No, I will die first.' So, seeing no other
way, She frankly declar'd, 'I will have J. B., if he will
have me.'"

And so, on October 3rd, these two muddled and bewildered people were joined together in Holy Matrimony.

Charles looked upon his work and saw that it was good.

V

Charles had ridden away without giving his brother
any hint of his intentions. When John discovered that he
had gone, he carried on quietly with his original programme. He was due to preach at Hindley Hill, so he
left Whitehaven, and on Wednesday evening drew up
before the cottage at Hindley Hill where he had left
Grace Murray. What follows is best told in his own
words:

"Hannah Broadwood, at whose house I left Sister
Murray, met me at a little distance from it, and said,
'Mr. Charles left us two hours since, and carried Sister
Murray behind him.' I said, 'The Lord gave, and the
Lord hath taken away: blessed be the name of the Lord!'
Soon after James Broadwood came in; he looked at me,
and burst into tears. I said I must go on to Newcastle.
James said, 'No; I will go, and with God's help bring her
back.' In a quarter of an hour he took horse, and I calmly
committed the cause to God!"

"Business as usual" was Wesley's motto in a crisis.
The business of God must go forward. Wesley reeled,
but he did not collapse under the blow. That evening, he
preached as usual, and the following day he set apart for
fasting and prayer and for self-examination, in the manner of his earlier diaries and journals.

"I now closely examin'd myself touching what was so
confidently laid to my charge, viz, Inordinate affection.
And this I clearly perceiv'd, That I had never before had
so strong an Affection for any Person under Heaven.
. . . But yet I cou'd not perceive it was inordinate by
any of the Marks which use to attend such an Affection.
For, 1. Inordinate affection leads from God. But this
continually led me to Him. 2. Inordinate Affection makes

us less desirous of doing the Works of God, less zealous to pray, preach, or do Good in any kind. But this increas'd my Desire of doing Good in every kind, and my Zeal to do all the Works of God. 3. Inordinate affection makes us cold and dead, in preaching, praying, or any other Office of Religion. But this made me more alive in all: more Sensible of the Power and Presence of God. 4. Inordinate affection creates Jealousy toward Rivals and Resentment toward them that oppose it. But I never felt a Minute's Jealousy, even of J. B. nor a minute's Resentment toward those who tore her from me. 5. Inordinate affection necessarily creates Uneasiness in the Absence of the Object of it. Whereas I never was uneasy, neither *in* parting, nor *after* it; no more than if she had been a Common Person. For all these Reasons (and I might mention several more) I could not conceive, That mine was an Inordinate Affection."

Next day, he returned to Whitehaven. "I need add no more," he writes in his Journal, "than that if I had had more regard for her I loved than for the work of God I should now have gone straight on to Newcastle, and not back to Whitehaven."

Should he turn north and follow Charles, or should he ride south where his work called him? He turned his horse's head to the south leaving behind him the last human love of his life. "The storm was exceeding high, and drove full in my face, so that it was not without difficulty I could sit my horse; particularly as I rode over the broad, bare backs of those enormous mountains which lay in my way. . . . But I knew where help was to be found, in either great difficulties or small."

He did indeed. "For God," adds Dr. Leger, "was after all the only lasting, absorbing passion of John Wesley." [4] For a moment, perhaps, he rebelled, but as he rode, he

[4] "John Wesley's Last Love."

transmuted into verse "of grave-like rhythm and tone" the experiences through which he had passed.

> "Unsearchable thy Judgments are,
>   O Lord, a bottomless Abyss!
> Yet sure thy Love, thy guardian Care,
>   O'er all thy Works extended is.
> O why didst thou the Blessing send?
> Or why thus snatch away my Friend?
>
> What thou hast done I know not now!
>   Suffice I shall hereafter know!
> Beneath thy chast'ning Hand I bow:
>   That still I live to Thee I owe.
> O teach thy deeply-humbled Son
> To say, 'Father, thy Will be done!'"

This last prayer, at least, was answered.

VI

Methodism was now faced with the possibility of disruption, for a violent quarrel between John and Charles Wesley would have been a mortal blow to the movement. The survival of Methodism is indeed due first and foremost to the saintly magnanimity of John Wesley, and secondly to the tact and wisdom shown by George Whitefield. The schism which George Whitefield prevented would have been far more serious than the Calvinistic schism which he provoked.

The marriage of Grace and John Bennet took place on October 3rd, after which Grace, her husband and Charles Wesley "all rode on contentedly to Leeds," as Wesley tells us, "to give me the Meeting there, as well that I might have the pleasure of seeing the Bride, as 'that I might acknowledge my Sin' (those were my Brother's Expressions) before J. B. and them all. But this I was not altogether ready to do."

John Wesley reached Leeds on the evening of the 3rd and met George Whitefield. Here is his description of what followed:

"I lay down by him on the bed. He told me, 'My brother would not come till John Bennet and Grace Murray were married.' I was troubled. He perceived it. He wept and prayed over me, but I could not shed a tear. He said all that was in his power to comfort me, but it was in vain. He told me, 'It was his judgment that she was my wife, and that he had said so to John Bennet: that he would fain have persuaded them to wait, and not to marry till they had seen me; but that my brother's impetuosity prevailed and bore down all before it.'

"I felt no murmuring thought, but deep distress. I accepted the just punishment of my manifold unfaithfulness and unfruitfulness, and therefore could not complain. But I felt the loss both to me and the people, which I did not expect could ever be repaired. I tried to sleep, but I tried in vain; for sleep was fled from my eyes. I was in a burning fever, and, more and more thoughts still crowding into my mind, I perceived if this continued long it would affect my senses. But God took that matter into His hand, giving me, on a sudden, sound and quiet sleep.

"*Thur.* 5. About eight one came in from Newcastle, and told us, 'They were married on Tuesday.' My brother came an hour after. I felt no anger, yet I did not desire to see him. But Mr. Whitefield constrained me. After a few words had passed, he accosted me with, 'I renounce all intercourse with you, but what I would have with an heathen man or a publican.' I felt little emotion. It was only adding a drop of water to a drowning man, yet I calmly accepted his renunciation, and acquiesced therein. Poor Mr. Whitefield and John Nelson burst into tears. They prayed, cried, and entreated, till the storm passed away. . . . We could not speak, but only fell on each other's neck.

"John Bennet then came in. Neither of us could speak, but we kissed each other and wept. Soon after I talked with my brother alone. He seemed utterly amazed. He clearly saw I was not what he thought, and now blamed her only; which confirmed me in believing my presage was true, and I should see her face no more."

John Wesley was never more Christian than in his controversies. "If I had any strength at all," he wrote, a few years later in his Journal, "and I have none but what I have received, it is in forgiving injuries." This was no more than the bare truth. And those who tax Wesley with domineering arrogance forget his meekness under intolerable injuries.

Wesley was human, and his brother's behaviour left a wound. "For ten years" (he wrote a short time afterwards to a friend) "God has been preparing a fellow-labourer for me by a wonderful train of providences. . . . I fasted and prayed and strove all I could, but the sons of Zeruiah were too hard for me. The whole world fought against me, but, above all, my own familiar friend. Then was the word fulfilled, 'Son of Man, behold I take from thee the desire of thine eyes at a stroke.'"

He forgave, but he found it less easy to forget. A few days after John and Charles had been reconciled, Charles wrote, "George Whitefield and my brother and I are at one, a three-fold cord that shall no more be broken." This was taking things too lightly. The two-fold cord between John and Grace which Charles had broken, could never again be repaired.

"I can forgive," wrote John Wesley, "but who can redress the wrong?"

CHAPTER XXII

WESLEY'S MARRIAGE

"**I** CAN forgive, but who can redress the wrong?" Many, we may be sure, were anxious to try, and it is a little difficult to discover why Mrs. Vazeille, the widow of a London merchant, was eventually selected to fill the position which Grace ought to have occupied. Mrs. Vazeille is never mentioned in Wesley's Journal until he records the fact of his marriage, and even then she is not mentioned by name. We know that she nursed Wesley during an illness, but we also know that Wesley found it difficult to avoid proposing to any lady who nursed him with sympathy and care.

Wesley, having determined to marry, consulted nobody. "The Twelve Rules of a Helper" were ignored. This time he was taking no risks, and Mrs. Vazeille became Mrs. Wesley before his brother Charles had been apprised of his intentions.

A laconic entry in his Journal records the event:

"*Sat. Feb. 2*. Having received a full answer from Mr. Vincent Perronet, I was clearly convinced that I ought to marry. For many years I remained single, because I believed I could be more useful in a single than in a married state. And I praise God, who enabled me so to do. I now as fully believed that in my present circumstances I might be more useful in a married state; into which, upon this clear conviction, and by the advice of my friends, I entered a few days after."

The very next entry is as follows:

"*Wed. 6.* I met the single men, and showed them on how many accounts it was good for those who had received that gift from God to remain 'single for the kingdom of heaven's sake;' unless where a particular case might be an exception to the general rule."

It would be interesting to discover what happened on the 3rd, 4th and 5th, days for which there are no entries in the Journal. Perhaps, these unrecorded happenings might help to explain why Wesley's particular case was not an exception to the general rule.

Wesley's honeymoon correspondence, however, was more romantic than his Journal:

"Testworth, 42 miles from London.
March 28. 1751.

"My dear Molly,
Do I write too soon? Have not you above all the People in the world a Right to hear from me as soon as possibly I can? You have surely a Right to every Proof of Love I can give, and to all the little Help which is in my power. For you have given me even your own Self. O how can we praise God enough, for making us Helps meet for each other! I am utterly astonished at His Goodness. Let not only our Lips but our Lives shew forth His Praise!

If any Letter comes to you, directed to the Rev. Mr. John Wesley, open it: It is for yourself. Dear Love, Adieu!"

The honeymoon did not long remain unclouded, nor was Mrs. Wesley entirely to blame for what followed. She has, indeed, received rather less than justice from Methodist biographers, few of whom seem to realise the difficulties of her position. Wesley was forty-eight years of age when he married, and he had no intention of allowing marriage to interfere with the routine of his itinerant life.

"I cannot understand," he writes a few weeks after his marriage, "how a Methodist preacher can answer it to God to preach one sermon or travel one day less in a married than in a single state. In this respect surely 'it remaineth that they who have wives be as though they had none.'"

In other respects, Wesley's views on marriage would have met with the cordial approval of eastern husbands. A wife's duties, he remarked many years later in a little tract, can be summed up quite briefly. "She must recognise herself as the inferior of her husband, and she must behave as such."

He did not keep these views to himself. He communicated them with that "openness" on which he laid so much stress, to his wife. "Be content," he wrote to her, "to be a private insignificant person, known and loved by God and me. . . . Leave me to be governed by God and my conscience. Then shall I govern you with gentle sway and show that I do indeed love you even as Christ the Church."

But, of course, Mrs. Wesley did not want to be loved "as Christ the Church." Still less did she wish her husband to lavish his spiritual affections on other ladies.

Wesley, as we have seen, was firmly determined not to reduce the number of sermons which he preached or the number of days which he travelled, in consequence of his marriage. The number of ladies with whom he corresponded remained equally unaffected.

Wesley was one of the big public figures of the day, and as such, the natural target for a particular type of woman; the type which will go to almost any lengths in order to get on to terms of intimacy with prominent people. It was a tribute to Wesley's modesty that he never questioned the sincerity of those who sought his spiritual

advice. There were few people to whom, and few subjects
on which, he was not prepared to give advice, as his lady
friends discovered and played very skilfully on this weakness. "It is certain," writes his great friend Alexander
Knox, "that Mr. Wesley had a predilection for the female character; partly because he had a mind ever alive
to amiability, and partly from his generally finding in
females a quicker and fuller responsiveness to his own
ideas of interior piety and affectionate devotion. To his
female correspondents, therefore (as it strikes me), he
writes with peculiar effluence of thought and frankness
of communication. . . . To interesting females especially
this affection continually showed itself."

It did indeed, and that was what started the trouble.

Wesley was far from wise in his choice of those whom
he honoured with his more intimate confidences. Consider,
for instance, the case of Sarah Ryan.

Sarah Ryan was a woman of no education; indeed, at
one time she had been a domestic servant. She must have
possessed unusual charm, for she married in rapid succession three husbands without the intervening formali-
ties of a divorce or a funeral. Her first husband was already married to another woman, still alive, so it will be
perceived that Sarah Ryan had a genuine vocation for
trigamy.

She heard Wesley preach and was duly converted.
The problem of her three husbands perplexed her much
as a similar problem perplexed the Woman of Samaria.
Finally, she decided to retain the name of the second
husband, and to live apart from all three. Fortunately,
they were all out of the country, the Irishman whom she
first married, the Englishman, her second husband, and
the Italian, the last of the trio.

Wesley entertained for Sarah Ryan the same affectionate interest that a doctor will entertain for a patient

whom he has saved at death's door. It was a very interesting case, a museum piece, a shining example of the
efficacy of justification by faith. "If she abides in her
integrity, she is a jewel indeed:" he writes, "One whose
equal I have not yet found in England."

Wesley appointed her Bristol and Kingswood housekeeper. As such, she sat at the head of the table surrounded by preachers. This was too much for Mrs. Wesley on one of her visits to Kingswood. "The ———"
she exclaimed, "now serving you has three husbands
living."

Wesley was much upset by this painful outburst, but
his sympathy should have been more discreetly expressed:

"January 20, 1758.

"My Dear Sister,

How did you feel yourself under your late trial? Did
you find no stirring of resentment; no remains of your
will; no desire or wish that things should be otherwise? . . . I never saw you so much moved as you appeared to be that evening. Your soul was then greatly
troubled; and a variety of conflicting passions, love,
sorrow, desire, with a kind of despair, were easy to be
read in your countenance. . . . Most of the trials you
have lately met with have been of another kind; but it
is expedient for you to go through both evil and good
report. The conversing with you, either by speaking or
writing, is an unspeakable blessing to me. I cannot think
of you without thinking of God. Others often lead me
to him; but it is as it were, going round about; you bring
me straight into His presence. Therefore, whoever warns
me against trusting you, I cannot refrain; as I am clearly
convinced He calls me to it.

I am

Your affectionate brother.

JOHN WESLEY."

Mrs. Wesley had already formed the habit of ransacking her husband's private correspondence. She found an affectionate letter to Sarah Ryan, perhaps the very letter which has just been quoted. The sequel surprised Wesley. It will not surprise the reader.

"January 27. 1758.

"My Dear Sister,

Last Friday, after many severe words, my —— left me, vowing she would see me no more. As I had wrote to you the same morning, I began to reason with myself, till I almost doubted whether I had done well in writing, or whether I ought to write to you at all. After prayer that doubt was taken away. Yet I was almost sorry that I had written that morning. In the evening, while I was preaching at the chapel, she came into the chamber where I had left my clothes, searched my pockets, and found the letter there, which I had finished, but had not sealed. While she read it, God broke her heart; and I afterwards found her in such a temper as I have not seen her in for several years. She has continued in the same ever since. So I think God has given a sufficient answer, with regard to our writing to each other."

Sarah was, of course, properly sympathetic. About a fortnight later Wesley writes again:

"February 10, 1758.

"My Dear Sister,

Your last letter was seasonable indeed. I was growing faint in my mind. The being continually watched over for evil, the having every word I spoke, every action I did, small and great, watched over with no friendly eye; the hearing a thousand little, tart, unkind reflections, in return for the kindest words I could devise,—

Like drops of eating water on the marble,
At length have worn my sinking spirits down.

Yet I could not say, 'Take thy plague away from me;'
but only, 'Let me be purified, not consumed.' "

It is not clear from the context whether "thy plague"
refers to Mrs. Wesley. If so his prayer was answered.

One sympathises with Mrs. Wesley. It was bad enough
to know that her husband was writing such affectionate
letters to a repentant bigamist; but it was even more intolerable to be insulted by women who resented her
sudden pre-eminence. Grace Murray, as we have seen,
shrank before the storm which her intended marriage
with John Wesley aroused among the fairer members
of the societies, who had determined to make things unpleasant either for the favourite of the moment or for
the wife of their leader.

In a long, pathetic letter Mrs. Wesley summarises the
petty insults to which she had to submit. "Honest John
Pawson makes it his business to slander me, wherever
he goes. . . . In this way, he and J. Allen, and your old
quondam friend, Mary Madan, did all they could to
render my life bitter while at Bristol. Mary Madan, the
very day you set off from Bristol, said, 'I hope Mrs.
Wesley is not to stay here till Mr. Wesley returns, for,
if she does, this society will be quite ruined.' "

Again, wedlock with John Wesley meant the choice
either between almost unbroken loneliness, or between
continuous travelling in all weathers and at all seasons.
At first she chose to travel. She went with him to Ireland
and was "extremely sick." She sampled the great variety
of English weather from snow to storm, and was exposed more than once to mob hostility. On one occasion,
she and her husband were saved by taking refuge in a
coach. The mob continued to hurl stones through the
window. "But a large gentlewoman," writes Wesley,
"who sat in my lap screened me so that nothing came

near me." One would like to know, as Dr. Leger remarks, whether Mrs. Wesley was screened by a large gentleman sitting in her lap.

No wonder that the poor woman grumbles at the hardships of an itinerant life. Wesley was pained by her complaints, and read into them a criticism not of English roads and inns, but a slight to God Himself. I have already quoted the opening sentences of a letter (see page 232) which concludes as follows:

"By the grace of God I never fret; I repine at nothing, I am discontented with nothing. And to hear persons at my ear fretting and murmuring at everything is like tearing the flesh off my bones. I see God sitting upon His throne and ruling all things well. Although therefore I can bear this also, to hear His government of the world continually found fault with (for in blaming the things which He alone can alter, we in effect blame Him), yet it is such a burden to me as I cannot bear without pain; and I bless God when it is removed. The doctrine of a particular providence is what exceeding few persons understand, at least not practically, so as to apply it to any circumstance of life. This I want: to see God acting in everything and disposing all for His own glory and His creatures' good."

This was no idle boast. "God's in His Heaven, all's well with the world" is a sentiment which most of us are more ready to endorse at the end of a long day's march than when buffeted by sleet or rain. Wesley, on the other hand, was unaffected by discomfort. He was one of those

> "That ever with a frolic welcome took
> The thunder and the sunshine."

But it was a little unreasonable of him to expect his sea-sick wife "to see God acting in everything and disposing all for His own glory and His Creatures' good."

Wesley's correspondence with Ebenezer Blackwell throws light on the growing estrangement between himself and his wife. Blackwell was a prosperous banker, and remained one of Wesley's closest friends for over forty years. . . . His country seat at Lewisham was the resting place to which John and Charles often retired.

"During forty years, John Wesley found there," writes Mr. Eayrs, "what his aristocratic cultured nature appreciated keenly, . . . Most of his best literary work was done there."

In 1758, Wesley went to Ireland without his wife, leaving Mrs. Wesley free to pour out her troubles to Mr. Blackwell. "Really, Sir," writes Wesley, "when you have so eloquent a person at your elbow, and I am two or three hundred miles off, I have little to say; it may be time enough when I return to London."

And again:

"Permit me to add one word to you. You think yourself a match for her; but you are not. By her exquisite art she has already made you to think ill of two very deserving women. And you have been more than once puzzled, what to think of me. Nor could you help thinking me *a little* in the wrong."

To this Blackwell wrote a charming reply:

"I this day received your favour of the 2nd inst. I am sensible of my incapacity either to speak or to write in that lively, concise manner which you do; but as well as I can I will paragraph by paragraph give a direct answer to your letter. . . . I do not think myself a match for Mrs. Wesley, or any one that studies to deceive me; but I deny that by any exquisite art, she has made me think ill of two *very deserving* women. I suppose you mean Mrs. Ryan and Mrs. Crosby. The first I know nothing of, having never seen her in my life, and hardly ever (for I won't say never) spoken of her to anybody, but yourself. The latter I only know from the letter wrote by yourself, which she owned to me was her handwriting, and which I think will plainly prove to everyone of common sense, that she is not that *very deserving* woman you think her; and permit me to add, I am afraid she has too much art for my dear *friend*."

Wesley, who never resented honest disinterested criticism, replied at once:

"You have never yet spoken to me with more freedom than was agreeable to me. Your freedom is the best proof of your friendship. There are not many that will deal freely with me. Nor indeed are there many from whom I would desire it, lest it should hurt themselves without profiting me. But I do desire it of *you,* and do not doubt but it will profit me, as it has done in time past."

After making all due allowances for Mrs. Wesley, the fact remains that she cannot be described as a sympathetic character. To Wesley at least, she revealed a very unpleasant side. John Hampson, who was certainly not biassed in Wesley's favour, and who criticised him severely and unjustly, described a terrible scene in which Mrs. Wesley took part. "Jack, I was once on the point of committing murder. Once, when I was in the North of Ireland, I went into a room and found Mrs. Wesley foaming with fury. Her husband was on the floor, where she had been trailing him by the hair of his head; and she herself was still holding in her hand venerable locks which she had plucked up by the roots. I felt as though I could have knocked the soul out of her." [1]

In the course of January 1771, Mrs. Wesley left her husband, taking with her a bundle of Wesley's most private letters. There is a laconic entry in the Journal which records the fact that Wesley had neither left nor

[1] Tyerman, II. 110–111.

dismissed his wife, and that he did not intend to recall her.

"Wed. 23.—For what cause I know not to this day, —— set out for Newcastle, purposing 'never to return.' *Non eam reliqui; non dimisi; non revocabo.*"

As a matter of fact, Mrs. Wesley did return, but not for long. We find her riding with Wesley through Yorkshire the following year, but the reconciliation was not permanent, and again she left him. Shortly afterward, she committed an unpardonable act of treachery.

The Calvinistic controversy was at its height. The Calvinists were attacking Wesley with the foulest of abuse and with the cruellest of insults.

Mrs. Wesley invited some of the leading Calvinists to meet her, and read to them letters which she had stolen from her husband, letters which she had deliberately mutilated and edited, in order to read into purely spiritual letters an expression of ardent physical passion. These letters, in their mutilated form, were published in Toplady's paper, "The Gospel Magazine."

A few months later Mrs. Wesley was apparently anxious to return once again to her husband:

"Things standing thus," wrote Wesley, "if I was to receive you just now without any acknowledgment or reparation of these wrongs, it would be esteemed by all reasonable men a confirmation of what you have said.

"It may be asked, 'What Reparation are you either able or willing to make?' I know not if you are willing to make any. If you are, what reparation are you able to make? Very little indeed, for the water is spilled, and cannot be gathered up again. All you can do now, if you are ever so willing, is to Unsay What you have said. For instance, you have said over and over, That I have lived in adultery These Twenty Years. Do you believe this, or do you not? If you do, how can you think of living with such a Monster? If you do not, give it me under your hand. Is not this the least that you can do?" [1]

Presumably, Mrs. Wesley did not return. There is only one further reference to her in his Journal which runs as follows:

"1781, Friday, October 12.—I came to London, and was informed that my wife died on Monday. This evening she was buried, though I was not informed of it till a day or two after."

[1] "Wesley Studies," 103–104.

CHAPTER XXIII

WESLEY AS A POLITICIAN

"WESLEY" writes Dr. Hutton, Dean of Winchester, "was very like most clergymen; he knew very little indeed about politics or war, but thought he knew a great deal; and did not hesitate to express his opinions vociferously, but with inadequate knowledge. An opinion he expresses after a debate among the Peers is eminently characteristic:

> Tues. 25 (January 1785). I spent two or three hours in the House of Lords. I had frequently heard that this was the most venerable assembly in England. But how was I disappointed! What is a lord but a sinner, born to die!

"His political pamphlets, it must be admitted, are not of great value."

This may be true, but one, at least, of Wesley's political pamphlets had far-reaching results.

Before the American War began, he was inclined to sympathise with the Colonists. "I do not defend the measures which have been taken with regard to America," he wrote, "I doubt whether any man can defend them either on the foot of law, equity or prudence." This was in 1771.

Four years later, forty-eight hours before the battle of Bunker Hill, he wrote an open letter to the Premier, Lord North, in which he argued strongly against the expediency of trying to coerce the Americans by force of arms. He showed more military insight than the War

Office of his day, which perhaps need not surprise us, in his forecast of the probable result of such a war. He proved himself a true prophet when he warned Lord North that twenty thousand troops fighting half-heartedly three thousand miles from home could never hope to conquer a nation of men defending their wives and children and their homes. He warned Lord North that his own preachers in America had convinced him that the Colonists were not peaceful farmers "ready to run at the sight of a red coat" but a well-trained and well-disciplined body of volunteers "terribly united."

Four months later, Wesley enraged those who had applauded, and delighted those who had reviled his first pamphlet by a complete change of ground.

His "Calm Address to our American Colonies" is a defence of the English rights to tax the Colonists without giving them representation.

Four-fifths of the English people, as Wesley pointed out, had no parliamentary vote, and yet they were all taxed. The colonists, he urged, could hardly claim to have acquired by emigration rights which they did not possess before they left England. And so on, and so forth.

Wesley's argument, in its forensic emphasis of legal rights, was unlikely to appeal to one who had taken up arms for liberty. "You tell us," the colonists might have answered, "that four-fifths of the English people, though taxed, are unrepresented in Parliament. This seems to us an excellent reason for leaving England, but no reason at all for reproducing in the New World, the worst features of the old."

Wesley was attacked, not only for inconsistency, but also for plagiarism, for he had, in fact, abridged and curtailed Samuel Johnson's "Taxation no Tyranny," simplified the argument, and reproduced the result as his own without acknowledgment to Johnson. He was less perturbed by the charge of plagiarism; but indeed, to both charges Wesley made the same disarming reply. "As soon as I received new light myself, I judged it my duty to impart it to others."

Wesley was probably the only man in England with sufficient courage to try his hand at improving and editing the works of the Samuel Johnson, but the great man, so far from resenting this liberty, declared that he was flattered to have made so distinguished a convert, and compared himself to the philosopher who was unperturbed by the departure of his audience and declared himself well satisfied seeing that Plato, at least, remained.

Early in 1776, Wesley issued a "Seasonable Address to the inhabitants of New Britain." He deplored the fact that men of the same race and language should be engaged in "murdering each other with all possible speed" in order to decide a quarrel over a method of taxation.

Soon after this pamphlet had been published the Americans declared their independence, and Wesley's tone changed. In his pamphlet, "A Calm Address to the Inhabitants of England" which was published early in 1777, Wesley declared his loyal support of the Government. He was a sound Tory and a loyal Englishman, and had no sympathy with pacifists or with those who would have been called "Little Englanders" had this expression been invented in those days.

Wesley called upon those of his countrymen who were so ill-advised as to condone rebellion, to remember their duty, to "fear God and honour the King." He declared that he could no more continue in fellowship with any Methodist who had forgotten his duty to King and Country, than he could "with drunkards or thieves or whoremongers."

Wesley had come to the conclusion that in an energetic prosecution of the war lay the best hope of peace. He was bitterly attacked for this pamphlet, by none more bitterly than by his Calvinistic opponents.

Once the war was over, Wesley accepted the inevitable with good grace. He lost no time in picking up the dropped threads of friendship with the American Methodists. It is a tribute to his political sagacity, and to his unchallenged personal ascendancy that his influence with American Methodism was virtually unimpaired by the war. And, as we shall see, he was prepared on their behalf, to imperil one of the last links which still united him to the Church of his baptism, the Church to which he was still devotedly attached.

II

Wesley has been described as a Tory Democrat. He was certainly a Tory; He was certainly not a Democrat. So far, at least, as the Methodist Societies were concerned, he never made the least pretence of introducing democratic or representative government.

There are, of course, many people who pay lip service to democratic ideals in politics, while modelling themselves on Mussolini in private life. Wesley was, at least, consistent. He disliked demagogues, and distrusted the mob. In the famous Wilkes controversy which divided England, Wesley was on the side of the King, and not on the side of the people.

John Wilkes, the member for Aylesbury, described in his paper, "The North Britain," certain statements about the peace of 1763, which occurred in the speech from the Throne, as false. The King ignoring the accepted convention of ministerial responsibility, treated these criticisms as personal, and ordered Wilkes's prosecution on the grounds that his attack constituted a personal insult to the Sovereign. Wilkes who had returned to Paris was outlawed and expelled from the Commons.

The King's victory was dearly bought. The wiser statesmen in both Houses realised that the theory of ministerial responsibility was doomed if the Speech from the Throne was to be regarded "as the personal declaration of an irresponsible sovereign enforcing his own interpretation of libel by general warrant." [1]

In 1768, Wilkes was triumphantly returned for Middlesex and when he surrendered to his outlawry, a great mob demanded his release from prison in order that he might attend the House of Commons. The King determined that Wilkes should not take his seat in the House. Lord Weymouth, Secretary of State, prepared to use force. A detachment of guards, sent to preserve order, fired on the mob without provocation, killing five or six men. Wilkes charged Weymouth who had been in command with planning a massacre, and the House of Commons, which had learnt nothing and forgotten nothing, voted that Wilkes's remarks constituted a seditious libel, and once again Wilkes was expelled. He was twice re-elected and twice re-expelled. Eventually, the House of Commons with magnificent effrontery resolved that Luttrell who received 296 votes against the 1143 recorded for Wilkes "ought to have been returned" and duly declared him the elected member for Middlesex.

By this extraordinary decision, the House of Commons "had deprived an undisputed majority of the electors for Middlesex of a freehold right, secured by the law, while they had awarded the seat to a candidate with an undisputed minority of votes. . . . 'Wilkes and liberty!' was no longer the cry of a demagogue with a grievance. It became the watch-word of all who valued constitutional

---

[1] "England under the Hanoverians," by C. Grant Robertson, p. 232.

government, and who saw what would follow if the King's victory was not challenged until it was reversed."

Wilkes, the representative champion of popular rights, was the idol of the hour. Franklin, who was in England at the time, declared that Wilkes if he had had an irreproachable character, might easily have driven the King from his throne. But it was the King who possessed all the domestic virtues, whereas Wilkes was a notorious profligate. He enjoyed a great success with the other sex in spite of his devastating ugliness. His case is often cited in support of the consoling theory that women do not take much stock of masculine good looks. Even with men, Wilkes had a certain charm, and on a famous occasion he disarmed the Tory prejudice of Dr. Johnson, but the tone and temper of his public utterances were deplorable. He plumbed the lowest depths of demagogic virulence.

Wilkes's wife was a Methodist, and Wesley was, no doubt, influenced by the shameful treatment which she had received at his hands.

In 1768, Wesley published "Free Thought on Public Affairs" in which he defended the exclusion of Wilkes from the House of Commons. He expressed his undisguised alarm at the growing disloyalty to the Throne. He insists at great length on the domestic virtues and piety of the King, but the contrast beween a King who read his Bible and who was faithful to his wife and Wilkes who did not read his Bible, and who broke the Seventh Commandment, was not a very convincing reply to the champions of popular liberty.

Nor was it very plausible to suggest that the agitation against so good and so pure a King could only be explained by "French gold." This being, of course, the eighteenth century equivalent to the "Bolshevik gold" of our own times.

Burke, who of course disapproved of Wilkes's private character, had the insight to perceive that the universal disaffection was due to the corrupt and unconstitutional proceedings for which the King was responsible. Burke's pamphlet "Thoughts on the Causes of the Present Discontent" traced the evil to its source. Wesley merely skimmed about on the surface of the problem.

Two years later the Junius Letters elicited from Wesley another pamphlet, "Thoughts upon Liberty," an eloquent reply to those foolish people who were clamouring for greater freedom. The English, so Wesley urged, already enjoyed more religious liberty than any other people. No stronger proof could be adduced of Wesley's ingrained Toryism, than the fact that he accepted without demur the religious disabilities under which his own preachers laboured—for, of course, they had to apply for licenses under the Toleration Act, as if they had been Dissenters—and that he resented any clamour for the greater extension of religious liberties from which the Methodists would have been the first to benefit. Civil liberty Wesley defined as "the liberty to enjoy our lives and fortunes in our own way—to use our property, whatever is legally our own, according to our own choice," "and who," he cried, "is robbed of this liberty?"

"Of course, the Whig could reply," as Mr. Winchester justly points out, "that the liberty which leaves my property and my person in the control of a government that will not seat the representative I have elected, or, having seated him, manages by corrupt influence to silence his voice and stifle his vote, is not civil liberty at all. The truth is, Wesley's ingrained conservatism would not let him see the real question at issue."

Wesley, in fact, cared very little for the principle of representative government which was at stake. He had a profound respect for law and order, and he contrived to inspire most of his followers with these sentiments. He loved the common people, but he had seen too much of them on his travels to have any respect for their political sagacity. He may, perhaps, have dimly foreseen the ultimate outcome of all democracy, the lack of self-respect on the part of the elected, and the lowering of standards by the crude simplification of all issues into catch-words and slogans. He did not make the mistake of putting Methodism on a democratic basis, which is one of many reasons why Methodism has succeeded.

III

Wesley, indeed, would have liked the Wilkeses of our own day no better than their eighteenth century prototypes. Nor would he have been impressed by that modern form of altruism which consists in voting away other people's money rather than in giving away one's own. He would have agreed with Rousseau that no man has a right to attack the rich until he himself is so prudent and thrifty as to have no need of riches. Both Rousseau and Wesley acted on this principle.

Wesley's politics might fairly be described as ultra-conservative. He did not understand the meaning of democracy. It is true that he urged the rich to give all that they could, but he did not incite the poor to take all that they could. He was never tired of extolling the importance of good citizenship, the virtues of which are definitely fostered by the kind of religion in which Wesley believed. Wesley distrusted mysticism, chiefly because the mystic was an unsociable person only concerned to save his own soul. He never forgot a remark made to him in his Oxford days: "You cannot serve God alone. You must, therefore, find companions or make them. The Bible knows nothing of solitary religion."

"The gospel of Christ," wrote Wesley in his preface to the Hymn Book of 1739, "knows of no religion but social, no holiness but social holiness . . . this command have we from Christ, that he who loves God loves his brother also."

That was the crucial test, not mere emotion, nor mystic ecstasy, but "faith working by love,"—practical, helpful love which found expression in the best because the most Christian type of good citizenship. He never failed to apply the great test "By their fruits ye shall know them" to all forms of religious experience. Wesley succeeded in curbing the flood of emotion let loose by the Revival. "It was Wesley's triumph," as Mr. Rattenbury remarks, "that his people, who saw visions and dreamed dreams, and sang heady and intoxicating hymns, should have been so sober, and that his organization should have rapidly become one of the most steadying influences in English social life."

When Wesley began to preach in Cornwall, he soon learnt that even devout Methodists often sold smuggled goods, indeed, the practice of buying uncustomed goods was well-nigh universal in those parts. Wesley promptly called his people together at St. Ives, and told them plainly that they would have to choose between putting away "this abomination" or seeing his face no more. Wesley's firmness had the desired effect, not only in Cornwall, but throughout Methodism. To Joseph Benson, who had expelled a smuggler from the Newcastle society, he wrote, "You did right . . . fear nothing . . . you must, at all events, tear up this evil by the roots."

Wesley opposed with equal firmness yet another common practice of the day, giving and receiving bribes at elections. The Secret Ballot had not yet been introduced, and open voting naturally lent itself to the development of a trade in votes. Thanks to Wesley, the Methodists soon became known as the most incorruptible class of voters in the kingdom.

The high standard of financial integrity which Wesley succeeded in enforcing on the Societies, is illustrated by the following well-known story. A woman who was charged at the York circuit with a capital crime, had been dismissed twelve months earlier from the Methodist Societies. John Nelson was subpoenaed to explain why this woman had been dismissed. He read the Rules, and after he had finished reading the Rule which forbids members to take up goods without a probability of paying for them, he stopped and said, "My lord, this was my reason for dismissing this woman from the Societies to which I belong." The judge said, "Good morality, Mr. Nelson," and asked that the rest of the Rules should be read. After hearing them he said with emphasis to the court," "Gentlemen, this is true Christianity."

This story is often quoted with ingenuous pride by Methodist writers, who have overlooked a possible criticism—that these Rules were more suitable to a trading corporation than to a Christian Society.

Of course, the judge was pleased. No doubt he had regarded the Methodists with dark suspicion. The Societies, so his lordship had understood, were infected by enthusiasm. They were the sort of people, so he supposed, who were fond of quoting the more unsettling portions of the Sermon on the Mount. But he was wrong. Credit was the basis of honest trade, as apparently none realised better than the Methodists. His lordship nodded his solemn approval. "Good morality, Mr. Nelson." . . .

It has, of course, always been a weakness of English Protestantism to equate, as did the judge, twenty shillings in the pound with true Christianity. But it is difficult to understand Wesley's decision to exclude bankrupts from his Societies. "I gave a fair hearing," he writes in his

Journal, "to two of our brethren who had proved bankrupt; such we immediately exclude from our Societies, unless it plainly appears not to be their fault."

The bankrupt is very properly asked to resign from a West End Club, but a church is not a club and should cater for the insolvent no less than for the prosperous.

Father Knox once remarked that it might be safer to leave one's umbrella in a Methodist chapel than in a Catholic church. "The Methodists are a picked lot, whereas the Catholic Church must cater for sinners no less than for saints." From which it would appear that the "umbrella test" is yet another "note" by which the true Church may be recognised. Lord Salisbury declared that he never used the Athenaeum Club in wet weather, because the bishops had a weakness for new umbrellas. So that, whatever may be the case with Methodism, the Church of England, at least, possesses the "umbrella note" of the true Church.

The Catholic Church, as Father Knox implies, realises that she cannot afford to be too exclusive. In the course of nineteen centuries she had made at least one great discovery, she has learnt that sinners sometimes sin. And as a result Catholicism is more successful than Protestantism in retaining the affectionate loyalty of the erring. . . . Protestant congregations are composed, in the main, of respectable and moral members of society. A Methodist, for instance, who started keeping a mistress, would almost certainly be lost to his chapel. A Roman Catholic, under similar circumstances, might continue to hear Mass, and even if he ceased to be a practising Catholic his loyalty to the Church as an institution and his pride of membership—*Civis Romanus sum* in a new form—would probably remain unimpaired.

The Protestant is, perhaps, more consistent. He feels that to maintain the outward practice of religion, while living in defiance of the religious code, is hypocritical. The Catholic Church, with a deeper insight into psychology, encourages the sinner to maintain the unbroken habit of outward observance, for habits, once broken, are difficult to resume.

In other words, Catholicism recognises, as Wesley never recognised, the value of the "half-Christians" or the "almost Christians."

"When I was at Oxford," writes Wesley, "I was never afraid of any, but the almost Christian." But in this wicked world we have to be content with what we can get, and we may be pretty sure that we shall never get a nation composed entirely of "whole Christians." The "half-Christian" is, indeed, a very useful member of society, and so long as he continues to form the backbone of a state, Christian ethics will not be challenged. Sinners will continue to sin, but they will, at least, have the decency to refrain from preaching what they practise, a much more serious offence than failing to practise what they preach. Lip-service to Christian ideals is better than no service, platonic respect for the Christian code of morality is better than official contempt. Czarist Russia, which was officially Christian, was less corrupt, less immoral and infinitely less degraded than Bolshevist Russia which is officially atheistic.

Wesley, as he grew older, became more tolerant in his attitude to "half-Christians." In 1770, we find him writing to a friend:

"I have frequently observed that there are two very different ranks of Christians, both of whom may be in the favour of God,—a higher and a lower rank. The latter avoid all known sin, do much good, use all the means of grace, but have little of the life of God in their souls, and are much conformed to the world. The former make the Bible their whole rule, and their sole aim is the will and image of God. This they steadily and uniformly pursue, through honour and dishonour, denying themselves, and taking up their cross daily; considering one point only, 'How may I attain most of the mind that was in Christ, and how may I please him most?' "

It is, of course, easy to defend the stringent rule which Wesley imposed on his Societies, once we realise that Wesley never intended to found a Church, but only an Order within a Church.

An Order, like a Club, has every right to lay down its own conditions of membership, and to exclude those who break its rules, however severe. Only Roman Catholics with a "vocation" are admitted to the monastic Orders, and only Anglicans with a "vocation" were admitted to the Methodist Societies.

It is, however, comforting to reflect that Wesley recognised that even those Christians "of the lower ranks," who remained outside his Societies, might be "in the favour of God."

CHAPTER XXIV

THE MIND OF WESLEY

WESLEY was the most consistent, and the most inconsistent of men. The formula which helps us to resolve the paradoxical contradictions of his mental processes must be sought for in Wesley's complete self-surrender to God. Wesley had only one interest in life, to discover and to do the Will of God. There was only one goal, but he followed different routes to that goal. He was consistent in his aim, but often inconsistent in his methods. Wesley was credulous and sceptical, emotional and hard-headed, a convinced believer in reason and logic to a point, and still more convinced that personal experience and experimental religion were the ultimate tests of truth.

Wesley's life was built on two, and on only two fundamental beliefs, the existence of God and the verbal inspirations of the Bible.

In the Preface to his Sermons, he writes as follows:

"I have thought, I am a creature of a day, passing through life as an arrow through the air. I am a spirit come from God, and returning to God: Just hovering over the great gulf; till, a few moments hence, I am no more seen; I drop into an unchangeable eternity! I want to know one thing,—the way to heaven; how to land safe on that happy shore. God himself has condescended to teach the way: For this very end he came from heaven. He hath written it down in a book. O give me that book! At any price, give me the book of God! I have it: Here is knowledge enough for me. Let me be *homo unius libri*."

Wesley never allowed himself to question these fundamental beliefs, the existence of God and the verbal inspiration of Scripture. He never exposed these beliefs to his critical faculty.

Wesley's comments on the historical and scientific works of the period were always shrewd and often sceptical. Had he not restrained his own critical faculties, he might, perhaps, have become one of the leading free thinkers of the age, but he foresaw this possibility and shrank from the consequences of unfettered research. "I am convinced," he wrote, "from many experiments, I could not study to any degree of perfection, either mathematics, arithmetic, or algebra, without being a Deist, if not an Atheist."

He believed that God had confined our knowledge "within very narrow bounds; abundantly narrower than common people imagine, or men of learning are willing to acknowledge."

At the age of sixty-five he preached a sermon in which he said: "After having sought for truth, with some diligence, for half a century, I am, at this day, hardly sure of anything but what I learn from the Bible. Nay, I positively affirm, I know nothing else so certainly, that I would dare to stake my salvation upon it."

Wesley, like other great religious leaders, is open to the charge that he kept his religious and his secular beliefs in separate compartments. It is, however, possible to defend the consistency of those who decline, as Wesley declined, to submit the basis of belief on personal experience to the erosive action of reason. Wesley, had he desired to rationalise his distrust of reason, might have defended his attitude as follows:

"I can no more doubt the existence of God than the existence of the world around me. This belief, based on personal experience, belongs to a higher order of certitude than any certitude arrived at by purely intellectual processes. Human reason is impotent when faced with the problem of infinity, and if I try to rationalise my belief in God, my faith will weaken, and I shall lose my hold on the eternal verities. Nothing could be more fundamentally irrational than to sacrifice truth on the altar of human reason. Nothing could be more essentially rational than to maintain intact and uncorrupted, truths which have been revealed to me by God, even if my limited understanding is unable to justify those truths by the normal processes of logic."

The arguments will be familiar to those who have studied "A Grammar of Assent," in which Newman tries to discredit reason and to prove its inferiority to the "illative sense"; this being Newman's name for that sense "to which we owe our certainty of the great fundamental truths of religion," such as "the divine origin of the Church."

Wesley would have sympathised with Newman up to a point, but he would have been puzzled by Newman's anxiety to rationalise his distrust of reason. Newman could not rest, until he had justified by reason his attacks on reason. He was a philosopher, and felt the need for a philosophical justification of his attitude. Wesley contributed nothing to formal philosophy, and disliked abstract speculations. His genius was for practical religion. His instinct told him that he could best serve God by not inquiring too closely into the intellectual basis of his faith, but he would have been profoundly shocked by Newman's aggressive attack on intellect itself. And he would have had no sympathy with sentiments such as those expressed in the following passages from Newman's Sermons:

"—What is intellect itself as exercised in the world, but a fruit of the fall, not found in Paradise or in Heaven, nor in little children, and at the utmost but tolerated in the Church and only not incompatible with the regenerated mind . . ."

"Reason, I say, is God's gift; but so are the passions! Eve was tempted to follow passion and reason instead of her Maker, and she fell. . . .

"To conclude: let us learn from what has been said whatever gifts of mind we have, henceforth to keep them under, and to subject them to innocence, simplicity and truth. . . .

"Faith and humility consist, not in going about to prove, but at the outset confiding in the testimony of others . . ."

The sermons from which I have quoted were preached when Newman was an Oxford Don. The university congregations to which they were addressed were in no danger of undervaluing reason, and perhaps required to be reminded of the claims of faith. Wesley, on the other hand, spent much of his life trying to equip men of little or no education for the evangelical campaign. To depreciate intellect is an easy way to win the applause of the uneducated. The text about the wise and prudent is popular with those too lazy or too stupid to learn. Wesley had no patience with the smug self-satisfaction of pious ignorance, and he would have had little sympathy with certain anti-intellectual tendencies of our own day. To a lay preacher he writes: "You are in danger of enthusiasm every hour . . . if you despise or lightly esteem reason, knowledge, or human learning; every one of which is an excellent gift of God, and may serve the noblest purposes. I advise you, never to use the words, wisdom, reason, or knowledge, by way of reproach. On the contrary pray that you yourself may abound in them more and more."

Here again, we are confronted with one of Wesley's many inconsistencies. The man who dared not study algebra "to any degree of perfection" lest he should be led into atheism, made no attempt to limit the studies of his preachers. They were all urged to read and he devoted a great deal of his time to providing the Methodists with books on a wide choice of subjects. The man who said, "It is so far from being true that there is no knowledge after we have quitted the body, that the doubt lies on the other side, whether there be any such thing as real knowledge till then," did his best to increase the sum of human knowledge by adding 231 original works to current literature. He tried to educate and reform unenlightened pietism. "Oh for light and heat united!" he exclaimed with reference to a fanatic Methodist. He believed that the heat of emotion should be guided and controlled by the light of reason. "Here indeed," writes Dr. Leger, "we reach the crowning and most paradoxical contrast in Wesley's nature and destiny: this highly emotional man was preeminently rational, both in his personal conduct and religion. The revival, in which he took a leading part, and which to many minds only conveys the idea of wild excitement and imaginative aberration, will ever be remembered under the sedate name of Methodism: that is to say, in the Oxford days, strict adherence to University statutes and to all the observances of the Church, doing things at regular hours, and punctually meeting on appointed days to transact carefully planned business; in later years, an elaborate network of minute, punctilious regulations that cover and control, throughout vast tracts of land, the whole activity of the members of Societies, closely bring them and hold them together, and, even in the turbulent atmosphere of American independence and the French Revolution, keep them under the strictest moral, social, and spiritual discipline, however lawless their former lives,

unruly their instincts, erratic the flights of their often
diseased fancy. The secret of it almost entirely lies in
John Wesley's personal influence, in the exactness of his
mind together with the ascendancy of his will."

II

Wesley has often been criticised for his credulity, and
with justice. We must, however, make due allowances for
the mental climate of the age in which he lived. Protestantism had substituted the infallible Bible for the infallible Church. Biblical criticism was almost unknown, and
Geology had thrown no doubts on Genesis. It is therefore
absurd to condemn Wesley as credulous, merely because
he accepted the inerrancy of Scripture and deduced
logical conclusions from that belief. Wesley's statement
that to give up witchcraft is "in effect giving up the Bible"
is often quoted as an example of his credulity. It is, of
course, nothing of the sort. It is an example of his logical
mind. There are many references to witches and to witchcraft in the Bible. *If* you believe in the Bible, you must,
therefore, believe in the possibility of witchcraft. This is
a blunt statement of incontestable fact.

It is usual to explain Wesley's alleged credulity by the
impression made on his youthful mind by the ghost that
disturbed the Epworth vicarage. We may, of course, believe that the Epworth Poltergeist, and indeed, all the
phenomena recorded in the annals of psychical research,
can be explained without invoking the supernatural, or
you may hold that there remains a residue of facts which
can be explained on no other hypothesis. Where the evidence is so nicely balanced, there is no room for the accusation of credulity.

The true nature of credulity is admirably illustrated

in an amusing anecdote of Cardinal Manning. Mr. W. H. Mallock in his Reminiscences writes as follows:

"The Cardinal went on to assert as a fact, supported by ample evidence, that the Devil at such meetings assumes a corporeal form, sometimes that of a man, sometimes that of a beautiful and seductive woman, the results being frequent births in the prosaic world around us of terrible hybrid creatures, half diabolic in nature, though wholly human in form. . . . On this delicate matter he descanted in such unvarnished language that the details of what he said cannot well be represented here. Of the truth of his assertions he obviously entertained no doubt—in the Cardinal's character there must have been a vein of almost astounding credulity."

That evil spirits intervene in spiritualistic séances is a plausible, if not a probable hypothesis. It is a belief which has the official support of the Roman Catholic Church. That their intervention takes the picturesque form described by the Cardinal, is neither plausible nor probable, and a man who accepts such a belief without overwhelming evidence, may fairly be accused of credulity. For credulity is in effect a failure to understand the proper relations between proof and probability. Now Wesley did not accept the improbable unless supported by what he deemed to be adequate proof.

"One of the capital objections," he writes, "to all these accounts (of witchcraft) is this: 'Did you ever see an apparition yourself?' 'No, nor did I ever see a murder yet I believe there is such a thing . . . the testimony of unexceptionable witnesses convinces me both of the one and the other.'"

And indeed, to a man of Wesley's age, the legal evidence for the existence of murder would appear to be hardly stronger than the legal evidence for the existence of witchcraft.

Lecky in his "History of Rationalism" writes as follows:

"The subject of witchcraft was examined in tens of thousands of cases in almost every country in Europe, by tribunals which included the acutest lawyers and ecclesiastics of the age . . . the judges had no motive whatever to desire the condemnation of the accused; and as conviction would be followed by a fearful death, they had the strongest motives to exercise their power with caution and restraint. . . . The evidence is essentially cumulative . . . it is very difficult to frame a general rationalistic explanation which will not involve an extreme improbability. . . . If we consider witchcraft probable, a hundredth part of the evidence we possess would place it beyond the region of doubt. If it were a natural but a very improbable fact our reluctance to believe it would have been completely stifled by the multiplicity of proofs."

Wesley as I have said required proof before believing in the marvellous, and where that proof was lacking, he remained unconvinced.

"I was desired to read part of Bishop Pontoppidan's 'Natural History of Norway.' I soon found he was a man of sense, yet credulous to an extreme; and therefore I was the less surprised when I came to his craken and sea-serpent. Of the former (an animal a mile round, to which a poor whale is no more than a gudgeon) he gives no proof, or shadow of proof; nothing but vague, uncertain hearsays. 'Two sailors,' he says, 'made oath of seeing part of the latter, seven or eight folds of his back. But I did not talk with them myself; so I can lay little stress on their evidence.' They might be weak men; they might be frighted (yea, they were, by their own confession); or they might be men of no conscience. On any of which suppositions their testimony is nothing worth."

Wesley, indeed, fills his note-books and journals with penetrating and critical comments on contemporary works of history or science. Here, for instance, are his comments on Mr. Dobbs's "Universal History."

"I cannot believe," he writes "that there was ever such a nation as the Amazons in the world. The whole affair of the Argonauts I judge to be equally fabulous."

He riddled with criticism a contemporary "History of St. Patrick," Dr. Leland's "History of Ireland" and the Abbé Raynal's "History of the Settlements and Trade of the Europeans in the Indies." He declared, indeed, that the Abbé's account of China is "pure romance." Even Livy did not escape. "We want history, not romance," he remarked, "though compiled by Livy himself."

His criticisms of contemporary science are no less acute. He anticipates many of the results of modern research.

His remarks on the Count de Buffon's "Natural History" covered several pages, but I must content myself with two quotations to illustrate his shrewd common sense:

"Many of his thoughts are quite singular. So: 'The upper stratum of the earth, from which all animals and vegetables derive their growth and nourishment, is nothing but a composition of the decayed particles of animal and vegetable bodies.' (Vol. i., page 12.) Impossible! Was it composed of decayed animals and vegetables before any animal or vegetable had decayed?"

" 'All animals but man are totally void of reason.' (Page 367.) You may as well say, they are totally deprived of sight. Only put the plain word understanding for the equivocal word reason; and can you say, They are all totally void of understanding? No man dares affirm it.

"Smiles and tears are peculiar to the human species." (Page 376). No; stags, and even oxen, shed tears. An ox will weep much, if separated from his yoke-fellow."

Fanciful speculations unsupported by evidence never appealed to Wesley. The Anglo-Israelites and the Pyramidites of our day had, of course, their counterparts in eighteenth century England, but Wesley treated their prophecies with cheerful contempt:

"Preaching in the evening at Spitalfields on 'Prepare to meet thy God,' I largely showed the utter absurdity of the supposition that the world was to end that night. But notwithstanding all I could say, many were afraid to go to bed, and some wandered about in the fields, being persuaded that, if the world did not end, at least London would be swallowed up by an earthquake. I went to bed at my usual time, and was fast asleep about ten o'clock."

III

I have tried to show that Wesley was by nature sceptical rather than credulous, but it is impossible to deny that his critical faculty often deserted him in his dealings with human beings, and that his power of unmasking fallacies, and of discriminating between valid and worthless evidence, a power which made him a keen critic of books, vanished in his dealings with his fellow men. His brother's remark that John Wesley was born for the benefit of knaves has already been quoted. John was quite unperturbed by this admitted weakness, and he claimed that Charles, who believed nobody, was more often deceived than he who believed everybody, but he produced no evidence in support of this contention. "I have neither more nor less faith in human testimony," he remarks when he had turned fifty, "than I had 10 or 15 years ago, I could suspect every man that speaks to me, to be either a blunderer or a liar. But I will not. I dare not till I have proof."

As Dr. Leger wittily remarks: "The outcome of this charitable resolution was, that he took people at their face, or mouth, value."

IV

In some moods, Wesley professed a vast respect for logic. In other moods, with his characteristic inconsistency, he exposed the unreliability of logic when applied to fundamental religious problems.

A love of logic was one of the many good things that Wesley carried away with him from Oxford. Despite "what the little wits and pretty gentlemen affirm" logic is good, says Wesley, "for this at least, (wherever it is understood) to make people talk less; by showing them both what is, and what is not to the point; and how extremely hard it is to prove anything."

He strikes a lyrical note in his praise of logic: "I have since found abundant reason to praise God for giving me this honest art. By this, when men have hedged me in by what they called demonstrations, I have been many times able to dash them in pieces; in spite of all its covers, to touch the very point where the fallacy lay; and it flew open in a moment. This is the art which I have used with Bishop Warburton, as well as in the preceding pages. When Dr. E. twisted truth and falsehood together, in many of his propositions, it was by this art I untwisted the one from the other, and showed just how far each was true. At doing this, I bless God I am expert; as those will find who attack me without rhyme or reason . . . I have answered Bishop Warburton plainly and directly, and so untwisted his arguments that no man living will be able to piece them together."

True enough. Wesley's training in logic was the basis of his admirable controversial technique. He made good

use of logic for destructive controversy, but his attempts
to construct a logical foundation for one of his basic beliefs, the inerrancy of Scripture, are less successful. Here
is a sample from a tract which Wesley was sanguine
enough to describe as "a clear and concise demonstration
of the divine inspiration of the Holy Scriptures."

This tract concludes with the following trilemma:

"The Bible must be the invention either of good men
or angels, bad men or devils, or of God. 1. It could not
be the invention of good men or angels; for they neither
would nor could make a book, and tell lies all the time
they were writing, saying, 'This saith the Lord,' when it
was their own invention. 2. It could not be the invention
of bad men or devils, for they would not make a book
which commands all duty, forbids all sin, and condemns
their souls to hell to all eternity. 3. Therefore, I draw this
conclusion, that the Bible must be given by divine inspiration."

Was Wesley himself much impressed by this argument?
Probably not, for his real view of logic flashes out in the
characteristically sceptical comment that logic shows people "how extremely hard it is to prove anything."

His views of the natural limitations of "the mathematical method of reasoning," that is, the logical method, are
convincingly expressed in his criticisms of Ramsay's
"Principles of Religion":

"The treatise itself gave me a stronger conviction than
ever I had before, both of the fallaciousness and unsatis-
factoriness of the mathematical method of reasoning on
religious subjects. Extremely fallacious it is; for if we
slip but in one line, a whole train of errors may follow:
And utterly unsatisfactory, at least to me, because I can
never be sufficiently assured that this is not the case.

"The two first books, although doubtless they are a fine
chain of reasoning, yet gave me the less satisfaction, be-

cause I am clearly of Mr. H——'s judgment, that all this is beginning at the wrong end; that we can have no idea of God, nor any sufficient proof of his very being, but from the creatures; and that the meanest plant is a far stronger proof hereof, than all Dr. Clarke's or the Chevalier's demonstrations."

Wesley would probably have criticised in similar vein the "Summa Theologiae," or indeed any other product of scholastic theology. Wesley, like Tyrrell, "was a sincere believer in unreasoned reason and a profound sceptic as to the possibility of demonstration where concrete truth is in question."

"St. Anselm," writes Tyrrell, "perhaps constructs God as inevitably as Euclid constructs his equilateral triangle; but the constructions are equally bloodless. Who cares about his three-cornered equilateral God? These demonstrations make millions of infidels, and never a single believer."

This is, in effect, merely a flippant echo of Wesley's views of the limitation of "mathematical reasoning" when applied to religious problems.

William Law once warned Wesley against confusing Christianity and philosophy. Twenty years later, Wesley reminded Law of his own words:

"At a time when I was in great danger of not valuing the authority of Scripture enough, you made that important observation. 'I see where your mistake lies. You would have a philosophical religion, but there can be no such thing. Religion is the most plain, simple thing in the world. It is only "We love Him, because he first loved us." So far as you add philosophy to religion, just so far you spoil it.'"

From which it follows that metaphysical speculation can contribute nothing of value to religion. Human reason is incapable of adding to the facts about God which

He Himself has revealed to us in the Scriptures. Wesley disliked fanciful speculation. "I would not," he writes to his brother Charles, "read over Dr. Watts's tract for a hundred pounds. You may read it and welcome. I will not, dare not, move those subtle, metaphysical controversies."

And again, "Some years since I read about fifty pages of Dr. Watts's ingenious treatise upon the 'Glorified Humanity of Christ.' But it so confounded my intellects and plunged me into such unprofitable reasonings, yea, dangerous ones, that I would not have read it through for five hundred pounds."

Wesley, it is often said, contributed nothing of value to the formal philosophy of religion. Perhaps not, but to define the limits within which speculation and research are profitable, is in itself a valuable contribution.

Wesley was one of the first to emphasise the distinction between religion and theology. "What is faith?" he asks. "Not an opinion, nor any number of opinions be they ever so true. A string of opinions is no more Christian faith than a string of beads is Christian holiness." Wesley did not demand "a string of opinions" as a test of membership in the Methodist societies. To join the societies all that was necessary was a desire for salvation. To remain a member of the societies, all that was necessary was a high standard of personal conduct. Wesley imposed an ethical, but not a doctrinal test.

Wesley hated Calvinism with a holy hatred, but he made no attempt to exclude Calvinists from his societies so long as they refrained from aggressive and ill-mannered controversies. "The distinguishing marks of a Methodist," he wrote, "are not his opinions of any sort. Whoever imagines a Methodist is a man of such and such an opinion is grossly ignorant of the whole affair; he mistakes the truth totally. . . . Who is a Methodist according to your own account? I answer—A Methodist is

one who has, 'the love of God shed abroad in his heart
by the Holy Ghost given,' unto him, one who 'loves the
Lord his God with all his heart, with all his soul, and
with all his mind, and with all his strength.' "

In other words, Methodism was a personal and experimental religion. Life and experiment must come first. The
philosophy of a religion must be deduced from experience.
Wesley was always testing and reshaping his creed in
congruity with the practical requirements of the evangelical mission field. He would have agreed with Newman
that "it is our duty to act upon the rules given us until
we have reason to think them wrong, and to bring home
to ourselves the truth of them by their fruits on themselves." This, of course, is pure pragmatism, and William
James, who invented this "new name for old ways of
thinking," would have cordially endorsed Newman's contention that "life is not long enough for a religion of in-
ferences; we shall never have done with beginning if we
determine to begin with proof. Life is for action. If we
insist on proof for everything we shall never come to
action; to act you must assume, and that assumption is
faith."

This passage is, of course, a glorification of the experimental religion in which Wesley believed, but Wesley
would never have followed Newman to Rome, and Newman would have been very shocked by Wesley's contempt
for mere orthodoxy. "Orthodoxy or right opinion," writes
Wesley, "is at best but a very slender part of religion, if
it can be allowed to be any part at all. I will not quarrel
with you about my opinion. Only see that your heart be
right toward God, and that you know and love the Lord
Jesus Christ; that you love your neighbour, and walk as
your Master walked; and I desire no more. I am sick of
opinions; I am weary to hear them. My soul loathes this
frothy food. Give me solid and substantial religion; give

me an humble, gentle love of God and man, a man full of
mercy and good fruits."

Wesley's catholic tolerance was due partly to his in-
nate scepticism. He was sure of God's love, but of very
little else. No great religious leader has revised his own
views so readily and so often. He was always submitting
his views to the test of experience, and re-shaping them
in the crucible of life.

To appreciate Wesley's tolerance, you must remember
the age in which he lived. The following passage from his
Journal would not be in the least remarkable had it occurred in the journal of a modern Methodist:

"I read to-day part of the 'Meditations of Marcus An-
tonius.' What a strange heathen! Giving thanks to God
for all the good things he enjoyed! . . . I make no doubt
but this is one of those 'many' who 'shall come from the
east and the west, and sit down with Abraham, Isaac, and
Jacob,' while 'the children of the kingdom,' nominal Christians, are 'shut out.' "

The doctrine of exclusive salvation was still flourishing when Wesley wrote. It is dead to-day, for even in
the Roman Catholic Church that particular doctrine is
emasculated and civilized out of all recognition. The passage I have quoted is perhaps an echo of that confession
of faith which Zwingli wrote shortly before his death,
and in which he described that future "assembly of all the
saintly, the heroic, the faithful, and the virtuous," when
Abel and Enoch, Noah and Abraham, Isaac and Jacob,
will mingle with "Socrates, Aristides, and Antigonus,
with Numa and Camillus, Hercules and Theseus, the
Scipios and the Catos," and when every upright and holy
man who has ever lived will be "present with his God."

Bossuet, the great Catholic apologist, pounced on this
passage with unholy glee, and quoted it as a crowning
example of the damnable heresies of the Swiss reformers.

Luther, on reading it, despaired of the salvation of Zwingli.

Even in Wesley's day, Roman Catholics and Protestants would have indignantly repudiated the Zwingli conception of a paradise from which Socrates was not excluded, and to which "upright and holy men" were admitted irrespective of the theological tenets which they had professed during their lifetime.

But Wesley's tolerance, of course, was not confined to conceding that virtuous heathens may conceivably be saved. Human nature being what it is, it is easier to be broad-minded about virtuous heathens than about virtuous Christians who worship the same God in a different chapel. Wesley, in one of the finest sermons ever preached, enforced on his followers the vital duty of "charity, tolerance and the Catholic spirit."

"I dare not," said Wesley in the course of this sermon, "presume to impose my mode of worship on any other. I believe it is truly primitive and apostolical: But my belief is no rule for another. I ask not, therefore, of him with whom I would unite in love, Are you of my Church? of my congregation? Do you receive the same form of Church Government, and allow the same Church officers, with me? Do you join in the same form of prayer wherein I worship God? . . . Let all these things stand by; we will talk of them, if need be, at a more convenient season; my only question at present is this,—'Is thine heart right, as my heart is with thy heart?'"

Wesley then proceeds to explain that the man whose heart is right will always believe in God and in the Lord Jesus Christ, that his faith will be filled with the energy of love, that he will love his neighbour as himself, and that his love of God and of his neighbour will be shown forth by works.

He is careful to warn his congregation that by the

catholic spirit he does not mean speculative latitudinarianism. "It is not an indifference to all opinions: This is the
spawn of hell, not the offspring of heaven. This unsettled-
ness of thought, this being 'driven to and fro, and tossed
about with every wind of doctrine,' is a great curse, not
a blessing; an irreconcilable enemy, not a friend, to true
catholicism."

Nor does the catholic spirit mean "any kind of practical latitudinarianism. It is not indifference as to public
worship, or as to the outward manner of performing it."

The man of catholic spirit "having weighed all things
in the balance of the sanctuary . . . is clearly convinced
that *this* manner of worshipping God is both scriptural
and rational. Therefore, without rambling hither and
thither, he cleaves close thereto, and praises God for the
opportunity of so doing."

While condemning this form of worship, he does not
necessarily condemn all others.

Wesley repeats his formula, "if thy heart is right as
my heart is with thy heart?" and concludes:

"I do not mean, 'Embrace my modes of worship;' or,
'I will embrace yours.' This also is a thing which does
not depend either on your choice or mine. We must both
act as each is fully persuaded in his own mind. Hold you
fast that which you believe is most acceptable to God, and
I will do the same. I believe the Episcopal form of Church
government to be scriptural and apostolical. If you think
the Presbyterian or Independent is better, think so still,
and act accordingly. I believe infants ought to be baptized; and that this may be done either by dipping or
sprinkling. If you are otherwise persuaded, be so still, and
follow your own persuasion. It appears to me, that forms
of prayer are of excellent use, particularly in the great
congregation. If you judge extemporary prayer to be of
more use, act suitably to your own judgment. . . . I have

no desire to dispute with you one moment upon any of the preceding heads. Let all these smaller points stand aside. Let them never come into sight. 'If thine heart is as my heart,' if thou lovest God and all mankind, I ask no more: Give me thine hand."

One more quotation from a private letter which proves that John Wesley was prepared to practise the tolerance which he had preached.

Charles Wesley's favourite and most gifted son had just joined the Roman Catholic Church, and Charles was grievously distressed. "I doubt not," writes John Wesley to his brother, "that Sarah and you are in trouble because Samuel has 'changed his religion.' Nay, he has changed his opinion and mode of worship, but not his religion; it is quite another thing. . . . What, then is religion? It is happiness in God or in the knowledge and love of God. It is faith working by love, producing righteousness and peace and joy in the Holy Ghost. In other words, it is a heart and life devoted to God . . . Either he has this religion, or he has not; if he has, he will not finally perish."

CHAPTER XXV

LEX ORANDI: LEX CREDENDI

WESLEY believed in the Love of God, but he also believed in the hate of God. His heart assured him of God's universal love, freely offered to all mankind. His mind deduced from certain scriptural texts the grim doctrine of God's eternal hatred of those who fail to avail themselves of that offer.

At that time there was no challenge to the doctrine of eternal and intolerable punishment. The absence of revolt against this belief is one of the strangest facts in the history of Christianity, a fact which is only partially explained by the reluctance which Christians felt to doubt any belief apparently based on the explicit words of Christ Himself.

A few quotations from a sermon which John Wesley preached, may help the reader to realise what the world has gained by the virtual disappearance of one of the most revolting doctrines that ever darkened the mind of man.

Wesley chose for his text: "Where their worm dieth not, and the fire is not quenched" (Mark ix: 48) and he begins as follows:

"Every truth which is revealed in the oracles of God is undoubtedly of great importance. Yet it may be allowed that some of those which are revealed therein are of greater importance than others, as being more immediately conducive to the grand end of all, the eternal salvation of men. And we may judge of their importance, even from this circumstance,—that they are not mentioned once only in the sacred writings, but are repeated over and over. A remarkable instance of this we have with regard to the awful truth which is now before us. Our blessed Lord, who uses no superfluous words, who makes no 'vain repetitions,' repeats it over and over in the same chapter, and, as it were, in the same breath. So (verses 43, 44), 'If thy hand offend thee,' if a thing or person, as useful as a hand, be an occasion of sin, and there is no other way to shun that sin,—'cut it off: It is better for thee to enter into life maimed, than having two hands to go into hell, into the fire that never shall be quenched: Where their worm dieth not, and the fire is not quenched.' So again (verses 45, 46), 'If thy foot offend thee, cut it off: It is better for thee to enter halt into life, than having two feet to be cast into hell, into the fire that never shall be quenched: Where their worm dieth not, and the fire is not quenched."

These opening sentences seem to me highly significant. To the Calvinists, Wesley had replied: "What will you prove by Scripture? That God is worse than the Devil? It cannot be. Whatever that Scripture proves, it never can prove this. . . . No Scripture can mean that God is not love, or that His mercy is not over all His works."

And yet, in the sermon that follows, Wesley steels himself to prove that God's mercy is *not* over all His works. What is the key to this inconsistency? Wesley apparently discriminated between doctrines that Scripture appeared to prove but which he rejected because they conflicted with the central fact of his experience—the love of God, and doctrines which he dared not reject because they were based on the *ipissima verba* of Christ. Wesley was not a Higher critic. He did not question the accuracy of St. Mark's report of Christ's words. Still less was he prepared to take their eschatological imagery in any but the most literal sense.

Wesley continues:

"And let it not be thought, that the consideration of these terrible truths is proper only for enormous sinners. How is this supposition consistent with what our Lord speaks to those who were then, doubtless, the holiest men upon earth?"

In other words, Wesley did not believe in a Hell tenanted only by Judas Iscariot and Nero. Even the apostles were in danger of hell, from which it was a fair deduction, that the number of the damned greatly exceeded the number of the saved.

Wesley then proceeds to describe in detail the sufferings of the damned. Few more impressive sermons can have been preached on this threadbare theme. In the Middle Ages "the crescendo of pious exaggeration," writes Dr. Coulton, "shows that Hell terrors had a tendency to wear dull among the multitude. The general mind tended to grow callous from excessive friction upon one spot." Familiarity robbed the most lurid imagery of its power to frighten the imagination. Repetition blunted the effectiveness of well-worn phrases. Wesley's unique sermon on Hell is impressive precisely because it is unique. He hated the theme too much to return to it. He never made use of Hell-Fire to precipitate a conversion, and even in this sermon he does not pile on the horrors. "Let us keep to the written word," he says. "It is torment enough to dwell with everlasting burnings."

And as the careful argument unfolds, we feel that every word is weighed, every phrase considered, and every deduction wrung from Wesley by relentless logic. The absence of rhetoric heightens the effect. Here is nothing but a reasoned summary of facts, beyond all possibility of dispute. From the major premiss, the words of

Christ which Wesley takes for his text, the argument moves irresistibly forward to its pitiless conclusion.

The punishment of the damned, says Wesley, will be "either pœna damni,—'what they lose;' or pœna sensûs,— 'what they feel.' "

First as to the pœna damni "the punishment of loss."

"The soul loses all those pleasures, the enjoyment of which depends on the outward senses. The smell, the taste, the touch, delight no more. . . . All the pleasures of the imagination are at an end. . . . And nothing new, but one unvaried scene of horror upon horror. . . . At the same instant will commence another loss,—that of all the *persons* whom they loved . . . for there is no friendship in hell." And finally, the damned have lost their place "in Abraham's bosom, in the paradise of God."

And yet the negative punishment of loss is mild and merciful indeed compared to the positive punishment of pain.

Secondly as to the fire of hell. Away with all reassuring delusions.

"It has been questioned by some, whether there be any fire in hell; that is, any material fire. Nay, if there be any fire, it is unquestionably material. . . . Does not our Lord speak as if it were a real fire? . . . Is it possible then to suppose that the God of truth would speak in this manner, if it were not so? Does he design to fright his poor creatures? What, with scarecrows? with vain shadows of things that have no being? O let not any one think so! Impute not such folly to the Most High!

"But others aver, 'It is not possible that fire should burn always. For by the immutable law of nature, it consumes whatever is thrown into it. And, by the same law, as soon as it has consumed its fuel, it is itself consumed; it goes out. . . . But here is the mistake: The present laws of nature are not immutable. . . . Therefore, if it

were true that fire consumes all things now, it would not
follow that it would do the same after the whole frame
of nature has undergone that vast, universal change.

"I say, if it were true that 'fire consumes all things
now.' But indeed, it is not true. Has it not pleased God
to give us already some proof of what will be hereafter?
Is not the Linum Asbestinum, the incombustible flax,
known in most parts of Europe? If you take a towel or
handkerchief made of this (one of which may now be seen
in the British Museum), you may throw it into the hottest
fire, and when it is taken out again, it will be observed,
upon the nicest experiment, not to have lost one grain of
its weight. Here, therefore, is a substance before our eyes,
which, even in the present constitution of things, (as if it
were an emblem of things to come,) may remain in fire
without being consumed."

Paley in his argument from design clearly overlooked
the true significance of asbestos.

Then follows a terrible illustration, an illustration
which proves that Wesley did not run away from the
grimmest consequences of his beliefs. The sermon is
nothing if not logical.

"So even the tortures of the Romish Inquisition are
restrained by those that employ them, when they suppose
the sufferer cannot endure any more. They then order
the executioners to forbear; because it is contrary to the
rules of the house that a man should die upon the rack.
And very frequently, when there is no human help, they
are restrained by God, who hath set them their bounds
which they cannot pass, and saith, 'Hitherto shall ye come,
and no farther.' Yea, so mercifully hath God ordained,
that the very extremity of pain causes a suspension of it.
The sufferer faints away; and so, for a time at least,
sinks into insensibility. But the inhabitants of hell are
perfectly wicked, having no spark of goodness remain-

ing. And they are restained by none from exerting to the uttermost their total wickedness. Not by *men;* none will be restrained from evil by his companions in damnation: And not by *God;* for He hath forgotten them, hath delivered them over to the tormentors. And the devils need not fear, like their instruments upon earth, lest they should expire under the torture. They can die no more: They are strong to sustain whatever the united malice, skill, and strength of angels can inflict upon them. And their angelic tormentors have time sufficient to vary their torments a thousand ways. How infinitely may they vary one single torment,—horrible appearances! Whereby, there is no doubt, an evil spirit, if permitted, could terrify the stoutest man upon earth to death."

And so he goes on, draining the last drop of horror from his theme.

"This is the sting of all! As for our pains on earth, blessed be God, they are not eternal. There are some intervals to relieve and there is some period to finish them. When we ask a friend that is sick, how he does; 'I am in pain now,' he says, 'but I hope to be easy soon.' This is a sweet mitigation of the present uneasiness. But how dreadful would his case be if he should answer, 'I am all over pain, and I shall never be eased of it. I lie under exquisite torment of body, and horror of soul; and I shall feel it *for ever!'* Such is the case of the damned sinners in hell. Suffer any pain, then, rather than come into that place of torment!"

II

In Wesley's day, torture was still legal in Europe, the Inquisition had not been abolished, and women were still burnt alive in England for petty treason. It was there-

fore easier for Wesley than it would be for us to believe
in a Creator who deliberately employed torture.

The belief in Hell still lingers in the Church of Rome.
But the modern Catholic so far from regarding hell as
an asset feels acutely embarrassed by this distressing
liability which he has inherited from the past. He does his
best to explain away a doctrine which it is no longer possible to defend. The medieval theologian was made of
stouter stuff, and he delighted in emphasising the select-
ness of heaven and the overcrowded condition of hell.
But hell is not what hell was. Depopulation is proceeding
at such a pace that Judas will soon be, not only the oldest
but also the only inhabitant. And we are beginning to have
our doubts even about Judas. "We must state first,"
writes Father Martindale, S.J., in a masterly collection of
Catholic essays entitled "God and the Supernatural,"
"that it is not revealed how many souls, or what proportion, are lost. Most Catholics would say that we know
that Judas is." Note the "most."

Father Martindale also points out (p. 323) that the
unquenchable fire and the undying worm are plainly meta-
phorical. Nothing is left of the old horrors,

> "Esse aliquid manes, et subterranea regna,
> Nec pueri credunt."

The most interesting evidence of the complete change
in theological climate is the evidence unconsciously provided by modern writers on Wesley.

The one sermon of Wesley's which is never quoted is
the one sermon which exposes his deepest convictions on a
subject which, to Wesley, seemed of supreme importance.

Not only have we ceased to believe in Wesley's hell,
but we find it almost impossible to realise that this belief
was ever real to Wesley.

Mr. Rattenbury, for instance, dismisses Wesley's sermon on hell as unimportant. This sermon has "more literary ornament and is less alive than most. It is an artificial document."

Mr. Rattenbury is a good judge of literature—witness his masterly chapter on the hymns as literature—and he is certainly competent to discriminate between literary ornament and genuine thought. But I am sure that if he re-reads this sermon, he will be tempted to revise his hasty verdict. He must have forgotten that it was in this very sermon that Wesley condemned severely Dante's attempt to embroider by "literary ornament" the horrors of hell. The subject, he says, is too awful "to wander from the written word." The whole weight of evidence is against Mr. Rattenbury's view that this sermon is "an artificial production." Every line represents real thought on a subject of vital importance. Mr. Rattenbury, I feel, would have been more impressed by the tragic sincerity of this sermon, had he not been biassed by a sub-conscious conviction that no man as good and as great as Wesley could ever have entertained so absurd and revolting a belief.

It is true, of course, that Wesley only preached one sermon on hell, and that he virtually made no use of hell-fire in his appeals to the unconverted. But it is a mistake to base any arguments on Wesley's reticences. He never allowed his mind to dwell for long on distressing subjects which he was unable to remedy. He focussed his attention on reparable tragedies. His practical sense forbade him to waste effort or even emotion on matters which he could not control or alter. Hell was a fact beyond his control, and he faced the grim implications of that belief, and passed on to consider how best to reduce the number of the damned, and to increase the number of the saved.

His reticence on the subject of hell proves no more than the reticence on the subject of his wife or of his brother's death. Weeks passed after his brother died before he alluded to him in his Journal, and even then, the references are brief and few, as are also (for a very different reason) the Journal references to his wife.

There is one significant sentence in the sermon, a sentence which has already been quoted. After alluding briefly to the variety of fanciful tortures described in Dante's "Inferno," Wesley adds: "But I find no word, no tittle of this, not the least hint of it in all the Bible. And surely this is too awful a subject to admit of such play of imagination. Let us keep to the written word. It is torment enough to dwell with everlasting burnings."

"It is torment enough" . . . No wonder that Wesley turned with relief to the thought of God's love, and though his imagination was too sensitive to permit him "to dwell with everlasting burnings" and though hell was seldom alluded to in his sermons, the urge to save himself and others from "the worm that dieth not" and "the fire that is not quenched" remained the supreme motive of his life.

And, of course, if men were governed by reason, those who believed in a hell such as the hell which Wesley described, would have consecrated, as did Wesley, every waking thought to the problem of saving themselves and their fellow men from eternal agony. Against a background of never-ending torture, even the most seductive of temptations would soon lose their savour. The life that Wesley lived was, indeed, the logical result of the beliefs that Wesley held. But few men are as logical as Wesley, and so the sinners who profess to believe in hell continued cheerfully to sin just as if Hell was nothing more than the product of a diseased imagination.

It is, of course, a commonplace that mankind is not much impressed even by the most appalling of prospects unless they are imminent. After the Messina earthquake, the inhabitants set to work to rebuild the town on the same place, and so perhaps it is not very surprising that the belief in hell, even when it was most general, never succeeded in eclipsing the gaiety of nations.

Wesley was different. He had no use for half-beliefs. If he accepted a doctrine, he behaved as if that doctrine was true. Undoubtedly he believed in hell, and undoubtedly this belief had a profound influence on his life.

The very word "Hell" has lost most of its old meaning, and it is necessary to emphasise the fact that throughout this chapter the word "Hell" is used in its original and proper sense as the place of *eternal* torment. . . . The belief in hell is revolting, not because it implies punishment beyond the grave, but because it postulates a Creator who punishes with no hope of improving (since *eternal* punishment can have no remedial effect) and who is not sufficiently civilized to reject torture as a mode of punishment.

It is necessary to distinguish carefully between the belief in eternal punishment and the belief in punishment beyond the grave, that is, between Hell and Purgatory. Christ undoubtedly taught that those who persisted in sin should suffer in the next world, but there is nothing in His teaching which compels us to believe in the eternity of such suffering. The cardinal blunder of Protestantism was to reject purgatory and to retain hell. The Protestants should have rejected hell and retained purgatory.

For if hell is a fiction but purgatory a fact, it is still worth while to avoid the punishment of sin, a punishment which is often extremely unpleasant in this world, and which, for all we know to the contrary, may be even more unpleasant in the next.

It is all a question of proportion. To what extent should we treat this life merely as probationary, and this world *merely* as a platform from which trains start labelled "Heaven" or "Hell" respectively. That these aspects are important, no Christian would deny. Are there, however, no legitimate interests in life excepting those which concern our eternal welfare?

To this question, Wesley would have replied with an unhesitating negative. He was not a Puritan by temperament. He had a natural love for beauty. He loved children and young people, and good talk and friendly folk, and all the innocent trivialities of life. But his belief in that particularly horrible hell, described in his sermon, coloured his outlook on beauty and on innocent pleasure. Among the Moravians, Wesley had heard a sour German proverb—"He that plays when he is a child will play when he is a man." And neither holidays nor play were included in the programme at his Kingswood school. The unfortunate children at this school rose at 4 A. M. both in winter and in summer.

Wesley believed, that from childhood upward every energy should be focussed, and every moment concentrated to the one thing which mattered in life, salvation from the wrath to come.

A gloomy, depressing creed. A creed which divorces grace from nature, and joy from God. It is a tribute to the sanity of John Wesley that in spite of his creed, he remained tolerant and large-minded. It would be a mistake to exaggerate, but it would be foolish to deny the influence on his life and character of the foulest doctrine ever grafted on the parent stem of the Catholic faith.

I agree with Mr. Rattenbury that "the dominant message of the Wesleys was love, not hell," but it is unsound to reject Wesley's belief in hell as a mere side issue in its effect on his life.

III

Life is full of problems, but to Wesley all of them admitted a simple solution. There were few situations in life which were not covered either by Christ's explicit commandments, or a logical deduction from those commandments. Useless to talk to Wesley of the "responsibilities of wealth," or to try to enlist his sympathetic consideration of the problems of the Christian's attitude towards money. "Where is the difficulty?" he would have replied, "provide yourself and your dependents with simple food and plain raiment, and give away the balance."

Wesley practised what he preached. As a young man he discovered that he could live on twenty-eight pounds a year. When his income was fifty pounds a year, he gave away twenty-two pounds, and when his income was four hundred (as it was often from the sale of his books) he still lived on twenty-eight and gave away the balance. "Money never stays with me," he wrote, "it would burn if it did. I throw it out of my hands as soon as possible, lest it should find a way into my heart."

This would not seem the proper place to quote his famous reply to the Commissioners of His Majesty's Excise who had written circular letters to all such persons who they had reasons to suspect had plate, etc. :

"Reverend Sir,
As the Commissioners cannot doubt but you have plate, for which you have hitherto neglected to make an entry, they have directed me to send you the above copy of the Lords' order, and to inform you that you forthwith make due entry of all your plate, &c.
N.B. An immediate answer is desired."

Wesley answered:
"Sir,
I have two silver tea-spoons at London, and two at Bristol. This is all the plate which I have at present;

and I shall not buy any more, while so many round me want bread.

I am, sir,

Your most humble servant,
JOHN WESLEY."

Wesley continued to hope that all Methodists and to assume that all his preachers would act on these principles. So far as his preachers were concerned, his confidence was justified. John Jane, when he died, left the sum of one shilling and four pence, and his realisable property did not suffice to pay his funeral expenses.

"One shilling and four pence—enough for any unmarried preacher of the gospel to leave to his executors," such was Wesley's curt comment.

Wesley's rule for the proper use of riches was extremely simple. "Gain all you can. Save all you can. Give all you can." To quote from his sermon on Riches, "I do not say, 'Be a good Jew; giving a tenth of all you possess.' I do not say, 'Be a good Pharisee; giving a fifth of all your substance.' I dare not advise you to give half of what you have; no, nor three quarters; but all!"

And by "all" Wesley meant everything that remained over after simple food and raiment had been provided for the household.

"O ye Methodists, hear the word of the Lord!" he continues. "I have a message from God to all men, but to *you* above all. For above forty years I have been a servant to you and to your fathers. And I have not been as a reed shaken with the wind: I have not varied in my testimony. I have testified to you the very same thing, from the first day even until now. But 'who hath believed our report?' I fear not many rich."

Wesley was both pained and puzzled by the fact that the richer members of his congregations did not at once perceive that his arguments were irresistible. "Lay not up for yourselves treasures upon earth. . . . How do the Christians observe what they profess to receive as a command of the Most High God? Not at all! . . . It might as well be still hid in its original Greek, for any notice they take of it. In what Christian city do you find one man of five hundred who makes the least scruple of laying up just as much treasure as he can?"

It was all so perplexing. Wesley always expected people to be guided by reason. The reasons against laying up treasures upon earth are unanswerable and yet the Methodists continued to grow richer and richer.

Shortly before he died, Wesley made his Will. "I left no money to anyone," he writes in his Will, "because I have none." This was not strictly accurate, for he named three preachers who had to divide "whatever money remains in my bureau and pockets at my death."

His books, of course, represented a valuable property. The first charge on his property both before and after his death, was the annuity to Charles Wesley's widow and children. John Wesley during the course of his long life gave away the balance in charity.

His attitude to class distinctions is yet another illustration of his indifference to all standards, excepting the eternal.

"Rank," said Jowett, "is not a dispensation of providence, but it is a fact," and it is a fact of which even devout Christians are seldom unaware.

There are many references to the "genteel vulgar" in Wesley's Journal, and few of these references are polite. "O how hard it is to be shallow enough for a polite audience" . . . "showed as serious attention as if they had been poor colliers." . . . "Even the genteel hearers were decent." . . . "The congregation was very large and very genteel and yet as well-behaved as any I have seen in

the kingdom." . . . "How unspeakable is the advantage
in point of common sense which poor people have over
the rich." . . . "I dined at Lady ——'s. We need great
grace to converse with great people. From which, therefore (unless in rare instances), I am glad to be excused.
Horae fugiunt et imputantur. Of these two hours I can
give no good account."

That, of course, was the trouble. For every hour that
passed, Wesley felt it necessary to account as accurately as
a bank clerk for every pound paid over the counter. Had
it not been for this haunting sense of vocation, Wesley
would have thoroughly enjoyed the society of his own
class. Few men were more capable of appreciating what
he himself has called, "that easy, open affability which is
almost peculiar to Christians and persons of quality." He
was a welcome guest on those rare occasions when he
condescended to waste time with his friends. Samuel
Johnson who disapproved of the Methodists, and who
was an excellent judge of social qualities, once said to
Boswell, "I hate to meet John Wesley; the dog enchants
me with his conversation, and then breaks away to go
and visit some old woman." On another occasion he remarked, "Wesley's conversation is good, but he is never
at leisure. He is always obliged to go at a certain hour.
This is very disagreeable to a man who loves to fold his
legs and have his talk out, as I do."

Wesley's irritable comments on the rich cannot be explained by envy. He did not envy them their wealth, for
such money as he himself made, he gave away. He had no
reason to envy them their birth or breeding, for he himself was a scholar and a gentleman. The rich irritated him
because of his unresting preoccupation with the problem
of salvation. He felt about the rich a kind of despair.
Their money made it so easy for them to exploit the

pleasures of this world, that it was difficult to persuade them to concentrate on the business of salvation from the wrath to come.

That a godly washerwoman is more deserving of respect than a godless duke, is a sentiment to which most Christians might pay lip service. Wesley acted on this belief. "Love," he says, "supplies all the essentials of good breeding without the help of a dancing master," a sentiment which is incorrect, and which on other lips than Wesley's would be, not only incorrect, but insincere. Wesley viewed life *sub specie aeternitatis;* the only hierarchy in which he was interested was the hierarchy of saints. The sentiment against miscegenation has perhaps been implanted in us by Nature for some good purpose. Wesley was so obsessed by the eternal values that he completely lost all sense of class barriers. Grace, whom he was so anxious to marry, had been a servant. Mrs. Ryan, to whom he wrote the most intimate letters, letters entirely free, perhaps too free, of any hint of social barriers between them, began life as a servant, and ended as housekeeper at Kingswood. The fact that Grace had been a servant did not weigh with Wesley once he had convinced himself that Grace was a saint.

Charles Wesley would never have fallen in love with a servant. In his attitude to class distinctions he was as conventional as John was unconventional. Charles married into a County family. His home was visited by many of the great people of the day, largely because of the musical precocity of his children. When Samuel, his most gifted son, decided to join the Church of Rome, no less a person than the Duchess of Norfolk was chosen to break the news to Charles.

John Wesley told people exactly what he thought of them, but there was no hint of condescension in his "openness." He never patronised people. "It was his habit," we are told, "to raise his hat to any poor person who thanked him for his kindness." Charles, on the other hand, could never forget that the lay preachers were not his social equals. He *tried* to be kind, and that, of course, started the trouble. "God is my witness," he wrote to Cennick, "how *condescendingly* loving I have been to you." John Wesley never *tried* to be kind, but the kindness of his heart pierces through the most abrupt of his letters. He did not spare people when he thought them wrong but the preachers who resented Charles's condescending manner accepted without question John Wesley's quiet assumption of autocratic powers.

IV

Wesley's sense of vocation would have been less oppressive had there been no other element in his religion than the love of God. The belief in the love of God was, indeed, the central fact in Wesley's religious life, but he also pictured God as a stern Judge Who would demand an account of every minute and moment of his life.

Wesley, in fact, had only one scale of values, the scale on which the eternal values were also marked. He applied this measure ruthlessly to every detail in life. He had an instinctive love for stately gardens and parks, and he never mentions a nobleman's country seat in his Journal without some reference to the fact that the nobleman will some day have to account for his trusteeship at the Great Assize. These remarks are not common form, the routine rhetoric of a revivalist. To Wesley, the Last Assize was the most real of menaces. He could not see the most innocent of hobbies excepting against a background of eternal judgment. He could not even leave hell behind him during a visit to the British Museum.

"At the desire of some of my friends, I accompanied

them to the British Museum. . . . Seven huge apartments are filled with curious books, five with manuscripts, two with fossils of all sorts, and the rest with various animals. But what account will a man give to the Judge of quick and dead for a life spent in collecting all these?"

If you believe as Wesley believed in hell, you would rejoice, as Wesley rejoiced, at the death of a young child. This is logical; for if the child lived he might go to hell, whereas if he dies he is bound to go to heaven. What are a few years more or less of life in comparison with the slightest risk of an eternity of frightful torment?

"When old Mr. Perronet heard that his favourite child, the stay of his old age, was dead, he broke into praise and thanksgiving to God, who had 'taken another of His children out of this evil world!' "

Mr. Perronet [1] had lost four children. No wonder he found it difficult to moderate his transports of joy. And so by a perfectly natural transition we reach the verse in a once-favourite hymn:

> "Ah, lovely appearance of death!
> What sight upon earth is so fair?
> Not all the gay pageants that breathe
> Can with a dead body compare!"

This hymn is Charles Wesley's, and the verse in question was quoted by John Wesley in his Journal with every mark of approval.

The attitude which finds expression in the verse just quoted, long since removed from Methodist hymn books, if, of course, rank blasphemy against the Lord and Giver of Life. I am sure that Wesley would never have approved of such an ungracious response to all the beauty and wonder and romance of life, had he not been obsessed by a false scale of values.

---

[1] Author of "All Hail the Power of Jesus' Name."

V

Tyrrell, in a brilliant essay, has pointed out the contrast between the Lex orandi and the Lex credendi, the law of prayer and the law of belief; in other words, the contrast between religion and philosophy. "In the measure," he writes, "that God is dehumanized by philosophy, he becomes unreal and ineffectual in regard to our life and conduct."

There is no place for a dehumanized God, or even for a dehumanized devil in Wesley's scheme. He was no philosopher, for the distinguishing mark of a philosopher is an intolerance of fundamental contradictions. Wesley simply dismissed the reconciliation of such contradictions from his thoughts. "If anyone asks, 'how is God's foreknowledge consistent with freedom,' I plainly answer I cannot tell." This, at least, is honest, and quite as helpful as the bewildering and unconvincing arguments with which the great scholastics vainly endeavoured to reconcile free-will and foreknowledge. And doubtless, had Wesley been challenged to reconcile the love of God with the existence of an overcrowded hell, he would have made a similar reply. Had the Calvinists, however, retorted, "If anyone asks how God's love is consistent with the gospel of election, I plainly answer I cannot tell," Wesley would have been very far from satisfied with the answer.

Indeed, the dictinction between Calvin's and Wesley's doctrine of Hell does more credit to Wesley's heart than to his head. "Wesley will not believe," writes Leslie Stephen, "that God has foredoomed nineteen out of twenty of His creatures to eternal torture. The escape, of course, from the dilemma is made by the doctrine of free-will. The doctrine that God has made twenty creatures with the certainty that nineteen will be damned, and has left the selection to chance, is capable to being presented in such a way as to avoid the shock to the imagination."

Wesley was a brilliant debater, so long as he was defending the outposts of his creed. . . . He scored a dialectical triumph in his controversy with Bishop Lavington. Indeed, he could defend Methodism far more convincingly than Christianity itself, for he had no ready answer to certain criticisms of the substance rather than the accidentals of his faith. A good illustration is his evasive, feeble reply to a certain "infidel" who perplexed Wesley with a line of attack, familiar to all students of Hyde Park theology.

"I spent an hour and a half in beating the air, in reasoning with an infidel of the lowest class. He told me roundly, 'I believe God is powerful, and the Creator of all things. But I am nothing obliged to Him for creating me, since He did it only for His own pleasure. Neither can I believe that He is good, since He can remove all the evil in the world if He will. And therefore it is God's fault, and no one's else, that there is any evil in the universe.' "

"I am afraid we could not deny this," adds Wesley, "if we allowed that God had 'from all eternity, unchangeably determined everything, great and small, which comes to pass in time.' "

No wonder that Wesley "beat the air" if he could think of no better reply than this. "My friends the Calvinists," said Wesley in effect, "would be dreadfully puzzled to answer your criticisms." "Of course, they would," retorts "the infidel of the lowest class," "but what is your answer?" Wesley does not tell us.

Our friend the low-class infidel would have found much to criticise in Wesley's Journal. He would not, for instance, have drawn the same conclusions as Wesley from the following anecdote which Wesley records in his Journal.

"James Thompson, sailor on board the *George and Mary*, a Sunderland collier, bound for Middleburgh, in September last, met with a gale of wind, which wrecked her on the Baynard Sands, off the coast of Zeeland. Here every soul perished save himself, who was for three days and three nights floating on a piece of the wreck, with another man dead by his side, in which time the poor sufferer had lost his senses. At length he was taken up by the *Dolphin* packet, and escaped safe to land. He is now willing to return hearty thanks to God, and to proclaim his deliverance to the world, that all who hear it may 'praise the Lord for His goodness, and declare the wonders that He doeth for the children of men.' "

The low-class infidel might have cynically suggested that "the children of men" is an obvious misprint, the plural being out of place, seeing that James Thompson was the sole survivor. The infidel might add, that widows and children of those who had perished in the wreck might be reluctant to join with James "in praising the Lord for His goodness" and might even cavil at James's immodest assumption that Omnipotence had intervened on his behalf while leaving James's shipmates to the mercy of wind and wave.

These are the kind of offensive comments which infidels of the lowest class are in the habit of making.

Wesley's solution, of course, was to give God all the credit when things went right, and the devil all the blame when things went wrong. Indeed, if the devil had not existed, Wesley would have found it necessary to invent him, if only to relieve the Creator of all responsibility for shipwrecks and similar disasters. Had Wesley been asked to draft an insurance policy, he would certainly never have permitted the phrase "Act of God" to stand. He would have substituted "Act of the Devil."

The omnipotence and omniscience of God is a belief

which belongs to philosophy rather than to religion; for religion depends for its vitality on an unacknowledged and unofficial dualism. Wesley believed in good and in evil spirits, and he was firmly convinced that Satan was not only very active, but very powerful.

Once when Wesley was out driving, the horses bolted down a steep hill. The coachman was thrown from his box, and after a succession of miraculous escapes the horses pulled up within a few yards of a precipice. "I am persuaded," writes Wesley, "that both good and evil angels had a large share in this transaction; how large we do not know, but we shall know hereafter." In other words the evil angels made the horses bolt, and the good angels pulled the horses up, a very fair division of labour.

Here is another instance. "Sat. June 15. As I was coming downstairs, the carpet slipped from under my feet, which, I know not how, turned me round, and pitched me back, with my head foremost, for six or seven stairs. It was impossible to recover myself till I came to the bottom. My head rebounded once or twice from the edge of the stone stairs. But it felt to me exactly as if I had fallen on a cushion or a pillow. Dr. Douglas ran out, sufficiently affrighted. But he needed not. For I rose as well as ever; having received no damage, but the loss of a little skin from one or two of my fingers. Doth not God give His angels charge over us, to keep us in all our ways?"

Perhaps, but a Guardian Angel who allowed a venerable old gentleman of eighty to tumble downstairs deserves little credit for a belated effort to minimise the result of his negligence. But alas, the good spirits whom one meets in Wesley's Journal, are all alike. Well-meaning, but not very alert. England, it has been said, wins only one battle in every war—the last. The same might be said of Wesley's good spirits.

"Satan," says Wesley, "is never allowed to go beyond his chain." This remark repeated more than once in his Journal, admirably expresses one of his fundamental beliefs. You picture Satan undismayed by frequent failures, bounding out to the full length of his chain. He frightens the horses, and gets the carriage nicely started towards the precipice, trips up an elderly saint and sends him down towards the bottom of the stairs; but at the last moment the good spirit intervenes, and Satan's intended victim escapes "with no damage but the loss of a little skin from one or two fingers."

The same restraining influences, so Wesley believed, are at work in the case of inanimate agencies of evil. He describes the fire which damaged the Kingswood school and adds:

"It is amazing that so little hurt was done; for the fire which began in the middle of the long room . . . was so violent that it broke every pane of glass but two in the window. . . . What can we say to these things but that God had fixed the bounds which it could not pass?"

VI

On a parapet at Bern, there is a tablet recording a marvellous escape from death. A runaway horse leapt this parapet, and fell 150 feet on to the cobbled road below. The horse was killed, but the rider escaped. The tablet marks the spot where the horse leapt into the street below, and records the rider's gratitude to Almighty God for his miraculous escape.

You may divide religious people into those who, like Wesley, would pass this story without comment, and those who, like Tyrrell, would wonder why Omnipotence should not have intervened a little earlier, thus saving not only the rider, but the horse from destruction. Clearly it would be easier to stop a horse bolting than to arrange a safe landing for a rider after so tremendous a fall.

But though it is difficult to find an answer to the criticisms of a Tyrrell, it is the paradox of religion, that if results be any test of truth, and sterile failure any criterion of falsehood, it is the Wesleys rather than the Tyrrells who must be awarded the verdict of religious history. Religion owes as much to men like Wesley as philosophy owes to men like Tyrrell, and whereas Wesley founded, directed, and led to victory one of the greatest of religious movements, Tyrrellism is always subtly disintegrating. It can, at best, provide intellectuals with an excuse for continuing to believe. It can bring no rest to those that travail and are heavy laden.

No man realised this more clearly than Tyrrell himself. He knew—none better—that prayer and praise must be simple, instinctive and anthropomorphic, and he defended this thesis in the brilliant essay which supplies the title to this chapter. Tyrrell was clever enough to discover and to explain the laws of prayer, but he was too clever to pray. "Knowledge about a thing," writes William James, "is not the thing itself . . . to understand the causes of drunkenness, as a physician understands them, is not to be drunk. A science might come to understand everything about the causes and elements of religion . . . and yet the best man at this science might be the man who found it hardest to be personally devout. . . . If religion be a function by which either God's cause or man's cause is to be really advanced, then he who lives the life of it, however narrowly, is a better servant than he who merely knows about it, however much."

The last sentence is a sentence which sums up the difference between Wesley and Tyrrell. Tyrrell explained and Wesley put into practice the lex orandi. Wesley's spiritual life was fed by prayer, Tyrrell gradually drifted into scepticism. In regard to prayer, he wrote: "I do not *know;* and that is the simple truth. As to my practice, I have gradually grown dumb. . . . Overmuch reflection on religious problems is bound to produce this paralysis. To use forms helpfully one must be able to forget that they are forms; to approach God as 'Our Father,' one must not be too conscious of the hopeless inadequacy of the appellation."

One more concluding extract from Tyrrell, an extract which provides an illuminating contrast to Wesley's simple view of Satan and his chain:

"A curiously weak letter of J. H. Newman to Father Whitty has come out in 'The Standard'—the same fanatical conviction of a *special* mission and work that appears so often, and yet a recognition of the thwarting circumstances as the 'Blessed Will of God.' What a muddle! If the work impulse is from God, the obstacle is from God only in the sense that the devil is from God. Is the devil's will the 'Blessed Will of God'? The truth is that God never pokes His finger into the clockwork one way or the other, and faith of the best sort begins with an appreciation of that ruthless fact."

Faith of the best sort? No. For dynamic faith is based on the conviction that Satan is not allowed to go beyond his chain, and that God is well able to repair the limited damage which Satan can inflict on the clockwork.

CHAPTER XXVI

WESLEY'S CLOSING YEARS

IN an earlier chapter I have quoted a vivid pen-portrait of Wesley as a young man. We owe to John Hampson the best description of Wesley in his closing years. Hampson was one of Wesley's preachers, but he left the connexion in 1784 because he had not been included by Wesley in the "Legal Hundred." He was, therefore, by no means prejudiced in Wesley's favour. Hampson writes:

"The figure of Mr. Wesley was remarkable. His stature was of the lowest, his habit of body in every period of life the reverse of corpulent, and expressive of strict temperance and continual exercise; and, notwithstanding his small size, his step was firm, and his appearance, till within a few years of his death, vigorous and muscular. His face, for an old man, was one of the finest we have seen. A clear, smooth forehead, an aquiline nose, an eye the brightest and the most piercing that can be conceived, and a freshness of complexion scarcely ever to be found at his years and impressive of the most perfect health, conspired to render him a venerable and interesting figure. Few have seen him without being struck with his appearance; and many, who have been greatly prejudiced against him, have been known to change their opinion the moment they were introduced into his presence. In his countenance and demeanour there was a cheerfulness mingled with gravity; a sprightliness which was the

335

natural result of an unusual flow of spirits, and was yet accompanied with every mark of the most serene tranquillity. His aspect, particularly in profile, had a strong character of acuteness and penetration. In dress he was a pattern of neatness and simplicity. A narrow, plaited stock, a coat with small upright collar, no buckles at the knees, no silk or velvet in any part of his apparel, and a head as white as snow, gave an idea of something primitive and apostolical; while an air of neatness and cleanliness was diffused over his whole person."

Wesley's last years were very happy. Active opposition to his work practically ceased after 1770. The bishops contented themselves with a few growls in their pastoral charges and a sullen neutrality. "I have no power to interfere," said the Bishop of London, when asked to stop John Wesley preaching in a London church, "Mr. Wesley is a duly ordained clergyman, and under no ecclesiastical censure."

The Evangelical Revival had begun to leaven the Church; many of the clergy approved of Wesley's ideals even if they did not like his methods. Moreover, the English have always been quick to recognise the value of any movement which raises the standard of personal probity. The authorities gradually discovered that the Methodist Societies, which had been founded in almost every large town, so far from doing any harm, had transformed numbers of drunkards and wastrels into decent, sober citizens. The Methodists indeed were distinguished from their neighbours, less by their opinions than by their conduct.

And doubtless, the personal character of John Wesley was a factor of vast importance in this revolution of opinion. There was no man in the three kingdoms so universally revered as John Wesley in his closing years. He, himself, was much puzzled by this change of front.

On January 26th, 1777, he writes in his Journal, "I preached again at Allhallows church, morning and afternoon. I found great liberty of spirit; and the congregation seemed to be much affected. How is this? Do I yet please men? Is the offence of the Cross ceased? It seems, after being scandalous near fifty years, I am at length growing into an honourable man!"

Five years before his death he wrote in his Journal, "The tide is now turned; so that I have more invitations to preach in churches than I can accept of."

II

During Wesley's lifetime, Methodism was a religious autocracy centering in Wesley himself. He appointed the preachers at the Annual Conference, and the Conference consisted, as Wesley explained, of those preachers he invited to confer with him. In the eyes of the law the Conference had no legal existence, and no right to acquire or to hold property such as the Methodist chapels.

In 1784, Wesley drew up a list of a hundred preachers who were nominated permanent members of the Conference with powers to fill vacancies in this body. Wesley defined their rights and duties, and enrolled this "deed of declaration" in the Court of Chancery. The Conference thus acquired legal existence and legal control of the chapels and other property of the Societies. The Conference continued to meet every year.

A list of no less than a hundred and ninety-nine preachers had originally been submitted to Wesley. The old autocrat quietly drew his line through ninety-nine names and summoned the remaining hundred. There was much heart-burning among the rejected. John Hampson, whose son wrote a bitter attack on Wesley, was one of the ninety-nine, and as stated above, in consequence of his exclusion from the Legal Hundred, he left the Methodist connexion.

III

The Deed of Declaration did not, of course, render separation inevitable. The Church of England might conceivably have discovered a modus vivendi with Methodism, and have placed Methodism as a separate order within the Church, had Wesley not assumed episcopal powers in order to provide the American Methodists with ordained ministers.

When the American colonies declared their Independence, all but six of those preachers who had been sent to America by Wesley, returned to England. Asbury, the greatest figure in American Methodism, alone remained.

Asbury had gone to America in 1771, and had been appointed by Wesley Superintendent of all the itinerant preachers in America in 1772.

Like Wesley, Asbury was a great itinerant. There is a magnificent statue of Asbury on horseback, in America, a statue which makes one regret that John Wesley has not been similarly represented.

Asbury often rode 4,000 miles in the year on the worst possible roads. He pushed his way to the very frontiers of civilization.

His difficulties were, of course, greatly increased by the war, and were not a little aggravated by Wesley's various tracts on that subject. Most of the Methodists in America sympathised with the colonists, but they were all compromised by Wesley's anti-American attitude.

Asbury throughout maintained an attitude of strict neutrality, but in war time the neutral is often regarded as a dishonest enemy without the courage of his convictions. In Asbury's case, the suspicion was intensified by his refusal to take the Oath of Allegiance on the ground that this Oath involved an undertaking to fight against England if so required. His life was often in danger at the hands of patriotic mobs, and on one occasion a shot narrowly missed hitting him.

But the charm of his personality and the saintliness of his character gradually overcame all opposition, and as a result of his untiring labours, American Methodism actually increased during the war. Asbury modelled the Constitution of the American Societies on English Methodism. The American Methodists were divided into Societies and Classes governed by Wesley's Rules, and controlled by an annual Conference which assigned itinerant preachers to the different circuits.

Before the war, the American Methodists, like the English, were theoretically members of the Church of England. They depended on the Anglicans for their Sacraments. After the outbreak of the war, the American Methodists did not include among their number a single ordained priest. The Anglican clergy, being loyalist in their sympathies, had left the country at the first sign of hostilities.

The American Methodists were, therefore, virtually left without Anglican priests or ordained ministers, and before long, they became insistent in their demands that their own preachers should assume the powers to administer the Sacraments. Asbury, however, persuaded them to take no overt action until they had had an opportunity of consulting with Wesley. Wesley urged them to be patient, and to avoid irregularity.

Wesley realised that the American Methodists could not be left indefinitely without the Sacraments. He did his best to persuade the Bishop of London to ordain one of his own ministers who was on his way to America, but the Bishop refused.

Thirty years before, Wesley had read a book which had made a great impression on him in spite of the youth of its author and the immaturity of its views. In his Journal for January 20th, 1746, he wrote as follows:

"Mon. 20.—I set out for Bristol. On the road I read over Lord King's 'Account of the Primitive Church.' In spite of the vehement prejudice of my education, I was ready to believe that this was a fair and impartial draught; but, if so, it would follow that bishops and presbyters are (essentially) of one order, and that originally every Christian congregation was a church independent of all others!"

Wesley had often quoted Lord King's views with approval since then, but he had never ventured to act on them. Many Methodists would have preferred to receive the Sacraments from their own lay preachers rather than from the hostile parish priests, but Wesley had always refused to tolerate such a radical departure from Church usage. The administration of the Sacraments by an unordained minister was, in his own words, "a sin which he dared not tolerate." Nor did he ever contemplate ordaining any of his own itinerant preachers.

Even in the case of the American Methodists, it is possible that his reluctance to assume episcopal functions might never have been overcome, but for the persistence of Dr. Coke, an ambitious and determined person who knew exactly what he wanted and meant to get it. Coke was an Anglican priest, an Oxford graduate, and a man of marked ability. Wesley had decided to send him to America, but he would not consent to go unless Wesley conferred upon him episcopal powers. "The more maturely I consider the matter," he wrote to Wesley, "the more expedient it appears to me that the power of ordaining others should be received by me from you, by imposition of your hand."

Wesley, once his scruples had been conquered, wasted no time on discussion. The Journal entry recording the most momentous decision in the early history of Methodism is characteristically laconic:

"Sept. 1, Wed.—Being now clear in my own mind, I took a step which I had long weighed in my mind, and appointed Mr. Whatcoat and Mr. Vasey to go and serve the desolate sheep in America.

Thur. 2.—(I added to them three more; which I verily believe, will be much to the glory of God.)"

Wesley's Journal, as I have elsewhere remarked, is highly significant in its reticences and omissions. It was not his practice to write at length about distressing or embarrassing subjects. In his brief Journal reference to the consecration of Dr. Coke, he omits to mention the name of the man whom he had made a bishop, just as in his brief Journal reference to his marriage he omits to record the name of the woman he had made his wife.

In both cases, the omission was doubtless due to a feeling of uneasiness.

The fact is, of course, that Wesley was torn between his devotion to the Church and his respect for Church order on the one side, and his practical realisation of the need of the American Methodists on the other side. Having done what he could to provide for the American Methodists, he would have been only too glad to have given no further thought to the manner in which their needs had been met.

Dr. Coke proceeded to America bearing with him Wesley's consecration certificate which read as follows:

"To all whom these Presents shall come.
John Wesley, late Fellow of Lincoln College in Oxford,

Presbyter of the Church of England, sendeth with greeting.
Whereas many of the People in the Southern Provinces of
North America who desire to continue under my care, and
still adhere to the Doctrines and Discipline of the Church of
England, are greatly distrest for want of ministers to administer the Sacraments of Baptism and the Lord's Supper according to the usage of the said Church. And whereas
there does not appear to be any other way of supplying them
with ministers. Know all men that I John Wesley think myself to be providentially called at this time to set apart
some persons for the work of the ministry in America.
And therefore under the Protection of Almighty God, and
with a single eye to his glory, I have this day set apart,
as a superintendent, by the imposition of my hands and
prayer (being assisted by other ordained ministers), Thomas
Coke, Doctor of Civil Law, a Presbyter of the Church of
England, a man whom I judge to be well qualified for that
great work. And I do hereby recommend him to all whom it
may concern as a fit person to preside over the Flock of
Christ. In testimony whereof I have hereunto set my hand
and seal this second day of September in the year of our
Lord one thousand seven hundred and eighty four.

JOHN WESLEY."

Coke, after arriving in America, ordained Asbury as
deacon and Presbyter, and then as Associate Superintendent, in other words as an associate Bishop, thereby
laying the foundation of the American Methodist Episcopal Church.

IV

Charles Wesley was acutely distressed by his brother's
action. He summed up his views in a bitter quatrain:

> "How easy now are Bishops made
>   At man or woman's whim;
> Wesley his hands on Coke hath laid,
>   But who laid hands on him?"

To Dr. Chandler, he wrote as follows:

"After having continued friends for about seventy years and fellow-labourers for above fifty, can anything but death part us? I can scarcely yet believe it, that in his eighty-second year my brother, my old intimate friend and companion, should have assumed the episcopal character, ordained * elders, consecrated * a bishop, and sent him to ordain our lay preachers in America. I was then in Bristol at his elbow; yet he never gave me the least hint of his intention. How was he surprised into so rash an action? He certainly persuaded himself that it was right.

"Lord Mansfield told me last year that ordination was separation. This my brother does not and will not see; or that he has renounced the principles and practice of his whole life.

"Thus our partnership is dissolved, but not our friendship."

John Wesley, in the course of his reply, said:

"I firmly believe, I am a scriptural episkopos as much as any man in England or in Europe. (For the uninterrupted succession I know to be a fable, which no man ever did or can prove.) But this does in nowise interfere with my remaining in the Church of England; from which I have no more desire to separate than I had fifty years ago. . . . What then are you frightened at? I no more separate from it now, than I did in the year 1758. I submit still (though sometimes with a doubting conscience) to mitred infidels. I do indeed vary from them in some points of doctrine, and in some points of discipline; by preaching abroad, for instance, by praying extempore, and by forming societies; but not a hair's breadth further than I believe to be meet, right, and my bounden duty. I walk still by the same rule I have done for between forty and fifty years. I do nothing rashly.

* Note the distinction. I have followed Charles Wesley by referring throughout to the *consecration,* not the *ordination* of Coke.

It is not likely I should. The high-day of my blood is over. If you will go hand in hand with me, do. But do not hinder me, if you will not help. Perhaps, if you had kept close to me, I might have done better. However, with or without help, I creep on. And as I have been hitherto, so I trust I shall always be,

Your affectionate friend and brother,
JOHN WESLEY."

To this, Charles answered:

"I do not understand what obedience to the bishop you dread. They have left us alone and left us to act just as we pleased these fifty years. At present some of them are quite friendly towards us, particularly towards you. The churches are all open to us, and never could there be less pretence for a separation. . . . I thank you for your intention to remain my friend. Herein is my heart as your heart. Whom God has joined let not man put asunder. . . . We have taken each other for better for worse, till death do us part—no, but unite eternally."

There was no real breach between the brothers. Charles attended the Conference in 1786, and was pleased by a Resolution, passed without one dissentient, to continue in the Church of England.

"My brother and I," he wrote, "and the preachers were unanimous for continuing in the old ship."

V

That bishops and priests belonged to the same order in the Primitive Church is a view which had the support of that great biblical scholar, Bishop Lightfoot, who held that "the episcopal office did not arise out of the apostolic by succession, but out of the presbyteral by localization.

Recently, Mr. Cohu defended a similar thesis with great skill." [1]

But all this has really no bearing on Wesley's consecration of Dr. Coke. Be the origin of the episcopacy what it may, the fact remains that for many centuries bishops had been regarded as an order superior to, and entirely distinct from the order of priests. On this point, every branch of the Catholic Church is at one. Historians may differ in their theories as to the origin of the various orders which compose the British peerage, but a viscount who conferred an earldom on a brother viscount would be regarded as highly eccentric by the House of Lords. No church which claimed to have preserved the apostolic succession could be expected to condone the attitude of any priest, however distinguished, who invited another priest into a back parlour and invested him with episcopal powers.

As Canon Overton remarks, "If bishops and priests were of the same order, what was the object of one priest laying his hands upon a brother priest? What could Wesley confer upon Coke, which Coke might not equally well have conferred upon Wesley?"

Wesley's action was, of course, hopelessly inconsistent. He was torn between his love for the Church of England and his realisation of the practical needs of the American Methodists. It would have been more consistent to have abandoned all pretence of maintaining the apostolic succession.

The vague suggestion of substituting a presbyteral for an episcopal succession is untenable and could lead to nothing.

John Wesley should have remembered his mother's re-

[1] "The Evolution of the Christian Ministry," by the Rev. J. R. Cohu, M.A., sometime Fellow of Jesus College, Oxford.

mark in reference to the first of his lay preachers: "John, take heed what you do with reference to that young man for he is as surely called to preach as you are."

He should have fallen back boldly on the theory that the validity of Christian ministry is proved, not by historic title-deeds, but by its results. "By their fruits ye shall know them" is a test which provides the Methodist Ministry with a more valid claim than any based on alleged identity of bishops and priests in the Primitive Church.

VI

Inconsistency is the privilege of a genius. Wesley's consecration of Dr. Coke did not herald his final and definite secession from the Church of England. Instead, Wesley's affection for the Church of his baptism was never greater than in the last years of his life. Nay more, his own church which might, with justice, have resented his high-handed assumption of episcopal powers, treated Wesley with the greatest reverence and affection in the sun-down of his life. Perhaps, they realised instinctively that the Grand Old Man was a schismatic *malgré lui,* and that his heart had never left the Church, for whose ritual, ceremonial services he continued to feel an affection which time only served to deepen.

As Wesley always compared gardens such as those he saw in Holland with the best-beloved gardens of Oxford, so he often contrasted in his Journal other church services with those of Anglicanism.

"Being informed that the Lord's Supper was to be administered in the West Kirk (Edinburgh) I knew not what to do; but at length I judged it best to embrace the opportunity, though I did not admire the manner of administration. How much more simple, as well as more solemn, is the service of the Church of England!"

Similarly, he preferred the Anglican funeral service to the Scotch. Again, "Glasgow, 1779.—I attended the Church of England service in the morning, and that of the kirk in the afternoon. Truly, 'no man, having drunk old wine, straightway desireth new.' How dull and dry did the latter appear to me, who had been acustomed to the former!"

To the end of his life, John Wesley disliked Dissenters. As an old man of seventy-four he visited the Isle of Man. "A more loving, simple-hearted people than this I never saw—and no wonder; for they had but six Papists and no Dissenters in the island."

He wrote to John Nelson: "John, I love thee from my heart: yet rather than see thee a Dissenting minister, I wish to see thee smiling in thy coffin."

A year before he died John Wesley, perhaps the greatest, and in his own queer, inconsistent way, one of the most loyal and affectionate sons of the Anglican Church, addressed to the Methodists the following valedictory letter. These are his last words on this subject:

"I never had any design of separating from the Church; I have no such design now; I do not believe the Methodists in general design it. I do, and will do, all in my power to prevent such an event; nevertheless, in spite of all I can do, many will separate from it, although I am inclined to think not one half nor perhaps a third of them. These will be so bold and injudicious as to form a separate party, which consequently will dwindle into a dry, dull, separate sect. In flat opposition to them, I declare, once more, that I live and die a member of the Church of England, and that none who regard my judgment will ever separate from it."

CHAPTER XXVII

THE END

WESLEY, in his closing years, became more mellow. His judgment softened. He discarded the last traces of that austere Puritanism which had wrecked his hope of happiness in Georgia. His interest and delight, as Tyerman observes, in scenes of natural beauty and historic buildings increased as he grew older. At the age of eighty-three, he decided that the time had come to take a holiday, and he accordingly visited Holland. It was a real holiday. For several days in succession he rose as late as 4.30 A. M.

Wesley must have been a charming old man. "The gaiety of his nature," writes his friend Knox, "was so undiminished in its substance, while it was divinely disciplined in its movements, that to the latest hour of his life, there was nothing innocently pleasant with which he was not pleased, and nothing naturally lovely, which in its due proportion, he was not ready to love."

His niece tells us that "he always showed peculiar sympathy to young persons in love." And not only to young persons in love, but to all young folk. There are many stories of his kindness to children and when we read his letters we find it easy to believe that the affection which he showered on youth was returned with interest. Here are a few passages from a letter written at the age of eighty-five:

"My dear Sister,

I should have been exceedingly glad to see you, for I have a tender affection for you. And I shall always be well pleased to hear from you, and to hear how your soul prospers. . . .

You will not take it amiss if I ask you another question. I know neither your father nor your uncle is rich; and in travelling up and down you will want a little money. Are you not sometimes straitened? Only let me know, and you shall want nothing that is in the power of, my dear Sally,

Yours affectionately."

As he looked back, darker passages of the past were transfigured by the golden light of his sunset years. Even his disastrous marriage suffered transformation in that golden haze. The following is a letter, which has never yet been published, written at the age of 86:

"London,
December 22nd, 1786.

"My dear Brother,

When I was quite worn down it pleased God to make my marriage a means of restoring my Health and Strength. I hope yours will have the same effect upon you: though not by Natural but by Divine Efficacy. But this cannot be unless you limit Preaching. I therefore positively require you for a month from the date of this not to preach more than twice in a week. If you preach less I will not blame you. But you shd at all hazards ride an hour every day, only wrapping yourself up very close. Take care not to lodge in too close a room, and not to draw your curtains. For Medicine I should strictly recommend Stewed Prunes and either Beef Tea or a small cup of Fresh Churned Buttermilk four times a day. Let my dear Friend, Sister Walton, take note of this. As we are just making up the affairs of the poor in London I want to know what has been done at Bristol and a particular account of the steps that have been taken there. May both assist and instruct our Friends here.

That Grace and Peace may be multiplied on you both is the Prayer of

Your affectionate Friend & Brother,

(sgd) J. WESLEY."

Thirty-five years had passed since Wesley declared that a Methodist preacher should not preach one sermon or travel one day less in a married than in a single state. "In this respect surely, it remaineth that they who have wives be as they who have none."

II

Charles was the first to go. He began to fail during February 1788, and on February 18th, John Wesley wrote to him and urged him not to economise at the expense of his health. "You certainly need not want anything," wrote John, "as long as I live."

A few days later John wrote again to Mrs. Charles Wesley recommending "ten drops of elixir vitriol in a glass of water," but there is no evidence that Mrs. Charles followed his advice, or that Charles Wesley's end was hastened by John's incorrigible habit of prescribing for his friends.

Charles died on March 29th, 1788. His brother was away at the time, and the letter announcing his death was misdirected and did not reach John Wesley until April 4th.

Charles was buried at his own request in the churchyard of the old church of St. Marylebone. Shortly before he died, he sent for the parson of the parish in which he lived and said, "Sir, whatever the world may have thought of me, I have lived and I die in the communion of the Church of England, and I will be buried in the yard of my parish church."

And so Charles Wesley went to his last rest borne by eight priests of that church which commanded to the last his undiminished loyalty and affection.

"Whom God hath joined, let not man put asunder. . . . We have taken each other for better for worse till death do us part—no, but unite eternally." So Charles Wesley had written, and at long last death had interrupted a partnership which had lasted for over fifty years.

John Wesley wrote least on the subjects on which he felt most deeply. The Journals are almost silent, and John Wesley's reference to his brother in the Minutes of Conference for 1788 are, at least, a model of terseness so far as obituary notices go.

"Mr. Charles Wesley, who after spending four-score years with great sorrow and pain, quietly retired into Abraham's bosom. He had no disease, but after a gradual decay of some months, 'the weary wheels of life at last stood still.' His least praise was his talent for poetry, although Dr. Watts did not scruple to say that the single poem, 'Wrestling Jacob,' was worth all the verses he himself had written."

A fortnight after Charles died, John Wesley was preaching at Bolton. He climbed slowly into the pulpit and began to give out the first verse of his brother's greatest hymn, "Wrestling Jacob":

"Come O thou traveller unknown
Whom still I feel but cannot see."

And as he gave out these lines, old memories came back like stars after a storm. Charles in cap and gown, and St. John's College gardens in May, the foam-flecked Atlantic breaking across the "Simmonds" and the thin line—which was America—stretched across the horizon, and the blue skies of Savannah. The evil, upturned faces of the crowd at Tyburn, and the great peace in the eyes of those whom Charles had helped to die, and Charles singing his own hymns. He forgot the things which might have wrecked a companionship less firmly welded, and he remembered the love which had endured to the end, and he brushed away something from his eyes, for the old man of eighty-five felt very lonely and his voice faltered as he gave out the next two lines:

> "My company before has gone
> And I am left alone with thee"

and then his voice failed, and he sat down in the pulpit and buried his face in his hands.

III

Until the curtain fell, Wesley retained almost unimpaired his vigour of mind and body. At the age of eighty-three, he was piqued to discover that he could not write more than fifteen hours a day without hurting his eyes, and at the age of eighty-six, he was ashamed to admit that "he could not easily preach more than twice a day."

We notice in his Diary an increasing tendency to lie in bed in the morning, sometimes as late as 5.30 A. M. But such lapses were uncommon. Wesley did not allow such insidious habits to get a hold on him. His Diary [1] would help to acquit him of a charge of idleness. Here is an entry which he made at the age of eighty-six:

"Saturday 13.
4.15. Prayed, sermon; 8 tea, conversed; 9 sermon,

---

[1] For the difference between Journal and Diary, see page 26. The diaries between 1741 and 1782 have been lost. The later diary continues until within a few days of Wesley's death.

garden; 2 dinner, conversed; 4 sleep, prayed, tea; 6 Matt. xxii: 39! garden, conversed: 9 supper, conversed, prayer; 10.15."

Observe the sermons and that on a weekday.

Wesley was over eighty-six before he began to notice the signs of the approaching end. On his eighty-eighth birthday he wrote as follows:

"For above eighty-six years I found none of the infirmities of old age; my eyes did not wax dim, neither was my natural strength abated. But last August I found almost a sudden change. My eyes were so dim that no glasses would help me. My strength likewise now quite forsook me, and probably will not return in this world. But I feel not pain from head to foot; only it seems nature is exhausted, and humanly speaking, will sink more and more, till—

"The weary springs of life stand still at last."

IV

But the mainspring of Wesley's life refused to "stand still." In his eighty-sixth year, he preached in almost every shire of England and Wales, and often rode from thirty to fifty miles in the day.

Wesley had planned out his usual journey through England for 1791, and he hoped to start on February 28th.

On Sunday the 20th February he was taken ill. He was well enough to leave his bed on Monday and to preach on the Tuesday and the Wednesday. It was, indeed, on Wednesday, February 23rd, at Leatherhead, eighteen miles from London that John Wesley preached his last sermon.

He spent Thursday at Balham with his old friend

Mr. Wolff. In the afternoon he took up his pen, for the last time, to write a message of encouragement to William Wilberforce on his "glorious enterprise in opposing that execrable villainy which is the scandal of religion, of England, and of human nature."

This was the last letter he ever wrote.

There is no greater blot on Whitefield's memory than his defence of slave-owning on the ground that "hot countries cannot be cultivated without negroes." Wesley never compromised with the evil thing. As a young man in Georgia his outspoken opposition to slavery was a contributing factor to his unpopularity. Perhaps old memories of Georgia crowded upon him as he took his pen for the last time. His hand trembled as he wrote, but the mind that guided the faltering hand was as active as ever, and his hatred of slavery burnt with all its intensity. And so the old *miles emeritus* who had fought his last fight sends his heartening message to the young crusader on the threshold of a great campaign.

"Go on, in the name of God, and in the power of His might, till even American slavery (the vilest that ever saw the sun) shall vanish before it."

Next day, Wesley returned to London, never again to leave his room in City Road. The end was very beautiful. He lingered for three days surrounded by those who loved him. No pain, only a growing sense of weakness, and a tranquil acceptance of the inevitable. He slept much and spoke little, but sometimes the dying flame flickered up, and the inner light which had changed the face of England glowed with its old intensity. On the afternoon before he died, he surprised his friends by bursting into song:

> "I'll praise my Maker while I've breath
> And when my voice is lost in death
> Praise shall employ my nobler powers."

He sang two verses, and then sank back exhausted.

To the widow of Charles Wesley who bent over him, he murmured, "He giveth His beloved rest."

As the afternoon wore on, his sight grew dim, and his voice failed. Suddenly he seemed to rouse himself. He could not speak, and he struggled pathetically to make those who stood round his bed understand what was in his mind. And then by a supreme effort, he marshalled his ebbing strength for one last effort, and the words of his farewell message, a message which was to become the watchword of Methodism, came clear and strong— "The best of all is God is with us."

At ten o'clock on the morning of March 2nd, 1791, he spoke his last word—"Farewell"—and his eyes closed for the last time.

V

Wesley in his Will insisted that there should be no hearse and no pomp at his funeral, and his wishes were observed. But at the desire of his friends, his body remained one day in the City Road chapel. Through that chapel ten thousand of his followers passed in sorrowful and single file to pay their homage to their lost leader. He lay there in his gown and bands, his fingers resting on an open Bible, a look of serene and radiant happiness on his face.

Those who were making the arrangements for the funeral, feared that they would be unable to cope with the crowd. They therefore decided to have the funeral at five o'clock and to issue the notices late on the previous evening. But those who had so often risen at five o'clock in the morning to hear Wesley preach, thought it no hardship to rise early to bid him farewell, and a great throng followed him to his resting place in the vault behind the City Road chapel.

Many years before, John Wesley at the burial of his mother had changed one word in the solemn sentence of committal—"Our dear sister" became "Our dear Mother." The Reverend John Richardson who read the burial office over Wesley may have been present on that occasion, but it was probably a mere coincidence that he too instinctively changed the sentence of committal and read:

"Forasmuch as it hath pleased Almighty God to take unto Himself the soul of our dear *Father* here departed."

"Our dear *Father*." . . . Those who stood beside the open grave could check their grief no longer and broke out into weeping unrestrained.

John Wesley had seemed to belong to the unchanging order of things that do not pass away. Few of them could remember a time when he had not towered above his contemporaries. His death seemed less an event in the natural course of Nature than a monstrous reversal of Nature herself. His life had all but covered the span of the dying century, and perhaps those who watched the lowering of his body into the empty grave realised in some dim, prophetic fashion that they were present at the burial, not only of a man, but of an epoch. For the old world did not long survive John Wesley. It was 1791, and the "rumble of a distant drum" had already proclaimed the blood-red dawn of revolution. England was to pass unscathed through those troubled years, but the tumbrils might well have been seen in the streets of London, had not a little man in gown and bands taken the world for his parish, and changed the hearts of men.

APPENDIX

A HITHERTO UNPUBLISHED LETTER

SMOKE WITHOUT FIRE

On the centenary of Wesley's death, a leading Methodist paper published a facsimile of Wesley's shorthand. The Editor was unaware of the true significance of the particular letter which he reproduced in shorthand. W. T. Stead, in all innocence, reproduced this facsimile in his paper, "The Review of Reviews." A few days later, a man was shown into Stead's office. "I am one of the few people in England," he said, "who can read Wesley's shorthand, and here is the translation of that letter, which I propose to publish unless you pay me five guineas."

He did not get his five guineas; for Stead understood the press and knew that no editor at that time would dare to publish the letter in question. In such respects, the Victorian press was very different from our own.

The sequel is an excellent illustration of the folly of suppressing interesting facts which are known to more than one person. All those who are familiar with the inside history of Methodism have heard of this famous letter, but in the course of time, the actual facts have been distorted. The story reached the present writer in the following form. Wesley, in this letter, was supposed to have defended himself against a charge of misconduct by alleging that the real reason for the breakdown of his marriage was the fact that the marriage itself had never been consummated. I heard this story on good authority, and was inclined to credit it. But I had begun to doubt it long before I was informed on even better authority that certain unpublished portions of Wesley's Diary entirely refute the possibility of such a letter and the implications which might be deduced from it.

I thereupon secured a copy of "The Review of Reviews," and asked my friend Mr. I. J. Pitman of the famous firm of Isaac Pitman & Sons, to get me in touch with an expert on eighteenth century shorthand. Thanks to his good offices, a facsimile of Wesley's letter has been translated by Mr. E. A. Cope, and the translation is reproduced below.

It is difficult to see why this harmless document should have been withheld from publication. This type of accusation is brought with such frequency against public men in general and against prominent clergymen in particular, that it never carries the least weight unless fully supported by evidence. The bringing of such charges against public men is, indeed, one of the most common symptoms of hysteria.

Wesley, one must admit, made things easy for his traducers. No man was more artless and innocent, and no man was more indiscreet in his relations with women. It is a tribute to his real saintliness that most people were as unperturbed as Wesley by the rumours occasionally circulated by his enemies. Like Wesley himself they realised that few people believed these slanders even during the years of active opposition. Since Wesley's death, every critic, even the most hostile, has dismissed these suggestions as beneath contempt. In this, as in other matters, there is a strange resemblance between John Wesley and Gladstone. Had Wesley been concerned for his reputation, he would not have written some of the letters which have been quoted in this book. Had Gladstone been more sensitive to public opinion, he would not have chosen rescue work among prostitutes as a channel for his philanthropic activities.

Both Wesley and Gladstone were indifferent, and perhaps too indifferent to their own reputations. John Wesley's reply to his brother has already been quoted. "Brother, when I devoted to God my ease, my time, my life, did I except my reputation?"

Gladstone was equally unmoved by scurrilous attacks. A lady once took the trouble to inform him by letter that a political opponent had seen him talking to a courtesan in the shadow of the Crimean Monument. Gladstone replied, "It may be true that the honourable gentleman saw me in such a conversation. But the object of it was not what he assumed, nor, as I am afraid, what he hoped."

No man gifted with the least flair for character could read Wesley's Journal or Gladstone's letters without being impressed by the unstained purity of their minds.

Of all stupid proverbs, the most stupid and the most unjust is the proverb which declares that there is no smoke without fire. . . .

Wesley's letter is characteristic. No rhetoric, no emotionalism. Another man might have filled pages; for wounded vanity and injured innocence are often verbose. Wesley states the essential facts with dignity and with restraint.

I publish this letter in the belief that many of those who have heard garbled versions of this letter based on hearsay, will be as relieved as I was to see an authentic translation.

Transcript of Shorthand Copy (as reproduced in "Review of Reviews," Vol. iii, page 288) of a Letter written by John Wesley.

Letter to the Bishop of London.

My Lord,

Sometime ago I was informed that your Lordship had received some allegation against me by one [1]   charging me with committing or offering to commit lewdness with her. I have also been lately informed that your Lordship has been pressed to say (that unless) I solemnly declared my innocence, I should be superseded. I therefore take this liberty, deliberately and prayerfully saying, I declare that never did I ever commit lewdness with that person, neither did I ever solicit her thereunto, but am innocent of any such failure as wishing this thing.

As there are other such slanders cast on me, and knowing, alas, there will be evil spoken of me, I must beg leave, therefore, to declare mine innocence as to all other women likewise. It is now near twenty years since I began preaching of my Saviour, in all which time the God in whose presence I spoke, has kept me from either committing any act of adultery or fornication, or soliciting any person whomsoever thereto. I never did the action; I never spoke a word

---

[1] Blank space left in original.

inducing any one to such evil; I never harboured any such
design in my heart.

If your Lordship requires any further abrogation, I am
ready to repeat this declaration *viva voce,* and to take oath
that it is the entire truth of it.

I am, My Lord,

Your Lordship's dutiful son & servant,

J. W.

At D—n—ry [2]

February 8th, 1744.

[2] (Possibly means "Deanery." Actually written "dnr" with sign
for vowel following "r".)

INDEX